How Welfare Worked in the
Early United States

How Welfare Worked in the Early United States

Five Microhistories

Gabriel J. Loiacono

OXFORD
UNIVERSITY PRESS

OXFORD
UNIVERSITY PRESS

Oxford University Press is a department of the University of Oxford. It furthers
the University's objective of excellence in research, scholarship, and education
by publishing worldwide. Oxford is a registered trade mark of Oxford University
Press in the UK and certain other countries.

Published in the United States of America by Oxford University Press
198 Madison Avenue, New York, NY 10016, United States of America.

Library of Congress Cataloging-in-Publication Data
Names: Loiacono, Gabriel J., author.
Title: How welfare worked in the early United States : Five microhistories /
Gabriel J. Loiacono.
Description: New York, NY : Oxford University Press, [2021] |
"Second manuscript"—Title page. | Includes bibliographical references and index.
Identifiers: LCCN 2020054630 (print) | LCCN 2020054631 (ebook) |
ISBN 9780197515433 (paperback) | ISBN 9780197515457 (epub) |
ISBN 9780197515464 (online)
Subjects: LCSH: Public welfare—United States—History. | Poor—United
States—History. | Poor laws—United States—History.
Classification: LCC HV91 .L63 2021 (print) | LCC HV91 (ebook) |
DDC 362.5/56097309034—dc23
LC record available at https://lccn.loc.gov/2020054630
LC ebook record available at https://lccn.loc.gov/2020054631

DOI: 10.1093/oso/9780197515433.001.0001

To Caroline Cox, from one of the many beneficiaries of her kind mentorship.

CONTENTS

Introduction

What Can We Learn From These Five Microhistories?

I have had similar conversations with different people recently. They usually go something like this. A friend or acquaintance asks:

"What are you up to these days?"
"I am working on a book; it's almost done," I reply.
"Oh! What's it about?"

Happy to be asked, I explain: "It's about how welfare worked in the early United States. I want to tell five good stories about welfare, through the lives of people who received it, or doled it out."

"Wait, how early are we talking about?" is a typical response.

"Right after independence, when George Washington was President."

Usually, my friend or acquaintance will give me a surprised, even skeptical look at this point, asking "What? We had welfare *then*?"

We did. Or, rather, the United States of America did. And that is what this book is about. More precisely, this book describes government assistance to the poor, from George Washington's presidency in the 1790s to the political crises of the 1850s. Government assistance to the poor, often called "welfare" in the present day, was called "poor relief" in the early United States. And while poor relief is overlooked in histories of

How Welfare Worked in the Early United States. Gabriel J. Loiacono, Oxford University Press. © Oxford University Press 2021. DOI: 10.1093/oso/9780197515433.003.0001

this era, it undergirded the lives of most early Americans, whether they needed it or not. This book will map out how poor relief shaped Americans' experiences by following five people, all of whom lived in Rhode Island. *How Welfare Worked in the Early United States* will tell five microhistories, each highlighting different aspects of early American poor relief.

Although these five microhistories are specific to these particular men and women, they can also teach us what poor relief was like nationwide. Public poor relief in this period was almost entirely a local government function. Empowered by state laws, local governments raised and spent the tax revenue they needed to provide cash, food, clothing, firewood, housing, and healthcare to the people they were legally required to help. The requirements of American poor laws, typically, were that local governments *must* care for any needy person "settled" in their jurisdiction, if that person's spouse, parents, grandparents, children, and grandchildren could not provide for them. Even though few today know it existed, it was the most expensive government service of the early United States. For the individual taxpayer, poor relief absorbed a larger portion of their tax payments than anything else, including the military, criminal justice or, until about 1830, schools and roads. For some recipients, poor relief gave sustenance for decades. For others, it saw them through the most difficult moments of their lives: illnesses, financial crises, family emergencies.

At the same time, poor relief was the most significant form of policing that most early Americans faced. The poor laws could be used to oust people from their homes, and even to split up families. Many local governments used the laws to banish people that needed help, or were "likely" to need help, but "belonged" to some other locale. They called this "warning out." In theory, warning out was a way to spread out the financial burden of poor relief, while guaranteeing relief for everyone. In theory, every person had some locale to which they "belonged" and which *had* to care for them in their need, no matter how long it took or how much it cost. This was because every American state had poor laws, which might vary in detail, but operated on the same broad principles. Except for Louisiana, American states' poor laws were all based on older, English laws, particularly the Elizabethan Poor Law of 1601.

Of course, poor laws did not always work in practice as they should have in theory. That is why microhistories are needed, like the ones in this book, to reveal what actually happened. A microhistory can be defined as "the intensive historical investigation of a relatively well defined smaller object, most often a single event, or 'a village community, a group of families, even an individual person.'" One benefit of microhistories is that tightly focused stories often provoke our curiosity about other people's lives: they are human interest stories. A second benefit is that they help us under-stand how true our big, historical generalizations were in individual lives. Each of these women's and men's lives were shaped dramatically—and yet differently—by how local overseers of the poor applied the laws.[1]

FIVE LIFE STORIES

In these five life stories, we begin to understand people quite different from ourselves. These are people who ate salted pork and hard cider for break-fast, if they could get it. They were shocked to see men wearing beards. When a foreign traveler asked to stay the night at a tavern, he would be given a bed to share with a stranger. Most women made their own clothes from scratch: spinning, weaving, cutting, and sewing: making gowns and petticoats out of fibers. A dance party usually required a fiddle, with someone to play popular hits on it. If they wanted to move from one town to another, they could be required to ask permission of both the town they were leaving and the one to which they were moving. These were a people whose everyday experiences, like the assumptions and ideas in their minds, were quite different from ours. Yet, their world shapes our world. Even if we have forgotten some of the fundamental realities of their lives, we recognize that the governments and cultures they lived with are building blocks for the governments and cultures we live with. Like us in the present day, early Americans also struggled to help those in need, manage welfare budgets, ensure broad-based buy-in to welfare policies, make healthcare affordable, and support single parents and their children. How they cared for the poor can help us better understand our own experiences, assumptions, and practices in poor relief. As the first—and still the longest—system of wel-fare in United States history, the poor laws offer examples of social services that are sometimes awe-inspiring and sometimes repugnant. As the most expensive and intrusive public service of the early American republic, poor relief is crucial to understanding how everyday life unfolded in the decades after independence. Government poor relief was always supplemented by private charitable efforts. Standing in their kitchen doorways, early Americans gave food to beggars. After the Revolution, Americans created one charitable society after another. But these private charitable efforts were always supplemental to government poor relief, never replacing it. This book will focus on what governments did, tracing how government poor relief shaped the lives of William Larned, Cuff Roberts, "One-Eyed" Sarah, Lydia Bates, and William Fales.[2]

Chapter 1 will introduce how the poor laws worked, including how generous and expensive they could be, through the life of William Larned. A "yankee," born in colonial Connecticut to a long-settled English family, Larned moved to Providence, Rhode Island on the eve of the American Revolution. Trying several careers, including Continental Army commissary and import merchant, Larned settled into town service around age forty. He was an overseer of the poor from 1792 until he died in office, in 1828. Overseers of the poor were elected officials whose job was to care for the poor of their municipality, while identifying those who did not have a right to poor relief in their town. Walking the streets everyday, looking at faces, interrogating newcomers, Larned was merciful to some, intimidating to others. For those with a right to Providence poor relief, Larned provided what they needed. For those with rights in another town, Larned's job was to find them and banish them. Larned's story helps us understand how central the poor laws were to everyday life, to municipal government, and to taxpaying in this period. His story shows both how benevolent the poor laws could be and also how frequently they were used to banish people from town.

One man who was banished by Overseer Larned is the subject of chapter 2. Cuff Roberts arrived in Providence after marching for five long years through the American Revolution. Like Larned, Roberts was a Continental Army veteran, a husband, and a father hoping to find opportunities in the growing town. Unlike Larned, he was not made welcome. Although Roberts was born free in rural Rhode Island, slavery and racism shaped his life from childhood in another family's home to burial in a "colored" cemetery in Boston. The poor laws also shaped his life. Roberts's story shows how local governments could bend the police powers of the poor laws to their own ends. Providence overseers of the poor—including Larned—repurposed the poor laws to drive out many of their Black neighbors, even veterans collecting a war pension like Roberts. But Roberts came back, again and again. He would forge a family and a community in spite of the power of the poor laws.

Unlike Cuff Roberts, "One-Eyed" Sarah was largely a beneficiary of Overseer Larned's power, and passed its benefits on to others. As chapter 3 will show, Larned hired her as a nurse, right around the time he first banished Roberts. Described as "Indian," Sarah's job was to give full-time nursing care to some of the poorest and sickest of her neighbors. Her work saved lives. Town tax revenue, passing through the accounts of the overseers of the poor, paid for it. Although I do not know her last name with certainty, or which Native nation she was a part of, Sarah's experience shows how far towns would go to help needy people, especially the ill.

Moreover, a newspaper controversy over her work reveals elite attitudes about welfare. Providing care for the poor, through the government, was uncontroversial around 1810. What was controversial was whether that care was humane enough, and whether taxes were going up. This chapter shows the tension between providing good care and being economical with the town's money. It also shows how much healthcare was a part of the poor laws' benefits. Finally, Sarah's chapter shows how much ordinary people—who were not themselves paupers—benefitted from the poor laws. In larger towns, scores of people like Sarah were paid to assist the needy each year.

Another woman whose work benefitted those in need is the subject of chapter 4. Lydia Bates was a pauper herself, who helped others avoid poverty. The terms "pauper" and "one of the poor" had legal definitions: both denoted people who received poor relief from their local government. As a young single mother, Bates and her daughter Rhoda were officially "paupers." Before becoming pregnant with Rhoda, Bates appeared to be a hired hand, living and working in one household after another. A closer look, however, suggests that she might have been a pauper then also, assigned as a temporary worker to each household in exchange for room and board, but no pay. Whether as pauper or hired hand, whether doing needlework or farm chores, or caring for an elderly couple, Bates's labor was as helpful to her hosts as they were to her. Lydia Bates's life shows how poor relief could take the shape of temporary contract labor in some towns. Overseers could find her a home and shore up struggling households all in one deft move. Her chapter also shows how much power overseers of the poor had to govern single women, hold unmarried fathers responsible for their children, and separate families. As young Rhoda's experience shows, overseers of the poor could intervene between children and parents in the most profound ways.

William Fales, the subject of chapter 5, was born the same year as Rhoda Bates-Hill. Like Lydia Bates, Fales's mother also struggled to keep him with her. In Fales's case, it was a debilitating illness which led to his needing the help of overseers of the poor. By the time he was separated from his mother, though, overseers in his town relied on a poorhouse to take care of their charges. Where Lydia Bates and Rhoda had received poor relief in the midst of their community, Fales was isolated in a poorhouse in Portsmouth, Rhode Island. Over the course of William Fales's and Rhoda Bates-Hill's childhoods, poorhouses had become more popular as ways to provide humane but economical care. Living in the poorhouse, though, was a psychological and spiritual trial for Fales. He documented his suffering after he met a local philanthropist, "Shepherd" Tom Hazard, who would go on to advocate for poor law reform. Chapter 5 illustrates how the tension between providing humane care and inexpensive care led to more institutionalization. Fales's experiences, and Hazard's efforts, show what was gained and what was lost as poorhouses became more popular again throughout the United States.

While each chapter examines the poor laws from a different angle, they combine to make a complete portrait of early United States poor relief. Prior to 1830, poor relief was typically the largest single expense in each municipality, usually half or more of a local budget before 1820. Since local taxes were the largest most people paid, that meant that poor relief was the single most expensive government service a taxpayer supported. And yet, prior to the 1820s, few argued that governments should not offer it. The only real controversies were how much it should cost and how humane it was in practice. In theory, it guaranteed that every American would have the life-saving food, medical care, warmth, or shelter they needed if their families could not support them. But the poor laws also required municipalities in several states to banish newcomers, suppressing mobility. And even for those who had a right to poor relief in the town of their choice, overseers and voters decided how they could obtain that relief. Overseers might deliver cash, clothes, and food to needy homes, as Larned often did, or they might separate families and fold the needy into neighbors' houses, as overseers did to Bates. Later, overseers were likely to segregate the needy from everyone else, as they did to Fales. This was a complicated system, different in different places, and different for different people.

HOW THIS BOOK BUILDS ON—AND ARGUES WITH—OTHER HISTORIES OF WELFARE

A major goal of this book is simply that more readers become familiar with early American welfare and how it shaped society in significant ways, for good and bad. The format of five chapter-length biographies is intended to make the story of welfare more compelling. Moreover, a chapter each on individual paupers—like Lydia Bates and William Fales—is more space in a book than the slim sources on paupers' lives usually allow. As far as I know, I am the only historian to tell these particular five stories. Nevertheless, this book is built on the foundation of scholarship by many other historians, over several generations, who have worked hard to understand and tell the history of early American welfare. Sometimes, this book will repeat, illustrate, and amplify what other historians have found. At other times, this book will emphasize different conclusions based on similar evidence. In a couple of ways, this book will point to new evidence about how welfare worked in the early United States.

Historians have been working to understand early American poor relief for about a century. Some of the most enduring studies were written in the 1930s, just as this long-lasting municipal poor relief system was being augmented and then superseded by New Deal national programs. Inspired by Edith Abbott, one of the founders of social work, scholars fanned out across the country. Diving into many of the same sources that I have read, this generation of social work historians documented each state's history of poor relief. Their histories laid the groundwork for the massive changes in welfare that were part of the New Deal. They also laid the groundwork for historians who came after them. A generation or two later, American social welfare history became a very active field again. It was in the 1960s and 1970s that the "social control" thesis—the idea that poor relief functioned at least in part as a way to control the working classes—became widely accepted. Unlike welfare history in Britain, which remains a popular topic for historians, early American welfare history has not been widely studied since the 1980s. A few really important books have explored the topic since 1990. But this scholarship is not widely known. American history textbooks, and other widely read histories of the period, barely mention poor relief or the power of municipal governments. Even scholarly investigations of government—or *"the state"*—in this period focus primarily on national government.[3]

One point of this book is that municipal governments loomed far larger in the lives of ordinary Americans than state or national governments did in the first few decades after independence. Not only did they tax more, but municipal governments exercised more power. Granted by state law, but exercised by local officials, municipal powers to regulate public health, moral order, and economic markets were extensive. Municipal powers surrounding poverty were exercised frequently and shaped people's lives profoundly. Consider the roles of United States president George Washington and Providence overseer of the poor William Larned, both in office during the 1790s. As president, Washington visited Providence once, in 1790, and it was a grand occasion. But what power did he have over anyone he saw there? Little. It was Larned, walking the streets each day, scrutinizing the people he saw, whose power most impacted Providencians. His opinion mattered. If he thought people were "likely" to need poor relief, or not raising their children right, or not entitled to live in town, he could intervene. He could save lives with poor relief or upend lives, by getting a family banished from town. He could separate children from their parents. What president could do that? In focusing so much on the history of the national government, and to a lesser extent on state government, we have forgotten the power of the mighty municipality.

Remembering the powers of municipalities also reminds us how much they exercised control, or "social control" as many scholars call it. This book illustrates that social control in a number of ways. Chief among these examples is the story of how Cuff Roberts—and scores of his neighbors each year—struggled with a town's power to control where they lived. Overseers of the poor and town councils used the power of "warning out," usually leading to banishment in Rhode Island and the mid-Atlantic states, as both a financial tool and a method of social control. They used it to balance municipal budgets, by requiring each town to take on a share of the costs of poor relief. They also used it to tell some Americans—often the poorest or those of color—where they could and could not labor, live, and build communities. Other historians have described the role the poor laws played in policing people of color and suppressing the mobility of the poor. This book brings these interpretations together by following Roberts for a lifetime, including more than two decades in which overseers of the poor tried to control his movement, while he worked to outwit and outlast them.[4]

Two other examples of control exercised by overseers of the poor can be seen in the life of Lydia Bates. For one, Lydia Bates herself was, almost certainly, separated from her own parents. Then, her daughter Rhoda was separated from her. Intervening in the most intimate relationships, overseers of the poor did not hesitate to enforce their own vision of what a family should look like, as social work scholar Mimi Abramovitz has described. While local authorities continue to exercise this power today, the Bates' stories give readers a chance to see how this power was exercised two hundred years ago, from the financial and social motivations of the overseers to how Lydia Bates and Rhoda responded.[5]

A second way that Bates experienced social control is one that I have not seen in other histories of poor relief: Bates appeared to be a temporary worker, assigned by the overseers of the poor to various households, whose owners were sometimes needy themselves. This interpretation of the evidence will help readers think afresh about an old argument: that poor relief was often purposefully stingy so that poor people would prefer to take low-wage work than demeaning relief from the government. None of the microhistories in this book support that argument precisely. But Lydia Bates's story does suggest that overseers operated a temporary labor pool, assigning adult paupers to neighbors to work, for a few weeks or months. Other historians have discussed the practice of "venduing"—or auctioning off—a pauper's care to the lowest bidder. The winning bidder also gained the right to the pauper's labor with his contract to care for them. This was a common practice in small towns like Bates's. A related practice was contracting for children's labor, formally or informally. But the periodic arrangement, for temporary assignments, of a young, healthy woman's labor, is something different. It is a system that benefited householders at least as much as a young woman like Bates. It shows that overseers of the poor acted as labor matchmakers: putting temporary households together for the benefit of everyone, pauper and householder alike. If this was a common practice, it means that poor law officials shaped the labor market far more directly than scholars had previously contemplated. This book, then, supports the long-standing social control interpretations, in part.[6]

But I also want to push back against the social control interpretations. While welfare *was* sometimes used for purposes of social control, we cannot let that blind us to how expensive and effective it was. Overseers of the poor were expected to ensure that no one starved or froze or went without medical attention on their watch. At the same time that they used poor laws to control where people lived or whether they could raise their own children, overseers also spent the largest piece, sometimes the majority, of each municipality's budget providing basic goods and services, including medical attention, for those in need. This help can be measured in the dollars spent and individuals assisted in one municipality after another, between independence and the twentieth century. In the time of George Washington, and for generations after, Americans poured resources into caring for their neediest neighbors. They did this through both private and public means, but locally administered government poor relief was the backbone of this care for the needy. And it typically included a guarantee of relief for "settled" residents of a municipality. In the present day, there is no such formal guarantee. It is worth reflecting on the point that, in theory, early Americans offered a more seamless safety net than Americans do in the present day.[7]

A related point is that this was not easy to do. Historians seldom consider how difficult it was to finance a theoretically unlimited safety net using property taxes, even if it was only guaranteed to needy people with a recognized claim on a municipality. Poor law administrators carried out their tasks in the midst of great tension between the goals of being "humane" and also being fiscally conservative. It is easy to miss this tension when reading sources from the point of view of reformers or state-level officials from the top down. More recently, we have started telling the story of welfare from the perspectives of people who received poor relief from the bottom up. These perspectives have been vitally important, but they too do not bring into focus this humanity/economy tension. The stories of William Larned and "One-Eyed" Sarah, by contrast, tell stories of welfare focused on the people who actually provided it. Not quite top down or bottom up, their perspectives on poor relief are from the middle out. They help us to understand the nuts and bolts of how poor law officials actually provided the care they were supposed to.[8]

This tension between humanity and fiscal conservatism also helps readers understand the recurring popularity of institutions often called poorhouses. Frequently characterized as institutions of social control, poorhouses were supposed to be institutions that combined humanity with cost savings. That was the hope. The actual result was less cost-efficient and less humane than intended. Of course, different institutions could be quite different. Some poorhouses gave rise to thriving communities, shaped as much by inmates as by supervising officials. As the experiences of William Fales show, on the other hand, poorhouses could sometimes be quite isolating. Their intentionally remote locations could lead to a loneliness among inmates. Approaching the rises and falls of poorhouses through Fales's experience gives us a new and eye-opening perspective on the trend towards institutionalization in the nineteenth century.[9]

One last important point is that poor relief served as an economic stimulant for broad swaths of the local population in each town, not just the needy themselves. Elna C. Green describes the benefits of poor relief to people who helped the needy in Richmond, Virginia as a "welfare/industrial complex." Coining a new term that echoes President Dwight D. Eisenhower's term "military industrial complex," Green's point is that many ordinary people benefitted from the dollars spent by the town government on poor relief. This book further illustrates Green's argument. Nurses, doctors, grocers, firewood splitters, shoemakers, tailors, farmers selling produce, homeowners, or tavernkeepers with a spare bed: all could earn cash by providing for the poor. We could call them *local government relief contractors*. Poor taxes provided income for countless ordinary people who served as relief contractors, as well as for those who were officially "paupers," the recipients of poor relief. "One-Eyed" Sarah, William Larned, Cuff Roberts, and the farmers with whom Lydia Bates stayed were all beneficiaries of poor taxes in this way. This helps explain why poor relief was so popular for so long.[10]

On these themes and others, this book enters into conversation with other histories of welfare in the early American republic. But how well do these five stories from Rhode Island represent experiences across the United States of America?

HOW THESE FIVE MICROHISTORIES FIT INTO THE
WELFARE HISTORY OF THE WHOLE UNITED STATES

Because welfare was almost entirely a local government responsibility in this era, this book will focus on one particular location: Providence, Rhode Island, and smaller towns nearby. Sticking with this one place between the American Revolution and the Civil War will help readers to know the history of welfare more deeply. Readers will get to see a few different officials applying the same laws, and a few different individuals living their lives under circumstances shaped by those same laws. But readers will wonder, no doubt, how representative of the early United States these stories are.

No one location can stand in for all others, local government being *local* government, intentionally particular to that locale. Nevertheless, Rhode Island poor laws had a lot in common with poor laws throughout the United States. For one, every state in the United States except Louisiana built their legal codes on a foundation of English law. Early English settlers had benefitted from the poor relief practices of many Native nations, most famously the Powhatanite and the Wampanoag nations. Before Rhode Island had that name, Roger Williams and other English refugees gathered there with protection from their Narragansett hosts. When it came time to write down their poor relief practices, though, English settlers would formally adopt the most current codification of English welfare: the Elizabethan Poor Law, a 1601 collection of innovations in social welfare made in the mid- to late 1500s.

From Maine to Georgia to Texas to Oregon, the Elizabethan Poor Law was the blueprint for welfare into the 1930s. All British North American colonies wrote a version of it into colony law before independence, and barely changed it after independence. New states copied what older states had copied from the Elizabethan Poor Law, even after Great Britain made a major reform called the New Poor Law of 1834. One by one, colonies and states modified their poor laws according to local circumstances and legislative preferences, beginning even before independence. Nevertheless, modifications were added onto the structure of the Elizabethan Poor Law. Only in the 1930s, when a new federal apparatus was built as part of the New Deal, did the old poor law structure begin to be less important to how poor relief worked.[11]

So, like Rhode Island, all states depended on local municipalities to collect poor taxes and administer poor relief before the 1930s. Whether parishes in Great Britain, towns in New England, or counties from New York to Georgia and west, local municipalities did most of the work of poor relief. Officials called "overseers of the poor" in New England would be called "guardians of the poor" in Pennsylvania, "managers of the poor" in Maryland, or churchwardens and vestrymen in the colonial South. In the South, too, churchwardens and vestrymen were replaced by "overseers of the poor" at various points: the 1780s for Virginia. These officials might share the job or do it solo. They might have responsibility for a whole town or a neighborhood. But in all cases, their job was to determine who was eligible for poor relief and decide how to get that relief to those eligible.[12]

All over the early United States, local governments collected the most taxes from individual taxpayers. Although more historical scholarship needs to be done, extant evidence shows that local taxes were the biggest tax burden shouldered by a property tax payer before the Civil War. Moreover, as readers will see in chapter 1, the single most expensive government service at any level—federal, state, or local—was poor relief, until about 1830. From Rhode Island to New York to Virginia, then taxpayers were paying more to local governments than to state and federal governments, and local governments were using those funds for poor relief more than for anything else. By 1830, in the larger towns and cities, roads, schools, and debt service grew to be as expensive as poor relief. But it would remain a big budget item through the nineteenth century.[13]

As a big budget item, the cost of poor relief was a political issue all over the United States throughout the nineteenth century. Providing poor relief, per se, was rarely controversial before the 1820s. How much that poor relief cost, though, was often an issue. Thus after attempting to economize on poor relief in a variety of ways, one municipality after another began turning—or returning—to institutionalization in the early or middle nineteenth century. Voters were persuaded that building or buying expensive poorhouses would provide care that was both more cost-effective and more humane. Some also thought that poorhouses might dissuade people from asking for poor relief in the first place. A strain of nativism and an increasing distrust of the needy were part of the poorhouse movement. But the central concern of the movement was rising poor relief costs.

In the nineteenth-century sources I have read, the word poorhouse was interchangeable with the words almshouse, asylum, poor farm, or town farm. Obviously, the names poor farm and town farm guaranteed that a farm was part of the institution. Poorhouses, almshouses, and asylums might or might not be attached to a farm. "Asylum," which is now usually assumed to be a mental health institution, was usually an "asylum for the poor" in the early nineteenth century. "Asylums for the insane" grew out of "asylums for the poor" in the mid-nineteenth century, as part of an international movement to make treatment of mental illness more humane. A "workhouse," or "house of industry," meanwhile, was a related institution. As the name suggests, inmates of a workhouse or house of industry were supposed to work, but these buildings also served as places providing housing and food for the homeless and destitute, like an almshouse. Even without the words "work" or "industry," though, any of these institutions might require inmates to work. Requiring work or not, any poor relief given inside an institution was called "indoor relief," as opposed to providing goods, services, or money to someone outside an institution: "outdoor relief."[14]

Called by whichever name, publicly funded poorhouses and workhouses existed all over the United States at the time of independence, and many more would be built in the century after. Both poorhouses and workhouses had been part of the Elizabethan poor law apparatus which Americans inherited from English law. Along with an array of privately funded institutions for the poor, these poorhouses and workhouses would expand and contract for a variety of reasons. Notable pulses of institution building took place in the decades just before and after the American Revolution. Beginning in the 1820s, though, was one of the largest of such waves of poorhouse building in the United States, coinciding with a push to ban "outdoor relief" in both Britain and the United States. Rhode Island poorhouse builders were a part of each of these waves of institutionalization. During each period, voters at the local government level were convinced that a poorhouse or a workhouse or both were the best way to provide good, cheap care. Typically, voters building a new poorhouse or workhouse also wanted to reduce or eliminate the "outdoor" poor relief they provided.[15]

As chapter 5 will show, poorhouses gave way, in part, to greater state-level involvement in poor relief. Colonial, and then state, governments had long taken partial responsibility for poor relief in different ways. For example, some colonies and states paid relief for people with no settlement in the colony or in the United States. Some paid poor relief for widows and orphans of soldiers. Moreover, the United States government became involved in welfare in two important ways: hospitals and asylums for sailors and federal pensions for veterans of the Revolutionary War and the War of 1812. But nationally funded hospitals and pensions, and most state-funded poor relief, targeted narrow segments of the population, and usually they were meant to ease the burden of poor relief for municipal governments. The vast bulk of poor relief, around the country, remained local through the Civil War. And while welfare was almost always administered locally, municipalities across the United States ran their miniature welfare states more similarly than not. In the recurring impulse to build institutions, and in the continuing importance of local government, Rhode Island was much like the rest of the United States. There were some significant differences between states, though, in 'warning out' and slavery.[16]

Warning out, the legal term for using the poor law to banish people from a municipality, worked quite differently in different places. In Rhode Island, it was practiced in 1830 largely as it had been in 1730. Local overseers of the poor watched out for new residents in their town. If they thought those new residents might ever need poor relief, the overseers made a 'complaint' to the Town Council, the highest government authority in town. The Town Council 'examined,' or interrogated the newcomer, and then decided where the newcomer had a 'settlement,' a legal right to poor relief. If the newcomer's settlement was in any other place, the Town Council could then 'warn out' the newcomer, telling that person to leave town, anytime from that day, to a week or two later, to some other specific date. Or, the Town Council could 'reject' the newcomer from settlement, but allow the newcomer to stay, for the time being. If the Town Council thought the newcomer would not leave on his own, they could order the Town Sergeant to jail the newcomer and then remove the newcomer, usually by horse and cart, to another town. They could even order the Town Sergeant to whip anyone who was warned out and came back to town without official permission.

Recent scholarship, though, has found that neighboring Massachusetts did not practice warning out this way by the Revolution, while Pennsylvania and other mid-Atlantic states did. Cornelia H. Dayton's and Sharon V. Salinger's 2014 *Robert Love's Warnings: Searching for Strangers in Colonial Boston* follows a Boston official named Robert Love, whose job before the American Revolution was simply to 'warn' newcomers to Boston. Unlike in Rhode Island, Love's 'warning,' was not meant to be taken literally. Newcomers warned did not actually have to leave. Rather, the warning had become a formality that meant only that the provincial government was financially responsible for the newcomer, not the Boston government: an innovation in how poor relief was financed. By contrast, Kristin O'Brassill-Kulfan's 2019 *Vagrants and Vagabonds: Poverty and Mobility in the Early American Republic* traces how local officials responded to newcomers in Pennsylvania, New York, Delaware, and Maryland. Unlike Massachusetts, but much like Rhode Island, the mid-Atlantic states regularly practiced warning out into the 1830s, and occasionally practiced it into the 1930s. This timeline matches Rhode Island's well. In the South, according to Timothy James Lockley's 2007 *Welfare and Charity in the Antebellum South*, warning out was less common than in the North. Thus not every state used warning out as much as Rhode Island did in the first half of the nineteenth century, but some did.[17]

One other major difference between Rhode Island and other states in the early United States is the interconnection between the poor law, slavery, and race. Rhode Island enacted gradual emancipation in 1784, as did Pennsylvania, Connecticut, New York, and New Jersey between 1780 and 1804. Massachusetts, by contrast, saw emancipation by a series of court decisions that started during the American Revolution. States from Maryland southward, of course, did not abolish slavery until the Civil War era. In most northern states, as in Rhode Island, the question of how freedpeople could gain access to poor relief was a politically fraught question, and states tried different answers, beginning in the 1780s. Rhode Island settled on a compromise, granting poor relief rights to some freedpeople while denying poor relief to others. At the same time, local officials used the poor laws to round up and banish people of color frequently in the two generations after emancipation. Both Joanne Pope Melish and Ruth Wallis Herndon have found that Rhode Island towns disproportionately warned out people of color through the late eighteenth and early nineteenth centuries. States to the West, such as Ohio, explicitly excluded Black newcomers from entering the state, as Stephen Middleton has shown. Similarly, Kunal Parker has found that slave states increased their efforts to regulate the movement of free African Americans through the first half of the nineteenth century. Comparing Rhode Island and other New England states to the West and South, racial discrimination was less likely to be written into law, but town officials used the poor laws in discriminatory ways.[18]

In general, though, there were more similarities than differences between the Rhode Island poor laws and those of other states. Rhode Island towns practiced warning out longer than municipalities in Massachusetts and more energetically than those in the South. Mid-Atlantic states, though, were similar to Rhode Island in this regard. Rhode Island's officials frequently used the poor laws in racially exclusionary ways, though they also gave assistance and jobs to people of color. This was similar to much of New England and yet distinct from the even more explicitly race-conscious poor relief of the South and West. These are some of the most obvious differences between Rhode Island relief and that of other states.

At the same time, the laws that shaped the lives of William Larned and "One-Eyed" Sarah were based on the Elizabethan Poor Law, just like those in every state but Louisiana. Like the rest of the country, Rhode Island's poor relief was similarly expensive and similarly local. So, while these five lives are unique, and cannot represent the experience of every other life shaped by the poor law, readers can use these stories to understand what poor relief in the early United States was generally like. Readers are welcome to read chapters out of order, but chapter 1, Overseer of the Poor: How William Larned Spent Public Funds on the Needy, will explain the basics of how poor relief worked. The chapters will proceed in roughly chronological order from there. The epilogue will sum up the lessons to be learned from these five lives, and bring the story to the year 2020.

The epilogue ends in 2020 because Americans still struggle with welfare. Whether we need assistance ourselves, or we are social workers trying to help, whether we are policy makers or taxpayers, we are rarely satisfied with welfare. Is it effective? Is it too controlling? Not controlling enough? What form should it take? How much should it cost? How intrusive should it be? Who should administer it? Should we do it in the first place? Understanding that welfare has a past much older than the twentieth century is crucial to helping policymakers, voters, and practitioners with these questions today. American political leaders frequently give their listeners history lessons when they are trying to persuade us to support a policy. Whether to inspire us or to chart a change in course, these leaders typically sketch out how Americans of the past have approached similar issues. On issues from foreign policy to individual rights, from race to the economy, political rhetoric is filled with references to the past, for good or ill. The problem with our understanding of the history of welfare policy is that we so often imagine that welfare started in 1935 with the New Deal. Before then, so many Americans assume, if people needed help from outside the family, then "Our neighbors, our friends, our churches would do it."[19]

As a result, many students, citizens, social workers, civil servants, policymakers, and historians work with a giant misunderstanding of the early American republic. We are right to assume that family help was important. Immediate family members were legally required to help, and often did. As historian David Danborn put it: families were early Americans' "premier welfare institution." We are also right to note the roles of neighbors, friends, and churches. But the part of the story we often miss is that neighbors and friends would often be reimbursed for their help by local government. Churches and benevolent organizations helped too. But in the early United States, churches and benevolent organizations were supplemental to a powerful, expensive municipal poor law system. For too long, we have focused our attention primarily on the national government, which barely taxed, and provided assistance chiefly to needy veterans and mariners. Since the national government did not provide much welfare, we mistakenly assume either that no government exercised these powers, or that local communities provided poor relief incompetently and cruelly. But that is a grossly incomplete picture of how early Americans addressed poverty. This book aims to put local government poor relief, the missing piece of the puzzle, back into our historical understanding of welfare.[20]

NOTES

1. There are many examples of microhistories, and also much written about microhistory as an approach. One influential example, for this historian, is John Ruston Pagan, *Anne Orthwood's Bastard: Sex and Law in Early Virginia* (New York: Oxford University Press, 2003). Explorations of the benefits and dangers of microhistory include Jill Lepore, "Historians Who Love Too Much: Reflections on Biography and Microhistory," *The Journal of American History* 88:1 (June 2001), 129–144, Cornelia Hughes Dayton, "Rethinking Agency, Recovering Voices," *The American Historical Review* 109:3 (June 2004), 827–843, Sigurður G. Magnússon and István M. Szijártó, *What is Microhistory? Theory and Practice* (New York: Routledge, 2013), and essays from Hans Renders and Binne De Haan, Eds., *Theoretical Discussions of Biography: Approaches from History, Microhistory, and Life Writing* (Boston: Brill, 2014), among them Richard D. Brown, "Microhistory and the Post-Modern Challenge," *Theoretical Discussions of Biography*, 119–128, Matti Peltonen, "What is Micro in Microhistory?" *Theoretical Discussions of Biography*, 105–118, and Carlo Ginzburg, "Microhistory: Two or Three Things That I Know About It" *Theoretical Discussions of Biography*, 139–166. The definition quoted here is from Magnússon and Szijártó, *What is Microhistory?*, 4.
2. For everyday social and cultural history, from the ubiquity of salted pork to the rarity of single-occupancy beds, I rely on Jack Larkin, *The Reshaping of Everyday Life, 1790–1840* (New York: Harper Perennial, 1989), 24–27, 121–127, 169–180, 184, 250–251. On asking permission of towns for coming and going, see below chaps. 1 and 2, as well as Kristin O'Brassil-Kulfan, *Vagrants and Vagabonds: Poverty and Mobility in the Early American Republic* (New York: New York University Press, 2019).
3. For a bibliography of the works of Edith Abbott, who often collaborated with her sister Grace Abbott and another Social Worker, Sophonisba Breckenridge, see Rachel Marks, "The Published Writings of Edith Abbott: A Bibliography," *Social Service Review* 32:1 (March 1958), 51–56. One superb 1930s study is Margaret Creech, *Three Centuries of Poor Law Administration: A Study of Legislation in Rhode Island* (Chicago: University of Chicago Press, 1936). On the historiography of welfare through the 1970s, see Clarke A. Chambers, "Toward a Redefinition of Welfare History," *Journal of American History* 73:2 (September 1986), 407–433. Early American historian Barry Levy wrote in 2010 that "Welfare history is hardly a popular focus among early American historians" and that "By ignoring welfare history for so long, early American historians have been part of the problem of present-day welfare inadequacies," in "Rediscovering the Lost City of American Welfare," *Reviews in American History* 38:3 (September 2010), 414, 419. Ten years later this is still true, but I see signs of hope for a renaissance in histories of early American welfare. It is hoped that this book will be part of that renaissance. For other reflections on the last few decades of early American welfare historiography, see Stephen Pimpare, "Toward a New Welfare History," *Journal of Policy History* 19:2 (2007), 234–252, and Maurizio Vaudagna, "Historians Interpret the Welfare State, 1975–1995," in Alice Kessler-Harris and Maurizio Vaudagna, Eds., *Democracy and the Welfare State: The Two Wests in the Age of Austerity* (New York: Columbia University Press, 2018). Recent works on "the state" largely focus on examples of national or state-level government. See Journal of the Early Republic, "Taking Stock of the State in Nineteenth-Century America," *Journal of the Early Republic* 38:1 (Spring 2018), 61–118, William J. Novak, "The

Myth of the 'Weak' American State," *American Historical Review* 113:3 (June 2008), 752–772, Brian Balogh, *A Government Out of Sight: The Mystery of National Authority in Nineteenth-Century America* (Cambridge: Cambridge University Press, 2009), 308, Steven Conn, Ed., *To Promote the General Welfare: The Case for Big Government* (New York: Oxford University Press, 2012), Gary Gerstle, *Liberty and Coercion: The Paradox of American Government from the Founding to the Present* (Princeton: Princeton University Press, 2015), 56, 69. One recent book with a strong focus on the powers of local government is O'Brassil-Kulfan, *Vagrants and Vagabonds.*

4. On the role of the poor laws in policing mobility, see O'Brassil-Kulfan, *Vagrants and Vagabonds.* On the role of the poor laws in policing race, see Ruth Wallis Herndon, *Unwelcome Americans: Living on the Margin in Early New England* (Philadelphia: University of Pennsylvania Press, 2001), 18–20, Kunal Parker, *Making Foreigners: Immigration and Citizenship Law in America, 1600–2000* (Cambridge: Cambridge University Press, 2015), 76, and Joanne Pope Melish, *Disowning Slavery: Gradual Emancipation and "Race" in New England, 1780–1860* (Ithaca: Cornell University Press, 1998), 190–191. For biographical treatments of people who faced this police power, see Gretchen Gerzina, *Mr. and Mrs. Prince: How an Extraordinary Eighteenth-Century Family Moved out of Slavery and Into Legend* (New York: Amistad, 2009), and Shirley Green, "Freeborn Men of Color: The Franck Brothers in Revolutionary North America, 1755–1820" (PhD diss., Bowling Green State University, 2011).

5. Mimi Abramovitz, *Regulating the Lives of Women: Social Welfare Policy from Colonial Times to the Present.* Third Edition (New York: Routledge, 2018), xiv–xv, 70–72.

6. While other works touch on auctioning pauper labor, two old works that focus on it are Benjamin Klebaner, "Pauper Auctions: The 'New England Method' of Public Poor Relief," *Essex Institute Historical Collections* 9:1 (1955), 195–210, and Thomas R. Hazard, *Report on the Poor and Insane in Rhode-Island; Made to the General Assembly at Its January Session, 1851* (Providence: Joseph Knowles, State Printer, 1851). Robert E. Cray, Jr., *Paupers and Poor Relief in New York City and Its Rural Environs, 1700–1830* (Philadelphia: Temple University Press, 1988) also discusses pauper auctions throughout. On children's labor contracts, which could sometimes closely resemble Lydia Bates's arrangements, see the essays in Ruth Wallis Herndon and John E. Murray, Eds., *Children Bound to Labor: The Pauper Apprentice System in Early America* (Ithaca: Cornell University Press, 2009). The classic work which interprets poor relief as social control focused on workers is Frances Fox Piven and Richard A. Cloward, *Regulating the Poor: The Functions of Public Welfare.* Updated Edition (New York: Vintage, 1993), xix.

7. This old debate on how benevolent or controlling social welfare was is described in Chambers, "Toward a Redefinition of Welfare History," as well as Conrad Edick Wright, "Review of Lawrence J. Friedman and Mark D. McGarvie, *Charity, Philanthropy, and Civility in American History*," in *American Historical Review* 109:1 (February 2004), 172, and Sharon V. Salinger, "Review of Simon Newman *Embodied History: The Lives of the Poor in Early Philadelphia*," *American Historical Review* 109:1 (February 2004), 176, among other places. A nice solution is Seth Rockman's insistence that poor relief institutions could simultaneously serve *competing* goals: "a civic culture of benevolence" towards the poor *and* "disciplin[ing] workers in the service of capitalism"; see Seth Rockman, *Scraping By: Wage Labor, Slavery, and Survival in Early Baltimore* (Baltimore: Johns Hopkins University Press, 2009), 197. Michael B. Katz makes a similar point in Michael

B. Katz, *In the Shadow of the Poorhouse: A Social History of Welfare in America* Tenth Anniversary Edition (New York: BasicBooks, 1996), xvi. Another helpful observation is David Wagner's that the "macro-level analysis" of welfare as a "secondary institution in support of a capitalist society" "does not explain (nor do I think it was meant to explain) how groups, towns, and other actors acted on a micro level" in David Wagner, *The Poorhouse: America's Forgotten Institution* (Lanham: Rowman & Littlefield, 2005), 157. One historian who, like me, remarks on how expensive poor relief could be is Tim Hitchcock, when he calls poor relief in eighteenth-century London "extensive, expensive, and remarkably comprehensive," in Tim Hitchcock, *Down and Out in Eighteenth-Century London* (London: Bloomsbury Publishing, 2005), 132.

8. Many histories cite the costs of poor relief in particular years. Usually, historians use these as a measure of how big or small a municipal government's willingness to help the needy was, or how great the need was. See, for example, Raymond Mohl, *Poverty in New York, 1783–1825* (New York: Oxford University Press, 1971), Cray, *Paupers and Poor Relief in New York City*, Elna C. Green, *This Business of Relief: Confronting Poverty in a Southern City, 1740–1940* (Athens: University of Georgia Press, 2003). One work that compellingly shows that tension between humanity and economy is Timothy James Lockley, *Welfare and Charity in the Antebellum South* (Gainesville: University Press of Florida, 2007), especially chap. 1.

9. On the possibility of communities inside poorhouses, see Wagner, *The Poorhouse*. Well-known studies of poorhouses, such as David J. Rothman, *The Discovery of the Asylum: Social Order and Disorder in the New Republic* (Boston: Little Brown, 1971), 191, 204, and Katz, *In the Shadow of the Poorhouse*, 25, mention inmates' isolation in passing, but focus mostly on the social control aspects of the institutions.

10. Green, *This Business of Relief*, 1.

11. Careful summaries of each state's poor laws, and their indebtedness to the Elizabethan Poor Law, can be found in William P. Quigley. "Reluctant Charity: Poor Laws in the Original Thirteen States," *University of Richmond Law Review* 31 (1997), 111–178., and William P. Quigley, "The Quicksands of The Poor Law: Poor Relief Legislation in a Growing Nation, 1790–1820," *Northern Illinois University Law Review* 18 (Fall 1997), 1–98.

12. For Philadelphia, see Billy G. Smith, *The "Lower Sort": Philadelphia's Laboring People, 1750–1800* (Ithaca: Cornell University Press, 1990). For Baltimore, see Rockman, *Scraping By*, chap. 7. On the South, see Lockley, *Welfare and Charity in the Antebellum South*, 4. For the churchwardens, vestrymen, and overseers of the poor in Virginia, see Edward L. Bond, "The Parish in Colonial Virginia," *Encyclopedia Virginia* <www.encyclopediavirginia.org/parish_in_colonial_virginia_the#start_entry>.

13. Historians could do much more to understand how municipal revenue and spending worked in comparison to state and federal revenue and spending. Based on newspaper advertisements in which town assessors printed how much individual taxpayers owed in overdue taxes, it seems clear that local taxes were greater than state or federal taxes for individual payers during the 1790s and 1820s. See for one of many examples, "Collector's Notice," *Rhode Island Republican,* 4 October 1815, 1. Economic historians Legler, Sylla, and Wallis, however, have found that municipal "local tax revenues per capita" were a bit smaller than federal tax revenues per capital in 1850, but outstripped that of states. In the next five decades, though, local tax revenues greatly outstripped federal revenues, both

of which left state revenues far behind (John B. Legler, Richard Sylla, and John J. Wallis, "U.S. City Finances and the Growth of Government, 1850–1902," *The Journal of Economic History* 48:2 [1988], 355). Moreover, looking at spending—not revenue—in the period 1820–1870, economic historians Holcombe and Lacombe argue that local governments accounted for 13.5% of government spending at any level in 1820, rising to 42.9% in 1870 (Randall G. Holcombe and Donald J. Lacombe, "The Growth of Local Government in the United States from 1820 to 1870," *The Journal of Economic History* 61:1 [Mar 2001], 189). . Robin Einhorn, *American Taxation American Slavery* (Chicago: University of Chicago Press, 2006), 219–221, finds local governments probably levied higher taxes in the North than in the South. All agree, though, that the picture remains unclear because the relevant data in uneven and not collected together.

14. By the time of American independence, "hospital" had mostly lost an early meaning. According to the Oxford English Dictionary, it had been synonymous with poorhouse or asylum in early modern England. In the period covered by this book, it was usually used in its modern sense: an institution dedicated to medical care. That said, doctors and nurses were still regular visitors to poorhouses.

15. On the eighteenth-century waves of poorhouse-building, see Gary B. Nash, "Poverty and Politics in Early American History," in Billy G. Smith, Ed., *Down and Out in Early America* (University Park: Pennsylvania State University Press, 2004) 4, and Ruth Wallis Herndon, "'Who Died an Expence to this Town': Poor Relief in Eighteenth-Century Rhode Island," *Down and Out in Early America*, 149–151, both essays in. See also Stephen Edward Wiberley, Jr. *Four Cities: Public Poor Relief in Urban America, 1700–1775* (PhD. diss., Yale University, 1975) and Jacqueline Jones, *American Work: Four Centuries of Black and White Labor* (New York: W.W. Norton & Company, 1998), chap. 5. For a summary of nineteenth-century poorhouse building, see Walter Trattner, *From Poor Law to Welfare State: A History of Social Welfare in America*. Sixth Edition (New York: The Free Press, 1999), chap. 4.

16. For examples of Rhode Island taking on some of these poor relief expenses, see Creech, *Three Centuries of Poor Law Administration*, 116–117. On marine hospitals, see John Jensen, "Before the Surgeon General: Marine Hospitals in Mid-19th-Century America," *Public Health Reports* 112:6 (1997), 525–527 and Gautham Rao, "Administering Entitlement: Governance, Public Health Care, and the Early American State," *Law & Social Inquiry* 37:3 (2012), 627–656. On pensions, see Michael A. McDonnell and Briony Neilson, "Reclaiming a Revolutionary Past: War Veterans, Pensions, and the Struggle for Recognition," *Journal Of The Early Republic* 39:3 (2019), 467–501 and Laurel Daen, "Revolutionary War Invalid Pensions and the Bureaucratic Language of Disability in the Early Republic," *Early American Literature* 52:1 (2017), 141–167.

17. Cornelia H. Dayton and Sharon V. Salinger, *Robert Love's Warnings: Searching for Strangers in Colonial Boston* (Philadelphia: University of Pennsylvania Press, 2014). O'Brassill-Kulfan, *Vagrants and Vagabonds*, Lockley, *Welfare and Charity in the Antebellum*, 21.

18. Melish, *Disowning Slavery*, 190–191. Herndon, *Unwelcome Americans*, 18–20. Parker, *Making Foreigners*, chap. 4. Stephen Middleton, *The Black Laws: Race and the Legal Process in Early Ohio* (Athens: Ohio University Press, 2005).

19. The quotation on neighbors, friends, and churches, comes from Congressman Ron Paul's remarks as a presidential candidate in the September 12, 2011 Republican debate hosted by CNN in Tampa, Florida. This assumption that there was no welfare before the 1930s is widely held among political leaders, though, and cuts

across party lines. For example, in answering press questions after introducing a major welfare reform act in 1996, President Bill Clinton talked about "when welfare was created" as being "60 years ago." See "Text of President Clinton's Announcement on Welfare Legislation" in *New York Times*, 1 August 1996, Section A, 24, available at www.nytimes.com/1996/08/01/us/text-of-president-clinton-s-announcement-on-welfare-legislation.html.

20. David B. Danbom, *Born in the Country: A History of Rural America* (Baltimore: Johns Hopkins University Press, 1995), 87. I came across this witty point in Daniel Blackie, "Disability, Dependency, and the Family in the Early United States," in Michael A. Rembis and Susan Burch, Eds., *Disability Histories* (Urbana: University of Illinois Press, 2014), 20.

CHAPTER 1

⤫

Overseer of the Poor

How William Larned Spent
Public Funds on the Needy

Stepping out of his house one morning, Mr. William Larned, Esquire, cuts a fine figure. Let's follow him as he walks on North Main Street, in Providence, Rhode Island. It is summer. The year is 1811. Mr. Larned walks briskly toward the grand Market House, just a few blocks from home. A young man is with him: one of his grown sons. A year shy of sixty, the elder Larned has outlived many of his contemporaries. Perhaps he wears knee breeches, which are out of style, but the way he carries himself projects confidence. He looks prosperous, even if he is not. He is not a rich merchant, not a Brown, one of whom has recently given $5,000 and his name to the local college. Nevertheless, he is aware of his own importance. He is a man trusted with important business of the town. Just a couple weeks ago, he was elected to a key government post—Overseer of the Poor—for the twentieth time. Few of his neighbors could boast that, not even the Browns.[1]

North Main Street is full of horses, wagons, carriages, and pedestrians. Some people are smartly dressed, like Larned: wearing richly dyed colors, or elegant, shiny black. If riding in a carriage, their boots are high above the messy road, about the level of an adult's shoulder. They exchange courtesies with Larned: a doffed hat, or a small bow. Others, walking or riding in wagons, are more humbly dressed. Their drab-colored clothes are stained

How Welfare Worked in the Early United States. Gabriel J. Loiacono, Oxford University Press. © Oxford University Press 2021. DOI: 10.1093/oso/9780197515433.003.0002

with work and with the muck and dust of the middle of the road, an avenue of packed earth, topped with horse, dog, and pig dung. How do the drably dressed react to Mr. Larned? Some take no notice. Others acknowledge him respectfully. They recall that Mr. Larned sent them food or firewood—or business—when they needed it. For yet others of the drably dressed, Mr. Larned passing by brings a moment of fear. They know his powers: to get them food and clothes, or to banish them from town. For those recently arrived, or even those just born somewhere else, Mr. Larned could upend their lives. He could send them on the road, with whatever possessions they can carry, to who knows where.

That is Thaddeus Smith's fear. A hard-working "truckman," he carries loads from place to place in his wagon. He and Mrs. Smith also grow vegetables and fruits in their rented garden. But born in Shrewsbury, Massachusetts, Smith has never bought land in Providence, as Mr. Larned has. That is why Thaddeus Smith is also headed to the Market House, pictured in Figure 1.1, this day. Smith has been summoned, probably by Larned, to come and explain himself to the town council. Directed to a room on the second floor, Smith enters, no doubt with hat in hand. The gentlemen sitting at the table go through the usual formalities. They call the meeting to order. The town clerk is absent so they engage a substitute: that son of William Larned's, who walked here with his father. Henry Larned is about twenty, and anxious to impress. But he cannot be as anxious as the forty-something Thaddeus Smith, whose wife and seven children are waiting to hear the outcome of this meeting.

The men in the room turn their attention to Smith. Tell us about your life and where you have lived, they prompt. Smith tells how he was born and raised in Shrewsbury, Massachusetts, but married his wife in Roxbury. They moved to Providence six years ago. Of his seven children, three are still at home, ranging in age from six years to fifteen months. When he admits that he has never owned property in Providence, or anywhere else for that matter, he can see in the gentlemen's faces that this has decided his case.

The Town Council makes up its collective mind. Smith and his family will have to leave. With no real estate, poor enough that he *might* need poor relief in the future, the authorities want him out of their jurisdiction. Two weeks, the town council gives him, "to depart from out of this Town." Smith is crestfallen. What will happen to all the vegetables Mrs. Smith planted? In the weeks to come, he will try one last, desperate gambit. He will present a petition signed by people who know him to be a hardworking, sober man. They will ask that he be allowed stay at least until the Fall, when he and Mrs. Smith can harvest the garden. The petition will be granted. The Smiths will

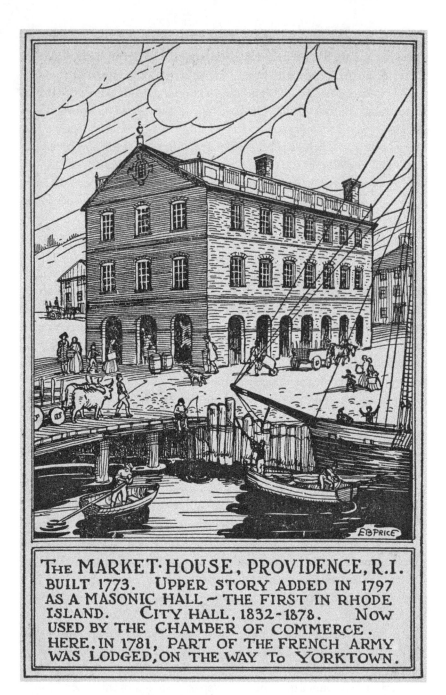

THE MARKET·HOUSE, PROVIDENCE, R.I.
BUILT 1773. UPPER STORY ADDED IN 1797
AS A MASONIC HALL ~ THE FIRST IN RHODE
ISLAND. CITY HALL, 1832-1878. NOW
USED BY THE CHAMBER OF COMMERCE.
HERE, IN 1781, PART OF THE FRENCH ARMY
WAS LODGED, ON THE WAY TO YORKTOWN.

Figure 1.1 This drawing of the Market House gives an idea of how it might have looked when William Larned and Thaddeus Smith met with the Town Council on the second floor in June, 1811. Edith Barringer Price drew this picture in the twentieth century, using records to imagine the Market House in the late eighteenth century. Although the tri-corner hats and knee breeches Price depicts would have been out of style by 1811, her artistic rendering gives an idea of the building's nearness to the river, and how much buying and selling happened there. One could imagine Larned as the man with the cane, or Smith as one of the men driving a wagon or a wheelbarrow. *This digital image of Edith Barringer Price's "Historicard" is reprinted courtesy of the Providence Public Library Digital Collections.*

be allowed to stay a couple months longer. That decision depends entirely on the mercy of the town council. Mr. Larned and his fellow overseers have done their duty. They discovered an outsider who had no legal right to town poor relief. Before Smith even asked for poor relief, the overseers brought him to the attention of the town council. Preemptively, they have made sure that Providence's considerable poor relief budget will be saved for those the town is legally required to help, and not those like Smith whose rights are in some other town.[2]

HOW OVERSEERS OF THE POOR WERE LIKE
THE ROMAN GOD JANUS

The overseers of the poor were a bit like the ancient Roman god Janus. With two faces, Janus was said to look both forward and backward, guarding the entrances of ancient Rome. In a similar way, overseers of the poor had two faces: a merciful face to the poor from their town and a stern face to the poor who were not locals. Moreover, overseers were gatekeepers of their towns, like the faces of Janus carved into ancient Roman arches. These Janus-faced overseers of the poor were elected in every municipality of the early United States. George Washington had served as a churchwarden, the colonial Virginia equivalent of an overseer of the poor. Whether in the counties of the middle, southern, and western states or the towns of New England, they were powerful government officials, entrusted with spending the largest portion of tax revenue in most municipalities. At a time when state taxes were lower than municipal taxes, and federal taxes were rare, overseers controlled the bulk of all tax dollars in the early United States. They disbursed these dollars to the needy of their towns, but also to local shopkeepers, homeowners, and others who provided goods and services to the needy. Engines of the economy and police of the population, it is hard to overstate the powers of overseers of the poor.[3]

In this chapter, you will read the story of one of these powerful men: William Larned. Larned had an unusually long run as an overseer, from 1792 to his death in 1828. His life story helps us understand four important aspects of poor relief in the early United States. First, it was expensive, costing more than any other local government service before 1830. Second, because it was so expensive, Larned was often under pressure to keep costs down. His constituents wanted him to provide humane care for as little money as possible. Third, early American poor relief was intended to be a seamless safety net. With deep roots in early modern English laws, it was supposed to provide everything necessary for survival, for anyone in need, born in the state, whose family could not care for them. Fourth, overseers like Larned depended on lots of local women and men to do the actual work of relieving the poor. These local women and men, in turn, earned part of their household income from the town treasury: they were *local government relief contractors*. Thus in ways that we do not usually appreciate, citizens of the early republic enjoyed an expensive, extensive safety net, administered by their local governments. This safety net, in theory, would give housing, food, medical care, and fuel to anyone who needed it, while also putting money in the pockets of their neighbors.[4]

But Larned's powers could also be harsh. He was required by law to get families like Thaddeus Smith's warned out. For many of the needy, Larned's was not a face of benevolence, but a face of control, what some historians term "social control." He forced poor families out of town if they had no ancestors with a settlement in Providence. In so doing, he and countless local officials around the nation restricted the mobility of newly independent Americans. Moreover, Larned went beyond the letter of the law in forcing out families of African or Native ancestry. The racist application of the poor laws, as well as its effects on mobility, will be themes of chapter 2.[5]

As we trace these themes in Larned's career, we also learn that Larned himself was in need. He did not need poor relief, but he needed his job distributing poor relief in order to support his large, far from rich family. When voters thought he had failed to keep poor relief costs low enough, he lost his job and most of his income for half a year. In Larned's career, we can see the contradictory mixture of impulses behind early American poor relief: benevolence mixed with social control, humanitarianism mixed with taxpayer concerns about costs, neighborly concern mixed with racism. Hopes for a better and more harmonious community mixed with anxiety about needing poor relief oneself. All of these impulses shaped Larned's work as overseer of the poor. After all, anyone might find themselves under the scrutiny of the overseer of the poor, even William Larned himself.

MIGRATING TO REVOLUTIONARY PROVIDENCE AND BECOMING A "FREEMAN"

About forty years before meeting Thaddeus Smith, shortly before the Revolutionary War, Larned was a newcomer to Providence. Did the overseer of the poor scrutinize him? Did he feel vulnerable to the overseer's awesome powers? It is difficult to know. But Larned's situation had been similar to what Smith's would be. In the early 1770s, Larned was the one coming from a country town across colonial borders.

He was born in 1752, in what was then Killingly, Connecticut, about thirty miles from Providence, or a half-day's travel in the 1770s. Descended from English Puritans, who left England for Massachusetts Bay in the 1630s, his family was prominent in Killingly. When William was little, his father Samuel was commissioned as a lieutenant to fight in the French and Indian War. When Samuel returned, he resumed his work as a farmer, on land that his father had farmed before him. William's uncle, Simon, was a storekeeper in town, as well as the town clerk. With uncle or father, young William had likely made the trip to Providence frequently. It was the nearest big market for anything a farming household might grow or manufacture.[6]

Why leave Killingly, when the Larned family had achieved so much there? Perhaps it was precisely for that reason: successful Larneds were everywhere in Killingly. William was the fifth of ten children borne by his mother, Rachel, including five sons and three daughters who survived childhood. In fact, in that startling naming practice of colonial New Englanders, William was the second son to be named William, after an older brother of that name died at age two. Of the surviving siblings, William's two older brothers and one sister stayed in Killingly, but the rest scattered. After his father died in 1770, William was the first brother to go. He left the small town of 2,000, where he and his kin were well-known, to a larger town of 9,200 or so, where few would recognize him.[7]

When he arrived in Providence, the long struggle over taxation and representation was reaching a tense crescendo. But even in these unusual circumstances, the town's overseers of the poor should have been vigilant: challenging and warning out newcomers like Larned, who might fall on hard times. Larned would have been no fool about warning out. His uncles and father were active in Killingly town government. Indeed, William probably came equipped with a note from his own uncle, the town clerk, assuring Providence's overseers that Killingly would support William in his time of need, if that ever came.

In 1774, as Parliament passed the Boston Port Act in punishment for the Boston Tea Party, William married Sally Angell. Genealogists refer to her as "Mrs. Angell," suggesting that she was a widow when she and William married. Perhaps it had been the widow Angell who drew William to Providence in the first place. Probably, she had some property left from her first marriage that made it possible for William to escape the attention of the overseers of the poor, and get a start in business in Providence. Soon, William and Sally had two daughters, Teresa and Betsey.[8]

Providence was a stronghold of anti-Parliament sentiment. Already in the summer of 1772, local merchants had spearheaded the burning of a British customs schooner, the *H.M.S. Gaspee*. No longer would the *Gaspee* stop Rhode Islanders from smuggling imports past the customs collectors. In March 1775, radicals staged a Providence Tea Party. They instructed the town's official town crier to walk around at noon announcing that tea would be burned near the Market House at five o'clock. They burned three hundred pounds of tea and a copy of a speech by Lord North. A "son of liberty" went around town painting over any sign that had the word "tea" on it. That the town crier had started the proceedings showed that all of this destruction of property had the imprimatur of the town's government and "freemen," the men who owned enough property to vote. The message was clear: Providence was a "patriot" town. Two town councilmen who refused to sign a "test act," affirming the legitimacy of the Revolution, would be forced out of office in November, 1776.[9]

The rest of the powerful town fathers, including the councilmen and the overseers of the poor, were choosing resistance to Parliament and the Crown. If one's local government chose the patriot path, one would not be throwing off all government by declaring independence from the Crown. The town or county, the most immediate face of government a subject could meet, would provide continuity through the otherwise turbulent process of revolution. In both Larned's hometown of Killingly and his newly adopted town of Providence, local officials would lead their towns against the Crown. William's uncle Simon would remain clerk of Killingly right through the tax crisis, the Revolution, even up to George Washington's inauguration as president in 1789.

No Loyalist himself, William had a post with the Continental Army from 1778 to 1780, serving as a "Commissary of Forage for the State of Rhode Island." He used his business contacts to bring Continental Congress dollars or promissory notes to farmers or storekeepers while providing food, clothing, and other goods to Continental soldiers all over the new nation. This was a difficult job. The British Navy was on the lookout for rebel merchant ships buying goods from Europe, and the combined demands of the rebel, French, and British militaries was straining American farm and cloth production to the utmost. Continental commissaries were at a disadvantage compared to British commissaries, who could offer gold and silver coins. But successful commissaries grew rich and influential. By the time Larned took on the job, a new Commissary General had reorganized the department, offering more incentives to men who could get the job done. Taking commissions on purchases and wielding a lot of purchasing power (at least on paper), some Continental commissaries parlayed their work for the rebel cause into lucrative careers as merchants after the war. Indeed, as overseer of the poor, Larned would do a similar job: bring government dollars to householders and storekeepers he knew.[10]

Tragedy struck in June, 1780, when Sally Larned, née Angell, died. Records do not say why. But William was a widower at twenty-eight, with two daughters. He left his job as a commissary. One can only imagine his disappointment and uncertainty. The war was still raging. French forces arrived in Rhode Island in July to help the rebel cause, but there were still few victories for the Continentals. Meanwhile, Larned's private affairs were in tumult. Without his post with the Continental Army, and most of all without the vital labor of his wife, what could he do now?

He soon hit on a business plan, and Continental officers hit on a winning strategy. Rhode Islander Nathanael Greene confronted British forces under Lord Cornwallis in the Carolinas, always retreating, but denying Cornwallis a convincing victory. Meanwhile, Larned turned from being a buyer and seller for the Army into being a buyer and seller on his own account. By Spring, 1782, Larned was purchasing goods from around the Atlantic World and reselling them in Providence. Specializing in fabrics, he advertised that there were "EUROPEAN AND WEST-INDIA *GOODS to be bought worth the Money* At the STORE of *William Larned & Company*." Dazzling in diversity and descriptiveness, his list of fabrics for sale, reproduced in Figure 1.2, reads like a poem.

An ebullient salesman, Larned's pitch aimed at Americans who hoped to wear more than homespun. The war was not yet over, but rumors of peace were gathering. Americans had been largely cut off from imported goods for years. In other ads, Larned announced that "Good yellow Pine Boards, long Staves, Grain, Butter or Cheese, will be taken in Pay for the above Articles." The instability of currencies during the War made merchants eager to barter. Accepting farmers' goods instead of their cash also gave Larned some defense against critics. In the mid- to late 1780s, some argued that Americans were not truly independent from Britain if they still depended on British weavers and merchants for their clothing. Moreover, critics thought, imported goods were "luxuries," unnecessary and ultimately harmful to American character. Why not wear plain, American homespun instead of flower-bedecked chintz from India, those critics wondered. Keep American cash in the United States, they reasoned. Larned no doubt grew up wearing homespun cloth, woven by his mother Rachel or another relative. Probably, he helped in the spinning and carding process as a boy. But as a family man, he turned to imported cloth as a way to support himself and his daughters.[11]

He also found companionship again. In February 1784, newspapers reported the marriage of "Mr. William Larned, Merchant, to Miss Sally Smith, Daughter of John Smith, Esq." William was thirty-one. Sally was fifteen or sixteen. Later in life, this Sally Larned would put aside the nickname Sally

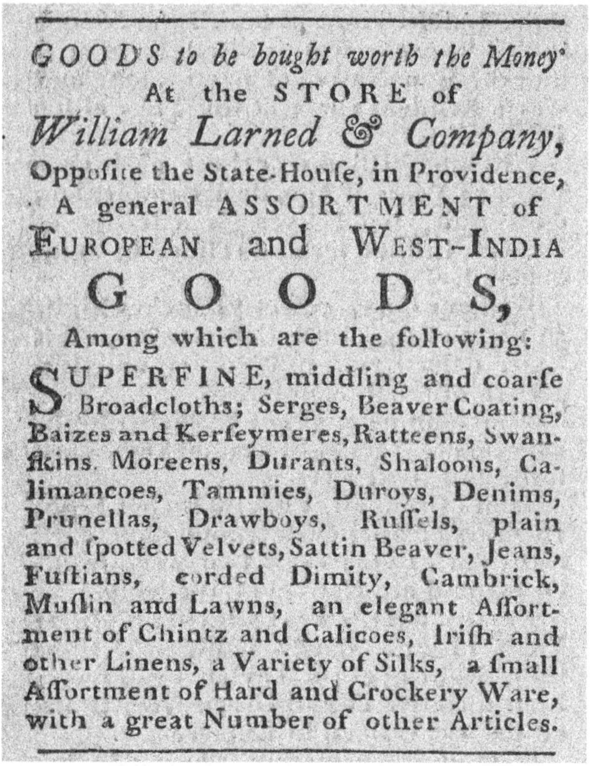

GOODS to be bought worth the Money*
At the STORE of
William Larned & Company,
Oppofite the State-Houfe, in Providence,
A general ASSORTMENT of
EUROPEAN and WEST-INDIA
G O O D S,
Among which are the following:
SUPERFINE, middling and coarfe
Broadcloths; Serges, Beaver Coating,
Baizes and Kerfeymeres, Ratteens, Swan-
fkins. Moreens, Durants, Shaloons, Ca-
limancoes, Tammies, Duroys, Denims,
Prunellas, Drawboys, Ruffels, plain
and fpotted Velvets, Sattin Beaver, Jeans,
Fuftians, corded Dimity, Cambrick,
Muflin and Lawns, an elegant Affort-
ment of Chintz and Calicoes, Irifh and
other Linens, a Variety of Silks, a fmall
Affortment of Hard and Crockery Ware,
with a great Number of other Articles.

Figure 1.2 This advertisement in the *Providence Gazette and Country Journal*, 8 June 1782, shows the variety of imported fabric Larned sold. Courtesy of the American Antiquarian Society.

and be known as Sarah, officially. But in 1784, as they began their household together, she was still Sally and was already expecting her first child. John Smith Larned was born August 15, 1784, six months to the day after Sally's and William's marriage, according to genealogists' records.[12]

His family suddenly growing again, Larned finally took steps to ensure that if they ever fell on hard times, his newly adopted town would take care of them. Having purchased real estate in Providence, Larned now applied to become a *freeman* of Providence. By becoming a *freeman*, Larned would get the right to attend town meetings and vote. Several times a year, a town official would walk around and announce a town meeting. In the eighteenth century a town "crier" announced the meetings while by the early nineteenth century, in Providence, the town sergeant used a drum to announce the meeting. Some meetings were called to address specific problems that came up. Other, more routine, meetings would elect town officers like the overseer of the poor, and still other meetings would elect state or federal officials, such as a representative to the United States Congress.[13]

Another right Larned would gain as a *freeman*, was something called a *settlement* in Providence for himself, his wife, their children and any of his descendants who did not acquire a *settlement* somewhere else. Having a *settlement* meant that you "belonged" to the town, in a legal sense. If you should ever fall on hard times, and your parents, grandparents, children, or grandchildren could not help you, your town would take responsibility for your well-being. Through the overseer of the poor, town taxpayers would foot the bill for your food, housing, firewood, doctor's bills, medicines, clothes, or whatever else was necessary to keep you alive and well. The overseer of the poor would spend what he thought was necessary, charge it to the Town Treasury, and every year, the Town Tax Assessor would add up all expenditures and include them in that year's property tax bill.

This often astonishes Americans living in the twenty-first century, but it is true: colonial and early republican Americans provided a robust, theoretically limitless social safety net for their fellow townspeople. If a neighbor with a *settlement* lacked food, and her family could not give it to her, the town provided it. If a neighbor with a settlement could not afford healthcare, and his family could not cover the costs, the town paid for doctors, nurses, and prescribed medicine. In fact, if your neighbor needed help and you gave it to them, chances were good that the town treasury would reimburse you for this help. Government-provided welfare, then, was not an invention of the twentieth century. Nor is government-sponsored healthcare a recent innovation. Both of these government services had been introduced into British North American colonies as some of the very first laws. Rhode Island and Providence Plantations, for example, had been created when four English towns united under one government and adopted a whole series of laws, including the Elizabethan Poor Law, in 1647.

The Elizabethan Poor Laws of 1598 and 1601 had summed up a series of legal innovations in English poor relief since the mid-1500s. These innovations had become necessary after Henry VIII took over English monasteries, which had traditionally provided much poor relief, and because a series of upheavals in the English economy drove more and more people to begging from town to town. After half a century of new policies to cope with poverty, Parliament had consolidated these reforms into one, big Elizabethan Poor Law. That law had made each local government responsible for its own poor, and had created the overseer of the poor position. The law insisted that parents, children, grandchildren, or grandparents be legally responsible for a needy individual. But if those relatives did not have the means, the local government had to provide the necessaries of life, somehow, to any needy person settled in that place. It was adopted wholesale by British North American colonies, as well as later American states, and structured American poor relief until the 1930s. When William Larned applied for the status of freeman and the legal settlement that came with it, he was doing what landowners in British North America had done for a century and a half already.[14]

If you did not have a settlement in the town you inhabited, like Thaddeus Smith in 1811, it was the overseer of the poor's job to have you "warned out" of town before you became "a charge on the town." These settlements, in theory, kept expenses even across jurisdictions, protecting any one town from being overrun with poor relief costs. In practice, overseers sometimes felt bound by humanity to provide assistance to anyone in very dire circumstances. If you were suddenly ill, and could not be safely moved, the overseers might absorb the cost of your care until you died or could be moved. To avoid these extra expenses, overseers would vigilantly assess residents of the town who did not have a settlement in order to warn them out at the first sign of potential need. For example, if William Larned had become seriously ill prior to gaining a settlement in Providence, the Providence overseers would have warned him out, legally requiring him to leave town in a certain amount of time. They also would have determined that his settlement lay in Killingly, where his father was settled.

After the Revolution, however, his place of settlement was changed to Providence. The September 1784 town meeting minutes note that Larned, "having purchased Real Estates in Providence," was "now nominated and propounded to be admitted as" a freeman. Likely, he had bought the small lot that he still owned in 1798, directly across from the State House, in downtown Providence, at the foot of College Hill. Seven months later, the town's freemen voted that "Messrs. William Larned and Israel Davis being duly Qualified are admitted freemen of the Town." At last, ten years after moving to the big town, Larned was "settled" in Providence. He could vote. He could run for town office. And, most importantly, if he or his wife or children ever were hungry or homeless or ill, they could depend on the town of Providence to *own* them, to take responsibility for their health and well-being, and take care of them as one of its own. William Larned now *belonged* to Providence. "Belonging to the Town," "Settled in the County," a "Charge upon the City," "Warned Out of the County," were all legal terms used frequently throughout the newly independent United States. These terms rolled off the tongues and pens of local officials throughout the country, filling the pages of municipal minute books. Soon, they would roll off the tongue of William Larned, as he quickly became involved in town government.[15]

In only the second election in which he could vote, at age 33, Larned was also a candidate and won two offices. He would be a member of the town's Fire-Engine Company No. 1, whose job it would be to fight fires in their ward of the town, as well as one of the seven Field Drivers. Called Hog Reeves in England, Field Drivers were a precursor to that villain of twentieth-century American cartoons: the Dog Pound Officer. Their job was to apprehend stray animals: cows, sheep, and horses. Not the most dignified of offices, Field Driver would be an entry-level position for William Larned. Within a year of becoming a Field Driver, the Rhode Island General Assembly appointed Larned to be one of Providence's justices of the peace. This was more a testament to the new freeman's political connections than to his legal expertise. It meant that he could add the honorific title "Esquire" to his name and that he could begin collecting some modest fees for his judicial work from the state. It also was a big expansion of the authority, rights, and privileges that Larned could exercise. As historian William Novak has pointed out, the status of early Americans was not so much a matter of whether they were "citizens," but a matter of how many of a "bundle of rights and privileges" they were able to accrue. This status included their ability to vote, of course, but also any offices they held; their membership in fraternal organizations; their standing in their church; and their authority over their own households, family, and servants. By this measure, William Larned was adding to his bundle of rights and privileges hand over fist in the late 1780s.[16]

He was also one of the hundreds of men statewide who provided continuity in local government, while national government underwent a period of great uncertainty. A new United States constitution was hammered out in Philadelphia in the summer of 1787. Providence freemen were overwhelmingly in favor of it. But by the spring of 1789, they had to watch a new United States form without them. The southern, rural part of the state had rejected the constitution and so Rhode Island was left out of the new country. Rhode Islanders had stormed out of the British Empire and then crashed out of the first United States of America in little more than decade. The most stable government they had was local government, which men like William Larned staffed whether there was a national constitution or not.[17]

By 1790, when Rhode Island finally rejoined the United States, Larned's work for town government was starting to become his most important source of income. That year, he was elected one of three Town Auditors, charged with evaluating the real estates and personal estates of all heads of household every year. This evaluation would be the basis on which each taxpayer would be assessed in the annual town tax, the largest tax which

Americans in this period had to pay. Elected by the very people whose property he had to assess, Larned had a delicate task. Two years after that, came a big promotion, one that would become part of his identity and provide income for his family for the rest of his life. It would also have a profound impact on many other lives.

AN OVERSEER OF THE POOR, ELECTED
THIRTY-SIX TIMES

In 1792, the town meeting selected William Larned and two other freemen to share the posts of Assessor of Rates and Overseer of the Poor. In other towns, these jobs were kept separate. But it made sense to combine them. Since overseers of the poor spent the most town money, few knew better than they how much in taxes would be needed to cover a year's public expenses. Combining these duties into one super-office symbolizes a truth that it has become easy to forget: Americans in the early republic paid more in taxes for the welfare of their needy neighbors than for any other government service.[18]

In 1789, for example, the year George Washington took office as US president in New York, that city spent £4,243 on "Poor-House" expenses out of a total budget of £10,364. The next largest expenses, paying for watchmen and lamp-lighting were each well under £2,000. For a comparison, Providence spent £200 out of a total town budget of £400 on poor relief that same year. The other half of the budget would be divided among bridges, highways, and debts. By 1800, the town of Providence was raising annual tax revenue of $12,000, of which poor relief was $3,471.24, the single largest item, though no longer near a majority. Of that poor relief sum, about $844 was recouped in a variety of ways: state support for "foreign paupers," and individual family members providing cash or bond for the care of relatives. The rest had to be covered by the town tax. The relative expense of poor relief could be even greater in small towns. In Scituate, a rural town near Providence, for example, the 1796 town expenses include $470 in poor relief out of a total town budget of $685. Historian Ruth Wallis Herndon has found a similar story in other small Rhode Island towns after the Revolutionary War: "the costs of caring for the poor dominated the budget, generally accounting for at least half of the town's disbursements." Southern jurisdictions, where responsibility for the poor was transferred from Anglican parish vestrymen to county authorities unevenly in the late 1700s, are harder to compare to other local expenses until after 1800.[19]

The poor's share of the town budget declined slowly over the years, but remained one of the greatest expenses. By 1825, Providence's annual town tax had grown to $30,000, of which Larned, as overseer of the poor, spent $7,367.35. That number was close to the costs of road and bridge improvement, schools, and paying off town debts. Other parts of the country were similar. Richmond, Virginia, a smaller city than Providence, spent roughly the same amount of money on poor relief in 1825. In New York City that year, almshouse and outdoor relief combined to make up between one fifth and one fourth of the whole city's budget, by far the greatest single expenditure. Thus William Larned's new office was of great importance to the town taxpayers. He and his colleagues would be responsible for the single greatest town expense. If they spent a lot, the town would be taxed a lot. If they spent little, the town would be taxed little. Tax records for the year 1825 show that Larned himself was still paying a small amount of property tax to the local government: $2.80, or $967 in terms of unskilled worker's wages at the time this book was published. Others paid far more. William Richmond, a town councilman by 1825, paid $30.80 that year, the equivalent today of $10,637. One of the wealthiest men in town, Sullivan Dorr, paid $257.60, the equivalent of $88,964. Where did all this money go?[20]

It is almost too obvious to say, but historians sometimes forget how much overseers helped people in need. Extant records of Providence from Larned's career are replete with examples of the help that overseers gave to settled Providencians. Thousands of receipts show overseers paying for everything from "meat," "supplies," "corn," "pork," and the "necessaries of life," to clothes, fabric, thread, firewood, rent, "shingles," and healthcare, including full-time nurses, doctors' visits, and medicine. One such receipt can be seen in Figure 1.3. During Larned's career as overseer of the poor, "outdoor relief," goods, services, or money given to people in their own homes, or their neighbors' homes, was his stock in trade. While he also oversaw people sent to the workhouse, as chapter 3 will discuss in more detail, these were usually people for whom no other arrangements could be made.[21]

Sometimes, overseers would give cash directly to the person or family in need, as when Larned asked the town treasurer: "Sir. Please to Advance Comfort Eddy one dollar to procure necessaries for his Family." In one unusual circumstance, after a contagious disease had swept through town, Larned gave cash or necessaries in the amounts of five to fifty dollars to a long list of sufferers. More often, the overseers would set up accounts for paupers with local merchants, especially grocers. For example, in the spring of 1804, grocer Samuel Thurber, Jr., presented a bill to the overseers, who approved it and gave it to the treasurer. In the bill, Thurber

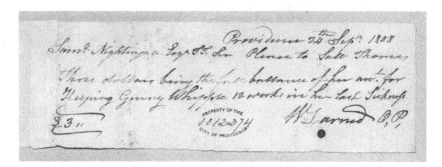

Figure 1.3 This 1808 scrip asks the Town Treasurer to pay Sall Thomas three dollars for 'Keeping Ginny Whipple 12 weeks in her last Sickness.' It is one of hundreds, if not thousands, of such requests signed by William Larned, to scores of local government relief contractors. Note that Larned included the initials "O.P." for Overseer of the Poor after his name. Courtesy the Rhode Island Historical Society (RHi X17 4215, Town of Providence, "Receipt to Sall Thomas for Keeping Ginny Whipple," 24 September 1808, Ink on Paper.").

detailed the groceries he had provided to four paupers: "Ruth Thurber alias Ruth Smith . . . or Ruth Tittenberry," "The Widdow Taber," "The Widdow Scranton," and "The Lame Negro." Altogether, Thurber had provided these four people with cheese, molasses, flour, fish, ginger, tea, medicine, wood, mutton, veal, potatoes, candles, and coffee. Considering that Providence was just coming out of its winter, and that potatoes were one of the few vegetables still available, this seems a rounded diet. Being a pauper did not mean you did not have access to good food. However, not all paupers were treated equally. Not only is the injured African American not given a name in the bill, he is also allowed the most basic diet: only meal and molasses each week.[22]

Receipts like these point to two very important truths about poor relief in the early republic. First, relief could be given out in a discriminatory way. Overseers might assume that people who have long been poor, or people of color, were entitled to a different standard of aid than those who only recently fell on hard times, or were of European descent. Overseers had a lot of discretion in how they administered relief. Second, poor relief was a major driver of the local economy.

LOCAL GOVERNMENT RELIEF CONTRACTORS

Overseeing the bulk of the town's budget, William Larned and his colleagues made arrangements with townspeople that could pay anywhere from a few dollars to hundreds in a year. In addition to setting up accounts with local merchants, overseers were constantly making temporary contracts with ordinary homeowners or healers which helped supplement a household's income. In the Summer of 1804, for example, Larned's distinctive flourish of a signature can be found on receipts to several different people. Nathaniel Sivich received twelve dollars for providing board, or meals, to Freelove Olney for twelve weeks. Elizabeth Convers, a landlady, received three dollars for three months' rent for Ruth Mitchel, who had since died. Lucy Cozzens received six dollars for letting Pamelia Atkinson live and eat in her house for an unspecified amount of time. A few years earlier, Amos Hawes had received the sum of fifty dollars "for taking James Drown, a poor Child, to bring up, and [take] an Indenture of him." While this was considered a good opportunity for young Drown, Amos Hawes got a great deal: a large amount of cash in return for feeding and housing and bringing up a boy who would likely repay him many times over with his labor for the Hawes household.[23]

These are just a few examples of how the overseers of the poor spent significant amounts of the town's tax money in ways that helped both the needy, and also helped townspeople who were not desperately poor, all of whom benefited from this robust network of help. As historian Ruth Wallis Herndon describes it: "Virtually all inhabitants could contribute to supporting the poor and thereby earn extra income in the way of payments from the town treasury." Herndon's list of what a townsperson could be paid for includes: making clothes, making shoes, providing food, delivering food, building a house, repairing windows and chimneys, delivering babies, nursing the ill, making coffins, digging graves, providing shelter and heat, and generally including the needy in one's household. Historian Elna Green describes this complicated tangle of people who were paid to help the needy as "the welfare/industrial complex." Although in the early republic it only occasionally involved factories, which is what we usually mean by "industrial," this label captures the important truth that is so often overlooked. Not only was poor relief extensive in the early republic, but it touched many, many people and bolstered the personal incomes of dozens if not hundreds of individuals in a given town in a given year.[24]

Few household incomes benefitted as much as those of the overseers' themselves. It is not totally clear how overseers of the poor were paid prior to 1819, when the town settled on a salary. Before that, the job was combined with the office of Assessor of Taxes, so the overseer enjoyed a small cut of the total town taxes collected each year. A rare printed budget exists for the fiscal year 1799–1800. As Tax Assessor, Larned received a share of the $480 in "Commissions for collecting &c. the $10000 Dollar Tax" of the previous year. The budget notes that $343.63 was paid for "the Services of the Justices of the Peace, Committees, Surveyors,

Town-Sergeant, Constables, etc." Larned and two colleagues also directed the huge sum of $3,471.24 listed as "Overseer of the Poor orders" in that 1799–1800 fiscal year. Perhaps the overseers' payments were part of the $1,187.73 that was vaguely accounted as "Remainder of Expences for the Town." As historian Nicholas Parrillo has explained, American government officials in this period got all sorts of ad hoc payments for the services they provided. Instead of a salary, they received bounties and what Parrillo terms "facilitative payments." Bounties were fees taxpayers paid per task, such as for capturing a criminal or escorting a warned-out pauper to the town line. Facilitative payments were fees that customers of the government paid for doing something they wanted, like granting a permit or reviewing an application. Receipts document countless small facilitative payments and bounties given to Larned from the Providence Town Treasury for a variety of small tasks, and for the big task of serving as overseer of the poor. By some account or other, overseers were receiving regular sums of money from the town. Extant receipts from 1808 show payments to the overseers in the significant amounts of twenty-five, forty, and even sixty dollars. While the receipts do not explain what the payment is for, they are paid to two of the overseers and to one of Larned's children.[25]

In addition to his pay, and the high profile of his office, there was another way in which Larned benefitted from being overseer of the poor. His importing store, the one that had sold fine fabrics and other goods, did a brisk business selling these goods to the town for use by the poor. In what might now be considered an unethical use of his government office, Larned was able to use his position to direct some of the town's business to himself. Larned, the importer of fine fabrics, sold fabric and thread to the poor of the town, with money controlled by Larned, the overseer of the poor. An 1808 receipt, reproduced in Figure 1.4, details the sales which Larned made to the poor, paid for by town moneys which were his to dispose of. This receipt accounts for almost a year of sales, expenses, and overseer-related errands, adding up to $223.27. It includes calico, other kinds of cotton, coating, and thread, as well as clothes that someone made. There are stockings and a shawl for Deborah Reed, a handkerchief and trousers for Tom Ingraham. Some, like Violet Matthewson and "the Portuguese in the Work house" got raw materials: thread, cotton, and molds. Whether they were making their own clothes or making clothes to sell is unclear. Larned also charged for "making" jackets for the "Portuguese in the Work House." In an 1806 receipt, Larned had charged for "Mending shoes for S Pitts & Child and Susan Stoakes Children" as well as "making shirts" for Mr. Gerong. A similar receipt exists for Larned's co-overseer, John Spurr, whose grocery store provided food to some of the town's paupers. Quite

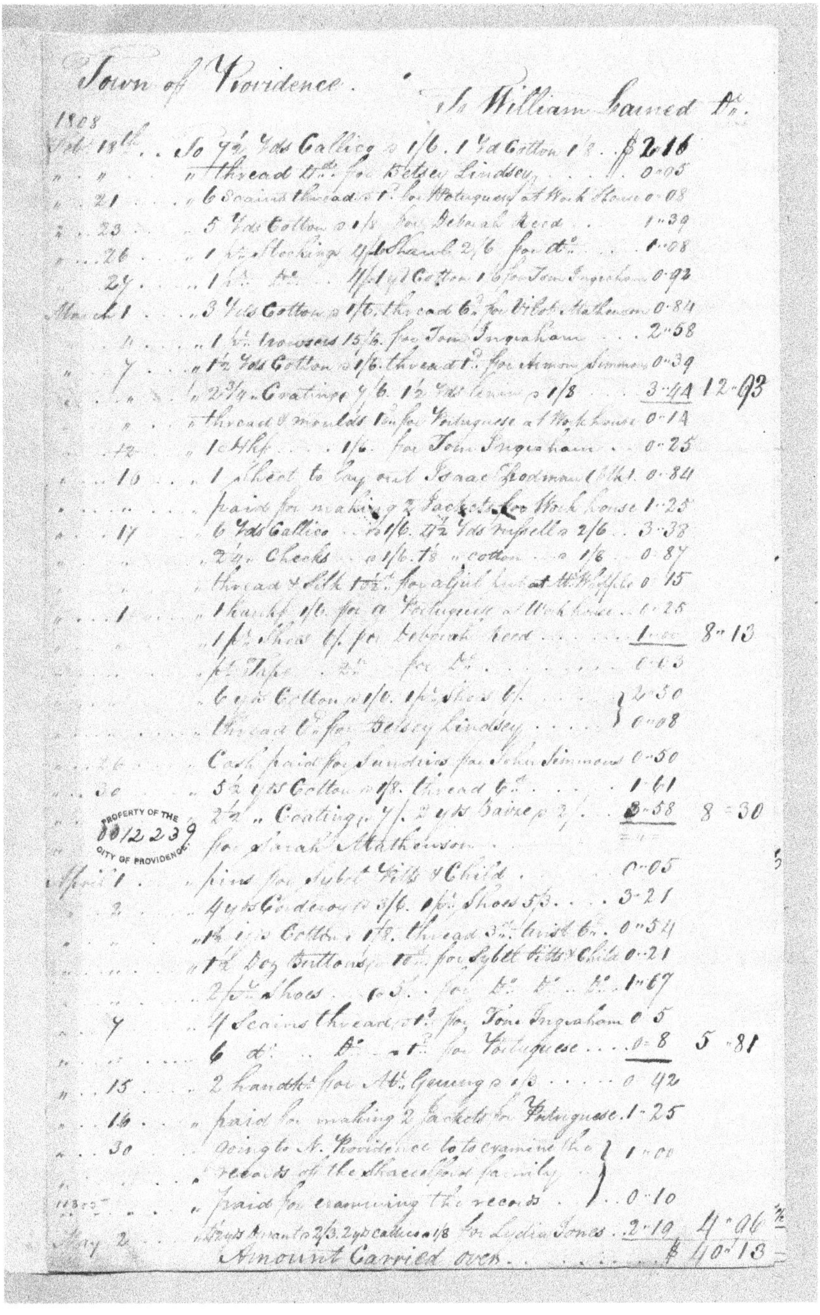

Figure 1.4 This is the first page of a lengthy account: Larned's summary of all of his money spent and goods given for the paupers of Providence, for which he expects reimbursal. Continuing for pages, and covering most of the year 1808, it adds up to $223.27. Courtesy the Rhode Island Historical Society (RHi X17 4216, Town of Providence, "Town of Providence to William Larned," 1808, ink on paper).

literally *trading* on their positions as overseers, Spurr and Larned found multiple ways to use the post to add to their families' incomes.[26]

Who did the jacket-making and shoe-mending for which Larned was paid? His wife, Sarah Larned? His daughters, Teresa or Betsy Larned? A servant in the Larned household? It is hard to know. The goods and services women provided to the poor were not often publicly recognized. They were paid for, but paid to husbands, fathers, masters, whose names alone were written on the receipts. In some ways, William Larned was a middleman in the shirt transaction between the women of his household and Mr. Gerong. And the women of his household were not unique: In countless houses, women did the hard work of clothing, feeding, and cleaning not only their own families but other people in need.[27]

Sarah Larned's labor was part of the household's survival, then, in both paid and unpaid ways. Sarah's and William's marriage was a particularly fertile one. It bore more similarity to the marriages of their Puritan New England ancestors than to marriages of the early republic, which tended to produce fewer children. Over the course of a forty-four-year marriage, as young Sally became known as matronly Sarah, Sarah and William had fourteen children together. They lost three in childhood: Eliza, their fifth child, in 1791; Daniel, their eighth child; and another Eliza, their fourteenth child. Including William's two daughters with Sally (Angell) Larned, Sarah and William were parents to at least sixteen children, raising thirteen to adulthood. By the twelfth time Sarah had given birth, to Sophia Larned in 1801, she had been pregnant for 108 months, the equivalent of nine years of her seventeen-year marriage to William. At no point in her marriage so far had she not been caring for children. Besides William, Sarah undoubtedly had some help. The census of 1790 had noted the presence of five "free white females" and one "slave" in the house. This suggests that there was one "free white female" apart from Sarah and her daughters, and one enslaved person, though it is not clear whether this was a man or woman, boy or girl.[28]

Having an enslaved person in their household in 1790 made the Larned family unusual for Providence. One of Larned's grandsons, Edwin Channing Larned, would become a noted antislavery lawyer in Illinois, said to have tangled with Stephen A. Douglas over the issue. But a long lifetime before that, in 1790, William Larned appeared not to share his neighbors' growing antislavery sentiment. Rhode Island had introduced *gradual emancipation* in early 1784. Few Rhode Islanders hung on to slaves despite after that. In 1790, there were only forty-eight enslaved people in the town of Providence. Roughly three percent of Providence households had any enslaved people in them.[29]

By the next census, in 1800, there were no slaves in Larned's household or in the entire town of Providence. But Larned now had a household of twelve, including one person under the category "All other free persons except Indians not taxed." This meant one person of the twelve in Larned's house was classified as not "white" by the census taker. Whether the Larneds had manumitted their former slave and kept him or her on as a servant, or whether this was a new person, is not clear. Freed slave or newly bound servant, this "other free person" was most likely a woman or girl of color, brought into the household in order to help Sarah with the children and the laborious tasks of washing clothes, cleaning floors, plucking chickens, pickling vegetables, and perhaps mending the clothes of the poor.[30]

How did Larned get the power to spend town money on his wife's, daughter's, or servants' work? He accumulated political capital. Larned had been building a public reputation and cultivating friends for years before he became an overseer. After becoming an overseer in 1792, his influence and power only increased further. By 1801, a Jeffersonian Republican newspaper in Providence was bemoaning Larned's influence in the Federalist-dominated town. Derisively terming the Federalists the "Anglo-Feds," a letter writer who called himself "EEL POT" complained that the Federalists were banking on a majority of five hundred votes in Providence alone. EEL POT asked the freemen of Providence, "where are your Rights, Liberties, and Sentiments to act for yourselves?" Implying the answer to his own question, EEL POT suggested that leading Federalists abused their power and patronage in order to ensure votes from people who needed jobs, business, or favors from them. Specifically naming only two Providence Federalists, John Dorrance and William Larned, EEL POT sarcastically laid out the consequences of refusing to defer to these two men

> if you do not obey . . . you will be waited on by one of the drag-committee, and if you then refuse to obey their mandate, you will forever lose their clemency; and Oh! What an awful situation you will then be in.[31]

Despite EEL POT's sarcasm and bravado, he seemed to feel real intimidation from John Dorrance and William Larned. He believed they could and would punish less powerful men who did not support them politically. That an overseer of the poor and cloth merchant should inspire such fear is another testament to the power of the position of overseer of the poor. Indeed, EEL POT's claim is perfectly plausible. Votes were not secret in the town meetings that chose town officers and government officials. Would Larned direct poor relief business to a grocer or doctor who had voted against him or against the Federalists? Republicans found it difficult to unseat Federalists in Providence town politics. Indeed, not long after EEL POT's complaint, Larned gained a new political office: representative to the Rhode Island's legislature, the General Assembly, elected in 1803 and again in 1804.[32]

By the 1810s, Larned depended on government offices for his income. There is no more evidence that he was in the cloth import business by that decade. In addition to being overseer of the poor and assessor of taxes for thirty-five years all together, Larned was also, at various points, a representative to the state legislature, a justice of the peace, the manager of various public and private lotteries, a public auctioneer, a notary public, and a member of countless committees to investigate "nuisances," or other matters that came up. All of these positions brought Larned public reputation and privileges. Most also brought income in the form of "facilitative payments" or fees. Hustling—for years—Larned could patch together an income from this hodgepodge of jobs. The job of overseer of the poor eventually brought the most stable form of income of all: a salary.

All these "offices" also earned Larned an actual, physical office: a room in which to do business. An 1814 ad for Larned's work as a commissioner of probate told readers that he could be found every other Saturday in "the office of Wm. Larned, in the southwest room in the market-house chambers." The Market House, the building on the far right of Figure 1.5, had just been built when Larned moved to Providence. It served as both a market and offices for town officials. Given the way the advertisement carefully describes the location of this office, it may be that William Larned had only recently moved in there. As the years went by, though, this room in the southwest corner of the Market House would become known as "William Larned's office." From this office, he would walk around town, scrutinizing newcomers. From this office, Larned would collect the fees he needed to support his many growing children. Maintaining his connections to the Federalist political establishment, Larned worked hard to keep this office.[33]

Although support for Federalists nationally sharply declined after the War of 1812, they remained strong in pockets of New England. Disappointed with another Federalist victory in 1817, the editor of the *Providence Patriot & Columbian Phenix* accused Federalist leaders in Newport of outright bribery in winning the election. In particular, he alleged, "The office of an overseer of the poor was offered to one" potential swing voter in Newport. That the office of overseer of the poor could be considered a bribe suggests how many perquisites came with it. It also suggests that lots of people might want the job, and helps explain how William Larned finally lost an election for overseer of the poor.[34]

Figure 1.5 By the end of the War of 1812, at the latest, Larned had his own office for government business on the second floor of the Market House, the building on the far right of this engraving. Depicting the Market House around 1823, this rendering gives an idea of how the buildings around the Market House had changed in the two generations since the depiction in Figure 1.1. The Market House was still a place of buying and selling on the ground floor, town government business on the second floor. As it remains in the twenty-first century, it was just steps from the Providence River. This image, entitled "Beehive of Providence, Market Square, circa 1823" is a fragment from a bank membership certificate, engraved by Annin & Smith, Boston, reproduced courtesy of the Providence City Archives. I am also grateful to the Quahog Annex blog *A Rhode Island Thing* for collecting images of the Market House over the years.

HOW WILLIAM LARNED LOST HIS JOB AND THEN REGAINED IT

1819 was a famously bad year for the United States economy. In 1818, the Bank of the United States, the repository for the United States government, had begun to call in loans and sharply contract the credit it gave to other banks. In a domino effect, Americans began to lose confidence in their local banks, asking for withdrawals from their savings accounts in gold and silver coins. These local banks, in turn, called in loans to make sure they had enough gold and silver, or they refused to pay in gold and silver. Many banks were forced to close as a result of the crisis of confidence. Historians have long called this the Panic of 1819. More recently, some have called it "the Great Hard Times." Prices for factory goods and farm produce dropped dramatically. It took credit to keep factories and ships afloat. As credit dried up, wages fell and unemployment rose, especially in cities. While most of New England fared better than the South and West, Rhode Island saw a lot of bankruptcies. Banks had not been as conservative there as in other New England states, and so the Panic of 1819 hit hard.[35]

One Rhode Islander who saw his loans called in was Samuel Larned, the son of William. Samuel was working as a merchant in Cadiz, Spain. Even there, the long arm of his creditor found him. Samuel owed a great deal of money to a big importing and exporting firm in Providence called Brown & Ives. While he was in Cadiz, his father tried to negotiate some way out and he wrote Samuel about it in October of 1819. "My dear Son," he wrote, "I am unable to write you so favorably as I wish," even if "I however dont entirely dispair." William had tried to visit Brown and Ives: "I call'd at their Counting Room . . . but neither of them was there. . . ." During other visits to the Counting Room, William had had to listen to the merchants' anger at his son: "the debt is large though nothing for them, yet it makes them sore, and at first [they] were very crusty about it," Larned admitted. He concluded on an upbeat note: "they have since show'd some tokens of a lissening ear so that I have some hope." For this powerful overseer of the poor, though, to endure the crustiness of these merchants underscores how much at their mercy he and his family were. As overseer, he usually held the power in his interactions with fellow townspeople. In the counting room, he was the one without power. The best he could tell Samuel was that the merchants "have both repeated[ly] assured me that they never would hurt nor distress you in any manner or way about it for they had no expectation you could ever pay them." In other words, the merchants would not be sending the law after Samuel because they did not think it would do any good: Samuel could not repay his debt. He was bankrupt. Already, in April of 1819, Samuel had paid off creditors in Cadiz by signing over "his estate and effects." Now, there seems to have been nothing left. Clearly, his father did not have the kind of money that could protect his son from debt collection either.[36]

Not only that, but Samuel had been engaged to be married in Cadiz. Letters from William to Samuel refer to a future daughter-in-law for William as early as January of 1817. But Spanish-language letters from Mariana Fudela to Samuel make it clear that he had broken off this long engagement by early 1819, probably because of his finances. Achingly, Mariana wrote to Samuel in February of 1819 that she forgave him and that no one in her house had any bad feeling for him. With much emotion, she closed her letter thus: "I remain, with great sincerity and good affection, your truest friend." Without a doubt, 1819 had been a bad year for the Larned family, both professionally and personally. William urged Samuel to cut his losses and come home: "I really think you had better come home and try some other course." Besides, William added warmly, "it is not possible for you to conceive my dear son the real heartfelt pleasure it would give your Parents and all the rest of the dear family to see and embrace you once more." Without even a pause for punctuation, William added "I am growing old now Sixtysix altho I enjoy good health and hold my Age remarkably well, yet I am . . . on the down hill side of life yet it seems as if it would considerably renew my age if I could be bless'd with the pleasure of beholding you again." William missed his son sorely, and also worried mightily for Samuel's ability to provide for himself. But Samuel was not the only Larned to hit uncertain times in 1819.[37]

As the Panic of 1819 unfolded, William Larned lost an election and lost his job. Alarmed at the spike in poor relief costs, some Providence freemen decided to make a significant change in the office of overseer of the poor. Through word of mouth, a plan was proposed that would reduce the number of overseers of the poor/assessors of taxes from three to one, and this one overseer/assessor would receive the considerable salary of $1000 per year. This salary, when compared against an unskilled laborer's wage, and estimated in twenty-first century dollars, could be considered the equivalent of more than $200,000. When rumors of this plan circulated, though, a number of voters were instantly suspicious.[38]

The rumors were printed in a newspaper editorial only two days before the annual town meeting in which town officers were elected. The editor of the *Providence Patriot* made the proposal sound positively conspiratorial: "it is whispered," he wrote,

> that a project will be offered to the freemen, by virtue of which it is intended to unite the offices of assessor and overseer in one person, instead of three; which person shall receive a fixed salary of about a thousand a year. Wm. Larned, Esq. is the gentleman spoken of by some, to sustain this important system.

If painting this "project" as a conspiratorial "whisper" campaign had not made the editor's thoughts on the matter clear, he made quite plain what he thought of it in the next sentence:

> Those who are disposed to favor the project, and *those who are not disposed* to place the whole fiscal administration of the town in the hands of this gentleman, are advised to attend the meeting.

Putting "*not disposed*" in italics, the editor hoped to rally opposition to the plan before it was too late. He emphasized how much the town's finances were shaped by the overseer of the poor, who spent such a large fraction of the town's budget, and the assessor of taxes, who decided how much each property owner should pay.[39]

Larned had, by then, been one of three overseers/assessors for twenty-seven years, longer by far than anyone else. He had enjoyed support from voters, but that did not mean he could be overseer as long as he wanted. The freemen expected the overseer to deliver two things: decent care for the *settled* needy, and a relatively low tax bill. Failure to deliver on either of those, especially the latter, would anger them. Perhaps Larned had not delivered a low enough tax bill. Perhaps he did not make a good case for why he should be in charge of this office. But for one reason or another, the town meeting of Monday, June 7, 1819, did not go as expected.

For one thing, it was packed. That did not usually happen. In the words of the editor of the *Rhode Island American*, the meeting "was attended by a larger number of the citizens than it is believed have ever before convened in this town, on a similar occasion." It was also unusual for elections to be contested. On that day, the offices of Town Treasurer and Overseer of the Poor were contested. This caused the meeting to be "adjourned at a late hour in the afternoon." Normally, there was little turnover in town officers. As for the "whispered . . . project" to put William Larned, alone, in the job of assessing taxes and overseeing the poor, it must have generated much discussion. None of this discussion was recorded in the newspapers, except that the contests were conducted "without any improper heat." The end result for Larned was a loss. George Olney was elected to be the town's one and only overseer of the poor. But things were not as bad as they could have been. The freemen decided not to combine both the office of assessor and overseer into one person. Instead, they maintained the three assessors of taxes, and William Larned as one of them. The new overseer got only half of the proposed salary: $500 per year. Still, this was a substantial, stable salary. After years of hustling, Larned missed out on it.[40]

Why had William Larned been turned out of office and replaced with George Olney? He spent too much on poor relief, or so voters thought. As the editor of the *American* noted, when explaining why he was printing his newspaper on cheaper paper: "*Retrenchment* seems to the order of the day in every department of business." In the midst of these "Great Hard Times," government and private businesses were trying to spend less. Providence voters thought that with one overseer, whose salary was contingent on saving money, they could keep poor relief costs in check. They also thought that Olney, who had not held the job before, would be more inclined to make new cuts. And Olney set out to do just that. He took out a newspaper advertisement reminding ship captains of their duties to report all passengers they brought to town to him, so that he could quickly warn out any potential claimants on town poor relief. After three months, he started doing the job out of his own house, to avoid renting an office. He also began requiring inmates of the workhouse to do the tedious task of picking oakum. The job was to take old rope and pick it apart, strand by strand, into its constituent fibers. These fibers could then be mixed with tar and used to caulk ships. Sale of the oakum, Olney hoped, would help reduce expenses.[41]

Within just a few months, though, something went awry. In September, three months into the post, Olney announced that he would step down in December, six months into what was normally a one-year term. In November, Olney printed an explanation. He made two big complaints. First, it was too hard to reduce expenses while being humane to the poor. Second, partisan politicians in Providence had stymied his efforts. Olney did not name names, in this latter complaint, but it was clear that Larned or his friends had not been cooperative. "It is cause of serious regret," Olney chided, that those who knew poor relief best, "should be so far influenced by any motives, whether of party spirit or disappointment, as to withhold from me the *necessary* information . . . to facilitate useful arrangement, and render the business less perplexing and embarrassing." In other words, Larned and his political allies had frozen Olney out. They refused to help him do the job of overseer of the poor. They even seem to have denied him an office in the Market House, as Olney first rented an office and then worked out of his house.[42]

On top of the politics, though, Olney just found the role difficult. He had never had the job before, thought he could do it better than Larned, but concluded that he could not. The only cost-cutting plan he could think of, he wrote, "benefitting the town, without adding to the distress of the poor by reducing their allowances . . . would fall far short of the expectations and wishes of the freemen." He could not think of a "more efficacious way of favouring the publick interest, in this article of heavy expenditure." He tried. He failed. It was partly due to his political enemies frustrating him. But, he had to admit, it was also really difficult to save money on poor relief while still doing a reasonably decent job. This is a rare insight into the work of overseers of the poor, from an outsider who tried it out. Frustratingly for Olney, it was a political office in which "the gain is so inadequate to the vexation and trouble, and its duties so adverse to my habits and feelings." Moreover, Olney realized, however "correct may be my conduct," he would never achieve "any thing like *general satisfaction*." Voters would never be totally happy with their overseers of the poor. The voters expected efficient, effective help for their neighbors and low taxes. Achieving that was an elusive goal.[43]

William Larned was vindicated, then, and would soon be overseer of the poor again. When he lost the election, Larned had maintained his other offices in the town, and probably some of his income. He remained a town assessor, and would have been able to collect the fees from that position. In addition, he was appointed to a "Committee to prevent Nuisances" in the town, which could include such dangers to health as raw sewage, rotting offal, or other kinds of pollution thought to endanger townspeople's health. This, too, would have come with some small recompense. Then, after George Olney stepped down, Larned was quietly chosen to replace him by the town council. Now, the "whispered" project which the editor of the *Providence Patriot* had so disliked had almost come to fruition. Larned was not the only assessor of taxes and did not collect a salary of $1000. But he was still one of the assessors, and no doubt collected their fees as well as the salary of $500 that came with being the only overseer of the poor in the growing town.[44]

Moreover, Larned had learned an important lesson after having been briefly thrown out of office. The lesson was this: anxious taxpayers vote for officials who promise to keep taxes low. When he next made a report of poor relief expenses to the town meeting in the summer of 1820, no fewer than three newspapers approved of his cost-cutting. The combined reports of Olney and Larned, gave the *Providence Gazette*'s editor a "belief that considerable reductions are making in this department of the town expences." The *Providence Patriot* and the *Rhode Island American*, usually on opposite sides of the political fence, sang in chorus that the overseers' reports "indicated a retrenchment of expenditure in that department." The *Providence Patriot* added, somewhat guardedly, that "it is hoped [the cuts] may be realized." Larned knew the right word to say to his constituents: "retrenchment." He knew that he had to demonstrate a vigilance, lest he spend too much on the poor. For the rest of his life, he was successful at this, never losing another election as overseer the poor. In fact, in 1822, he won a raise from $500 to $700 per year, based on how much work he had to do.[45]

This financial anxiety on the part of taxpayers is a common theme in the history of poor relief. Even the life of William Larned himself can help us understand it. Although he never needed poor relief, there were times when he or his sons got close to needing it. Samuel went bankrupt. William's property was repeatedly assessed as close to the lowest in value of all taxpayers. In 1793, the year after he was first elected overseer of the poor, William Larned's share of that year's £6000 total town tax was just seven shillings and one penny. This was slightly more than his fellow overseer and assessor of taxes William Richmond. Much wealthier men, however, like the brothers Moses and John Brown paid upwards of £11 and £20 respectively. Decades later, in 1825, Larned paid $2.80 on real and personal property combined. His old colleague William Richmond now paid $30.80 while local grandees like Sullivan Dorr paid $257.60. Though not a pauper himself, Larned was by no means a wealthy man.[46]

Over the next few years, Larned's work continued as usual. He carefully kept poor relief expenses in the range of $8000 per year, even as other town expenses steadily rose. In 1826, expenditures for "Highways and Bridges" were $11,079.43, far surpassing "Support of the Poor" at $7,797.62. Poor relief remained the third largest item in the town budget, about $1,000 less than "Engines and Pumps," but about $1,000 more than schools. In 1825, the Town Meeting had instructed Larned to start advertising for a "town physician" to care for the poor, instead of hiring physicians on an as-needed basis. The town remained committed to providing healthcare to its neediest settled members, but they hoped for a better deal.[47]

One way taxpayers thought they could save money was by building a poorhouse. Throughout the first century after independence, but especially in the 1820s, poorhouses were a popular idea in larger towns across the country. In Providence, a poorhouse became more realistic when a wealthy donor, Ebenezer Knight Dexter, willed his farm to become land for an "asylum for the poor." The town freemen would spend the next few years trying to figure out the best way to use Dexter's money, without spending too much of theirs. The result, in 1828, would be a magnificent new asylum for the poor, and a dramatic change in how Providence's paupers would be cared for. The kind of relief that Larned had provided—mostly food, firewood, and doctor's visits, supplemented by a small workhouse, and supervised by an overseer of the poor who hustled about town—would not be required once a new, large poorhouse was built.

Larned must have wondered how his role in the town would change as a result of Dexter's donation. But perhaps he was not too concerned. After all, Dexter was about a generation younger than Larned. That he should die before Larned was a reminder that Larned was unusually old: seventy-two when Dexter died in 1824. Two years later, when John Adams and Thomas Jefferson both died on July 4, 1826, William Larned would be named to a committee to celebrate these men. This was a tribute to Larned being one of the few revolutionary war veterans still around. The following summer William and Sarah proudly watched as their son Samuel, who had gone bankrupt in Spain, was given an important promotion in the United States foreign service. He was appointed Charge de Affaires to the Republic of Chile in 1827. Providencians celebrated their native son's accomplishment in local newspapers. As one editor noted, "This is the only diplomatic appointment now held by a citizen of Rhode Island." Larned could bask in his son's glory, and hope that the rest of his children would be as well provided for.[48]

Even at seventy-five, Larned continued to "hold" his age well, walking around town to perform his duties as overseer, holding office hours in the

Market House and overseeing the expenditure of more than $8,500 in the fiscal year 1826–1827, more than one fifth of the town's entire budget that year of about $41,000, not even counting their spending on the new Dexter Asylum for the Poor, which would add another $15,000 to poor relief expenses that year. Then, in the winter month of February, 1828, Larned became ill. After three weeks he died, a month before his seventy-sixth birthday. Reaction to his death had to be swift. The office of overseer of the poor could not be left empty, so less than a week after Larned's death, an emergency town meeting was called. Several candidates for the post were nominated, and newspaper editor Walter R. Danforth, a member of the town council and author of an 1824 editorial on the connection between African Americans and the poor law, was chosen. The meeting also voted that Sarah Larned be paid all of the salary that the town owed him, without waiting for the next payday. Indeed, William Larned's probate records suggest that she needed the money urgently. With assets totaling $555.60 and debts of $595.94, the estate was insolvent.[49]

William Larned would be buried in the cemetery of St. John's Episcopal Church, just a block from his house. St. John's had changed its name from King's Church in 1794, only two years after Larned started as overseer of the poor, but almost two decades after the Declaration of Independence made this Anglican church name an uncomfortable one in the rebel town. Sarah Larned recalled being married by a Congregationalist pastor in her pension application. How William Larned left the Congregationalist churches of his ancestors, and joined the Episcopal Church after the Revolution, is a mystery. Less mysterious is how Larned's fellow town fathers wanted to remember him. The same day as the emergency town meeting to replace him, an obituary ran in the *Rhode Island American*, a newspaper that had always been supportive of Larned and his son Samuel. The obituary was a mark of distinction, a special honor, carefully composed and not printed lightly. "When a citizen whose years have been marked by public usefulness through a long life of activity, integrity and honor, is at length called from this world," it began, "something more than a mere record of his death" should be printed. The obituary was sentimental and long, spilling over onto a second page. It called Larned "a kind and honourable friend, a humane, exact, and vigilant officer, a patriotic citizen, and, in all the relations of life, a fair, upright and honest man."[50]

Providing a brief life story, the obituary noted Larned's birth in Connecticut, his coming to Providence and his quickly gaining the trust of the townspeople. It noted his service in the Revolution, his state offices of Quartermaster General and Representative in the General Assembly. It dwelt longest, though, on Larned's service as overseer of the poor and assessor of taxes, emphasizing that he was elected thirty-six times and "faithfully discharged their duties till his death." It praised his administration of the office by himself after 1819, asserting that "it is well known how happily he united a kind and diligent attention to the comforts of the unfortunate objects of his care, with a strict methodical economy in the application of the public money." In this one sentence, the author of the obituary summed up the inherent tension in the job of overseer of the poor. Larned, the obituary claimed, had somehow managed to complete both his tasks: to humanely care for the town poor while spending as little money as possible. In the words of the obituary, Larned was "a humane, exact and vigilant officer." If this was true, then Larned had become the perfect overseer of the poor.[51]

Continuing on to illustrate these qualities, however, the obituary writer chose not to give an example of Larned's humanity, but rather of his "strict and methodical economy in the application of the public money." During Larned's time as the only overseer of the poor, the obituary claimed, "there was an annual saving to the town of at least $2000, in the expences of supporting the poor." This writer's priorities reflected the priorities of the town's taxpayers. As a group, they were committed to humane support of the poor. They assumed this must be done. But the details they cared most about were how inexpensively it could be done. They wanted poor relief done well, but they wanted it done cheaply too. And getting it done cheaply was what the voters usually paid most attention to. The obituary offered another insight into the workings of the system. It seemed that, despite his good salary as overseer of the poor, William Larned was still not considered a wealthy man. As the author put it:

> To a numerous progeny that grew up under his paternal guidance, to occupy respectable and honorable stations in life, he has left, not indeed an inheritance of wealth—but a better inheritance in his unsullied name, and in the qualifications for usefulness and happiness, which he was careful to bestow upon them as children of his hopes and affections.

He left honor but not wealth, "not indeed" wealth, the writer emphasizes. That "not indeed" makes it sound as though the Larned family were far from being wealthy, or that no one would expect them to have money. This highlights again how financially vulnerable Larned himself was, and how little seems to have separated him from the paupers he oversaw.[52]

William Larned's obituary points to two of the most important things to understand about early United States poor relief. First, it struck an uneasy balance between guaranteeing support for the needy and protecting taxpayers from higher taxes. Second, the difference between those in need of assistance and those supporting the needy was not that great. Living in small towns and small cities, at close range to one another, paupers and taxpayers were closely connected. Taxpayers often knew, personally, the recipients of assistance. Sometimes, those taxpayers might be the very people providing help to their neighbors, and getting reimbursed for it. If need rose, taxes rose with it, within a year. And townspeople knew that if they needed it, poor relief would be their right too. That had been William Larned's job: to hustle around town, spending money and saving money. He found help, lifesaving help, for the people from his town. At the same time, he guarded his town's treasury by banishing people from other towns. Like the American poor laws, Larned combined generosity and control.

NOTES

1. On Larned's recent reelection, see Providence Town Meeting Minutes for 3 June 1811, PCHA. For Henry Larned's presence, see Providence Town Council Minutes, 17 June 1811, PCHA.

2. Details of Thaddeus Smith's life and his hearings in front of the Town Council are in Providence Town Council Minutes, 17 June 1811 and 1 July 1811, PCHA and "Petition to permit a transient to remain in town" 1 July 1811 in MSS 214 sg 1, Providence Town Papers Series 3, Volume 76, Document 0017783, RIHS.

3. On Washington, see Mary V. Thompson, *In the Hands of a Good Providence: Religion in the Life of George Washington* (Charlottesville: University of Virginia Press, 2008), chap. 3. For a study of scores of overseers of the poor in the seventy-five years before the Revolution, see Wiberley, "Four Cities," chap. 6. Wiberley finds overseers of the poor to be among the wealthiest of townspeople, which does not hold true for Larned.

4. Green, *This Business of Relief*, 1.

5. For a brief discussion of social control, Chambers, "Toward a Redefinition of Welfare History," 407–433. On the effects of poor laws in restricting mobility, see O'Brassil-Kulfan, *Vagrants and Vagabonds*, especially chap. 3.

6. William Law Learned, *The Learned Family* (Albany: Weed-Parsons Printing Company, 1898), 60–61.

7. Learned, *The Learned Family*, 60–61, 98–101. The nearest census figures to the 1770s for Thompson are the first Federal Census of 1790, when Thompson had a population of 2,267. A 1774 census of Providence counted 9,208 people in the Rhode Island town. John R. Bartlett, *Census of the Inhabitants of the Colony of Rhode Island and Providence Plantations . . . 1774* (Providence: Knowles, Anthony & Co., 1858), 239.

8. Learned, *The Learned Family*, 100.

9. On the "tea party," see *Providence Gazette* 4 March 1775, 3. On the ousted town councilmen, see Entry for 20 November 1776 in Town Meeting Minutes Book 6, 1772–1783, PCHA.

10. On Larned's war service, see Declaration by Sarah Larned, 5 November 1839, and Declaration by Ephraim Bowen, 31 August 1839, in Revolutionary War Pension File for William Larned and Sarah Larned, Number W21542, National Archives (viewed on microfilm at Philadelphia NARA office). On commissaries in general, see James A. Henretta, "The War for Independence and American Development," in Ronald Hoffman, John J. McCusker, Russel R. Menard, and Peter J. Albert, Eds., *The Economy of Early America: The Revolutionary Period, 1763–1790* (Charlottesville: United States Capitol Historical Society/University of Virginia, 1988), 68–81. On commissaries, see Robert Middlekauf, *The Glorious Cause: The American Revolution, 1763–1789* (New York: Oxford University Press, 1982), 412–419.

11. These ads are in *Providence Gazette and Country Journal* 8 June 1782, 4, and 26 October 1782, 4. On the politics of imported cloth, see Kate Haulman, *Politics of Fashion in Eighteenth-Century America* (Chapel Hill: University of North Carolina Press, 2011), chap. 6, and Linzy A. Brekke, "The 'Scourge of Fashion': Political Economy and the Politics of Consumption in the Early Republic," *Early American Studies* 3:1 (Spring 2005), 111–139.

12. *Providence Gazette and Country Journal* 21 February 1784, 3. Learned, *The Learned Family,* 100 and Declaration by Sarah Larned, 5 November 1839, in Revolutionary War Pension File for William Larned and Sarah Larned, Number W21542.

13. On the drum, see treasury order to Henry Bowen dated 12 March to 18 April 1804, Document 006322 in MSS 214 sg 1 "Providence Town Papers" Series 3, Book 55, RIHS.

14. For a summary of the law of welfare from colonial British America to the nineteenth century, see Trattner, *From Poor Law to Welfare State*, chaps. 1 and 2. For the Elizabethan Poor Laws, see Paul A. Fideler, *Social Welfare in Pre-Industrial England* (New York: Palgrave Macmillan, 2006), 99–101. For discussion of how the Elizabethan Poor Laws did and did not change charity and poor relief in England, see Steve Hindle, *On the Parish? The Micro-Politics of Poor Relief in Rural England c. 1550–1750* (New York: Oxford University Press, 2004), especially the Conclusion.

15. On Larned becoming a freeman, see entries for 20 September 1784 and 20 April 1785 in Town Meeting Minutes Book 7, "1782 to May 16, 1804," in PCHA. For the location of Larned's property, see Henry Richmond Chace, *Owners and Occupants of the Lots, Houses, and Shops in the Town of Providence, Rhode Island, in 1798* (Providence: Livermore & Knight, 1914), 17 and Plate III..

16. On Larned's first elections to office, see entries for 5 June 1786, 4 June 1787 and 2 June 1788 in Town Meeting Book 7, "1782 to 5/16/1804," in PCHA. See also *United States Chronicle* 15 June 1786, 29 May 1788, and 5 June 1788. On bundles of rights and privileges see William J. Novak, "The Legal Transformation of Citizenship in Nineteenth-Century America," in Meg Jacobs, William Novak, and Julian Zelizer, Eds., *The Democratic Experiment: New Directions American Political History* (Princeton, NJ: Princeton University Press, 2003).

17. The University of Wisconsin Madison's History Department hosts a webpage on the history of Rhode Island's ratification of the United States Constitution at this address: https://csac.history.wisc.edu/states-and-ratification/rhode-island/referendum/.

18. Entry for 4 June 1792 in Providence Town Meeting Minutes Book 7, PCHA.

19. On New York, see "Supplement to the Daily Advertiser, Nov. 2, 1789" in *Daily Advertiser* 2 November 1789. On Providence in 1789, see Entry for 24 October

1789 in Providence Town Meeting Minutes Book 7. PCHA. On Providence in 1800, see Broadside: "Schedule of the Expences of the Town . . . from August 1, 1799 to August 1, 1800" (Providence: Carter, 1800). On Scituate, see Creech, *Three Centuries of Poor Law Administration*, 165–166. Herndon, "'Who Died an Expence to This Town'," 154.

20. On Providence in 1825, see *Rhode Island American* 14 June 1825, 2 and Howard Kemble Stokes, *The Finances and Administration of Providence* (Baltimore: Johns Hopkins University Press, 1903), 147–157. On Richmond, see Green, *This Business of Relief*, 33. On New York, see Mohl, *Poverty in New York*, 91. Tax figures for 1825 come from MSS 214 sg 10, Providence Town Tax Records, Box 9, Folder 1 "Providence Town Tax, 1825," 17, 35, 47, RIHS. Estimates of what these figures would be in unskilled wages today are from Measuring Worth Foundation, "Purchasing Power Today of a US Dollar Transaction in the Past," available at *Measuring Worth* website <https://www.measuringworth.com/calculators/ppowerus/index2.php>.

21. For a quick overview of the range of goods which overseers provided in this period, I recommend browsing the helpful results of a Works Progress Administration project which attempted to provide an index to the extensive Providence Town Papers books, into which many of these old receipts were pasted: MSS 214 sg 1 "Providence Town Papers" WPA Index Boxes 27–31, RIHS.

22. On Comfort Eddy, see Document 006501 25 June 1804 in MSS 214 sg 1 "Providence Town Papers" Series 3, Book 69, RIHS. On the sufferers of a contagious disease, see Entry for 16 December 1800 in Providence Town Council Books, PCHA. For Samuel Thurber's receipt, see Document 006457 "To Supplies for Several of the Poor" 26 May 1804 in MSS 214 sg 1 "Providence Town Papers" Series 3, Book 69, RIHS.

23. On Sivich, Convers, and Cozzens, see Documents 006490, 006492, and 006493 in MSS 214 sg 1 "Providence Town Papers" Series 3, Book 69, RIHS. On Hawes, see Broadside: "Schedule of the Expences of the Town. . . from August 1, 1799 to August 1, 1800".

24. Herndon, "'Who Died an Expence to This Town,'" 142. On the "welfare/industrial complex," see Green, *This Business of Relief*, 1.

25. For streets committee, see receipt dated 2 June 1806, Document 009340 in MSS 214 sg 1 "Providence Town Papers" Series 3, Book 55, RIHS. For nuisance committee, see entry for 28 October 1811 in MSS Town Council Book 9, PCHA. For "Remainder of Expences," see Broadside Nicholas Parrillo, *Against the Profit Motive: The Salary Revolution in American Government 1780–1940* (New Haven: Yale University Press, 2013), 2. None of the receipts name William Larned, strangely, but rather the other two overseers and Larned's twenty-two-year-old, unmarried son, Thomas A. Larned. Receipts to Thomas A. Larned and the three overseers are four identical amounts, but do not make clear the time period for which they are compensating. See Documents 0012322 to 0012324 and 0012376 to 0012378 in MSS 214 sg 1 "Providence Town Papers" Series 3, Book 69, RIHS.

26. For Larned's clothing receipt, see "1806 The Town of Providence to Wm Larned Dr," Document 009362 in MSS 214 sg 1 "Providence Town Papers" Series 3, Book 62, RIHS and "1808 Town of Providence to William Larned," Document 0012239 in MSS 214 sg 1 "Providence Town Papers" Series 3, Book 69, RIHS. For Spurr, see Document 009443 in MSS 214 sg 1 "Providence Town Papers" Series 3, Book 62, RIHS.

27. On women's unrecognized and uncompensated work caring for the poor, see Monique Bourque, "Women and Work in the Philadelphia Almshouse, 1790–1840," *Journal of the Early Republic* 32:3 (Fall 2012), 383–414 and Laurel Daen, "'To Board & Nurse a Stranger': Poverty, Disability, and Community in Eighteenth-Century Massachusetts," in *Journal of Social History* (2020): 1–26..

28. For genealogical information on Larned's children, I consulted both Learned, *The Learned Family*, 100–101 and what is sometimes more accurate, Eugenia Learned James, *The Learned Family in America, 1630–1967* (N.P.: Setco Printing Co., 1967), 44–45.

29. Bureau of the Census, *Heads of Families at the First Census of the United States Taken in the Year 1790 Rhode Island* (Washington, DC: Government Printing Office, 1908), 9 for totals and 34 for Larned (spelled Learned in this census). Accessed digitally at <https://www2.census.gov/library/publications/decennial/1790/heads_of_families/rhode_island/1790j-02.pdf>. Also see the reproduction of the manuscript return, *First Census of the United States, 1790* (NARA microfilm publication M637, 12 rolls), Records of the Bureau of the Census, Record Group 29, National Archives, Washington, DC, 181, accessed digitally at Ancestry.com. On Edwin Channing Larned, see *In Memory of Edwin Channing Larned* (Chicago: A.C. McClurg & Co., 1886), 15.

30. On Larned's household in 1800, see manuscript returns of *Second Census of the United States, 1800,* NARA microfilm publication M32 (52 rolls), Records of the Bureau of the Census, Record Group 29, National Archives, Washington, D.C., 577, accessed digitally at Ancestry.com. On total numbers of slaves in Providence in 1800, see *Return of the Whole Number of Persons . . . One Thousand Eight Hundred* (Washington, DC: House of Representatives, 1801), 26, accessed digitally at https://www2.census.gov/prod2/decennial/documents/1800-return-whole-number-of-persons.pdf.

31. *Impartial Observer* 11 April 1801, 3.

32. *United States Chronicle*, 8 September 1803, 3 and *Providence Phoenix* 21 April 1804, 3.

33. On the southwest room, see *Providence Patriot or Columbian Phenix* 14 May 1814, 3. See also *The Providence Directory* (Providence: Brown and Danforth, 1824), 42.

34. *Columbian Phenix or Providence Patriot* 11 May 1811, 2 and *Providence Patriot or Columbian Phenix* 26 April 1817, 2.

35. Murray N. Rothbard, *The Panic of 1819: Reactions and Policies* (New York: Columbia University Press, 1962), chap. 1. Daniel Dupre, "The Panic of 1819 and the Political Economy of Sectionalism," in Cathy Matson, Ed., *The Economy of Early America: Historical Perspectives & New Directions* (University Park: Pennsylvania State University Press, 2005), chap. 9. The term "Great Hard Times" is from page 670 of Jessica M. Lepler, "Introduction: The Panic of 1819 by Any Other Name," in Panic of 1819 Forum, *Journal of the Early Republic* 40:4 (Winter 2020), 665–670.

36. William Larned to Samuel Larned 14 October 1819, in Folder 28—Correspondence—Letters Received 1817–1819, MSS 81, Series 2, Samuel Larned Papers, RIHS. The note from his Cadiz creditors, dated 4/23/1819 is in Folder 28—Correspondence—Letters Received 1817–1819, MSS 81, Series 2, Samuel Larned Papers, RIHS.

37. The letter from William Larned, 21 January 1817, and two from Mariana Fudela, 8 and 11 February, are in Folder 28—Correspondence—Letters Received 1817–1819, MSS 81, Series 2, Samuel Larned Papers, RIHS. Translation of the two

letters from Mariana Fudela from Spanish to English made by the author. William Larned to Samuel Larned 14 October 1819, in Folder 28—Correspondence—Letters Received 1817–1819, MSS 81, Series 2, Samuel Larned Papers, RIHS.

38. This estimate is using the unskilled wage index at the website measuringworth. com.
39. *Providence Patriot* 5 June 1819, 2.
40. *Rhode Island American* 8 June 1819, 3 and 11 June 1819, 2.
41. On retrenchment, see *Rhode Island American* 15 June 1819, 3. On ship captains, see *Rhode Island American* 13 August 1819, 4. On Olney's office and oakum, see *Rhode Island American* 21 September 1819, 1.
42. Olney's first resignation announcement is in *Rhode Island American* 21 September 1819, 1. His lengthy explanation why is in *Rhode Island American* 19 November 1819, 3.
43. *Rhode Island American* 19 November 1819, 3.
44. On Larned's appointment to the Committee on Nuisances, see *Rhode Island American* 13 July 1819, 3. On Larned's regaining the office in November, see *Providence Patriot* 1 December 1819, 3 or *Rhode Island American* 4 December 1819, 3.
45. *Providence Gazette*, 5 June 1822, 3.
46. Tax lists for Providence can be found in MSS 214 sg 10, Providence Town Tax, RIHS. William Larned's 1793 tax payment is listed in Box 3 "1793" while the 1825 payment is in Box 9, Folder 1 "Providence Town Tax, 1825," 35.
47. On 1826 budget, see *Rhode Island American* 13 June 1826, 2. On physician, see *Rhode Island American* 14 June 1825, 2–3; *Rhode Island American* 13 June 1826, 2; *Rhode Island American* 16 June 1826, 3. On ship captains, see *Manufacturers' and Farmers' Journal* 11 July 1825.
48. *Providence Patriot* 15 July 1826, 3. *Rhode Island American* 17 August 1827, 2. See also *Cadet and Statesman* 15 August 1827, 2.
49. On holding his age, see William Larned to Samuel Larned 14 October 1819, in Folder 28—Correspondence—Letters Received 1817–1819, MSS 81, Series 2, Samuel Larned Papers, RIHS. On 1826–1827 expenses, see *Manufacturers' and Farmers' Journal* 14 June 1827, 2. On Larned's death, see *Providence Patriot* 27 February 1828, 2 and Probate Records file A5155, PCHA.
50. Declaration by Sarah Larned, 5 November 1839, in Revolutionary War Pension File for William Larned and Sarah Larned, Number W21542, National Archives. *Rhode Island American* 26 February 1828, 2.
51. *Rhode Island American* 26 February 1828, 2.
52. *Rhode Island American* 26 February 1828, 2.

Timeline

William Larned, Cuff Roberts, "One-Eyed" Sarah, and Revolutionary America

Year	National & Local Events	William Larned	Cuff Roberts	"One-Eyed" Sarah
1752	More than a century after English colonization, a majority of "New England" is English-descended like Larned, some are Native like Sarah, some are African-descended like Roberts, some are still other ethnicities.	William Larned born in Killingly, Conn.		Three-year-old Sarah Hill bound out to a master in Uxbridge, Mass.
1761			Cuff Roberts born in Coventry, R.I.	
1767–1772	"Whig" movement against imperial taxes which began protests in 1765, continues.		About this age, Roberts bound out to a master in Coventry.	Hill free of service 1767, first moves to Providence 1772
1774	British Parliament passes "Coercive" Acts in response to Boston Tea Party.	Larned has moved to Providence, marries Sally Angell.		
1778	Revolutionary War, begun in 1775, enters third year.	Larned becomes Continental Army commissary.	Roberts becomes Continental Army private.	
1780		Sally (Angell) Larned dies, William Larned resigns as commissary.		
1781	Continental / French victory at Yorktown.		Roberts's regiment fights at Yorktown.	
1783	Treaty of Paris ends Revolutionary War.		Roberts discharged from Continental Army, returns to R.I.	

Year	National & Local Events	William Larned	Cuff Roberts	"One-Eyed" Sarah
1784	Gradual Emancipation law takes effect in R.I.	Larned marries Sarah Smith, gains a settlement in Providence.		Hill removed from Providence for first time.
1788	11 states ratify a new Constitution, not including R.I.		Roberts marries Elizabeth Grummuch in Warwick, R.I.	
1791–1792	Washington elected to second term as President of the U.S.A., 1792.	Larned elected to first term as Overseer of the Poor, 1792.		Hill removed from Providence for second time, 1791.
1795			Roberts and family living in Providence.	
1801/ 1802/ 1803	Children born free under Gradual Emancipation law begin turning eighteen, the age of majority for women, in 1802.	Providence Town Council interrogates daughters of Aaron and Sarah Olney of Smithfield.	At some point, Elizabeth (Grummuch) Roberts dies, and Cuff Roberts marries Janette.	Hill interrogated by Providence Town Council for 3rd time, but not warned out, 1803; Sarah Olney paid for keeping poor
1806		Larned compiles list of eighty "Black" people to be warned out of Providence.	Roberts family are first on Larned's list, warned out to Coventry.	"One-Eyed" Sarah is active as a nurse for Providence in this period.
1811	Against wishes of New Englanders, United States. prepares for War of 1812 against Great Britain and Native leaders	"Howard" criticizes Overseers and Sarah in newspapers.		"One-Eyed" Sarah described in papers; Sarah Olney's husband, Aaron, dies.
1818			Revolutionary War pension requires twice yearly trips to Providence.	
1819	Providence people of color organize African Union Meeting House. Financial Panic of 1819 begins.	Larned loses election, but six months later is appointed as *only* Overseer of the Poor.		

Year	National & Local Events	William Larned	Cuff Roberts	"One-Eyed" Sarah
1820	In this decade, many municipalities invest in indoor relief institutions again, trying to cut down outdoor relief costs.	Larned congratulated in newspapers for "retrenchment" of expenses.	Roberts removed from Providence to Coventry in Town Sergeant's wagon.	
1823–1824	Anti-Black "Hardscrabble riot" in Providence.		Roberts asks permission to reenter Providence.	
1828	Andrew Jackson elected President of the U.S.A.	Larned dies in office.		
1831	Anti-Black "Snowtown" riot in Providence; Abolitionist movements growing.		Roberts has moved to Boston and remarried, dying in 1831.	
1839		Sarah Larned requests Revolutionary War pension based on William Larned's service.		

CHAPTER 2

⤳

Warned Out

How Cuff Roberts Was Banished by Poor Law Officials

Was it embarrassing, riding out of Providence in the town sergeant's wagon? It is hard to know, at a distance of two hundred years. For Cuff Roberts, the fifty-nine-year-old Revolutionary War veteran, getting a lift from the town sergeant saved him the weariness of a half-day walk back to Coventry. In late winter, 1820, trudging through the roads would be more difficult, the journey even colder, than bumping along in the horse-drawn wagon.

But shame stuck to the wagon, like an unpleasant smell. This was the same wagon the town sergeant used to expel people from town. When the town council warned somebody out, and thought that somebody could not be trusted to leave on her own, they turned to the town sergeant and his horse and wagon. The sergeant might be tasked to carry that somebody back to her town of birth. Or he might simply unload that somebody, and any paltry belongings she could carry, at the town limits. Traveling by cart with the town sergeant was not unlike getting a night's lodging at the jail, which Roberts also had done on this trip to Providence: It brought some comfort, but not dignity.[1]

While his night in jail would be fresh in Roberts's memory, as the big wagon wheels negotiated the rutted road, another memory would likely come to him. Back in the fall of 1806, Roberts had made a journey like this

How Welfare Worked in the Early United States. Gabriel J. Loiacono, Oxford University Press. © Oxford University Press 2021. DOI: 10.1093/oso/9780197515433.003.0003

one, except with his wife and their children. They had just been banished from Providence, and were supposed to go back to the town where Roberts was born: Coventry. The overseer of the poor who had engineered their banishment was the very same William Larned who still held the job all these years later. And all these years later, Larned was still patrolling the town, still keeping his eye on newcomers, and still watching out for old familiar faces like Roberts's.

Now, in 1820, Roberts had come back to Providence to collect his Revolutionary War veterans' pension. Roberts was among the first veterans to get a pension. His long tour of duty, combined with his current poverty, had qualified him. But thanks to town officials, collecting his pension was not easy. Before he could make the journey to Providence from Coventry, both of which towns are depicted in Figure 2.1, he was supposed to get special permission from the Providence Town Council. An old combat veteran, he could not freely travel around the country he had helped make free.

Roberts's freedom to move, to work, to live where he wanted was circumscribed by the poor laws. In addition to providing an extensive social safety net, the poor laws also empowered municipal governments to control where citizens lived. Indeed, the ability to banish people from town was the financial flipside of the ability to help those in need. The administrative structure of the Elizabethan Poor Law still meant that American municipalities were, in most cases, the governments which had to finance any relief they gave their residents. One way to do that, as seen in chapters 1 and 3, was to worry about "economy," keeping payments for each recipient as cost-effective—and low—as was deemed humane. Even more important, though, was carefully policing which people a municipality was responsible for. By banishing—or "warning out"—needy people for whom other municipalities were responsible, each town or county could keep its own poor relief expenses in check. In theory, this would balance out the costs of poor relief evenly across all municipalities. Some states had found ways to balance costs of poor relief without forcing residents out of town, as will be discussed below. Others, including Rhode Island and the mid-Atlantic states, continued to rely on banishment as a fiscal tool, well into the nineteenth century.

This power of banishment, though, could be used for other goals. Cuff Roberts did not need municipal poor relief when he was banished, over and over, from the town of Providence. The first time he was banished, in 1806, it had been entirely because he was "Black," in the words of the town clerk. The poor laws were not written to regulate race. They were intended to provide relief for people with a "settlement" in a municipality, and force other needy people to their own towns of settlement. But men who knew the

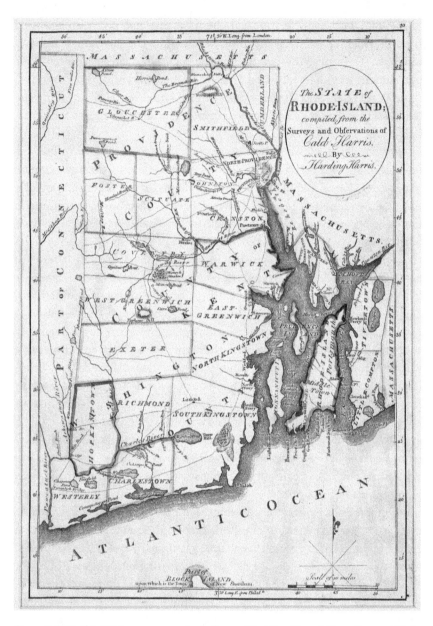

Figure 2.1 On this 1818 map, one can trace the road that Providence's Town Sergeant likely used when bringing Cuff Roberts to Coventry by cart, in February 1820. It would have been half a day's journey each way. The road was well-known to Roberts, since he had to travel from Coventry to Providence twice a year to collect his Revolutionary War pension. The map, surveyed by Caleb Harris and Harding Harris, appeared in *Mathew Carey's General Atlas, improved and enlarged* (Philadelphia: M. Carey & Son, 1818). Courtesy of the Norman B. Leventhal Map & Education Center at the Boston Public Library.

poor laws well knew how to use them for unintended purposes. Without violence, but also without clear legal authority, the overseers of the poor could bend the poor laws in service of driving people of color out of town. In one town after another, local officials used the poor laws explicitly to banish people of color, sometimes en masse. In this way, government officials tried to break up African-descended and Native communities.

The poor laws were versatile. They created a sustainable and, in many ways, generous safety net. They helped save lives. They housed the homeless and fed the hungry. They gave medicine and healthcare to the sick. But they could also be harsh, controlling where Americans could and could not live. Town officials had the power to say anyone was "likely to be chargeable" to the poor relief accounts. There was no appeal from that decision. Thus, the poor laws could be used as a broad police power, allowing overseers of the poor, backed up by town councils, to expel anyone deemed to be settled elsewhere. Following the life of Cuff Roberts, this chapter will trace how overseers of the poor policed and controlled people, especially people of color, under cover of the poor law. Readers may be surprised how unfree citizens of the early United States were. They could not move anywhere they wanted. Moreover, poor laws which were not, ostensibly, about race could be applied in racially discriminatory ways. Roberts resisted this racist application of warning out. Overseers kept banishing him, but he kept coming back. He built the life he wanted for his family in spite of the overseers.[2]

At first glance Cuff Roberts had little in common with the English-descended Overseer of the Poor Larned. "Black," with a father who had been enslaved, Roberts faced dangers and hostility that Larned did not. But like Larned, Roberts had also seized opportunities during the Revolutionary War, and later saw possibilities in the rapidly growing town of Providence. Where Larned had spent two years as a commissary officer for the army, Roberts had spent five years as a private. But what can we know about Cuff Roberts before he enlisted in the Continental Army in 1778?

FORGING A FAMILY IN THE FACE OF SLAVERY

Born in 1760 or 1761, young Cuff Roberts was not allowed to grow up with his parents. Town authorities would see to that as they did for other children, especially those of African or Native ancestry. In two interrogations by the Providence town council in 1819, Roberts remembered that his father was enslaved, in Coventry, to a man named Thomas Brayton. His mother was a free woman, though Roberts was not sure where she had been born: either

Warwick or Cranston. The town clerk recording the interrogation did not write down either of his parents' names. In a second interrogation, though, the town clerk *did* write down the names of two of Roberts's grandparents. Jack Prophet, his grandfather, had been enslaved to a man in Warwick. His grandmother, whose last name was Collins, lived in Cranston. While it is not explicit which grandparents these were, maternal or paternal, it seems likely they were his mother's parents: They lived where he thought his mother was born. Also, he probably got the surname Roberts from his father. He got his freeborn status from his mother. Not being raised by his mother or father, though, what else could he have gotten from them? He got a network of kin, spread around Rhode Island: grandparents, cousins, a community of color, who went to great lengths to connect with one another across town lines. And they must have given him his first name.[3]

His first name, Cuff, which today might be spelled Kofi, is an Akan-language name, from the region around present-day Ghana, in western Africa. Often called a "day name," Cuff or Cuffee denoted a boy born on a Friday. Moreover, it connected the baby to his ancestors, at least one of whom had been born in western Africa and endured capture and enslavement, torture and transshipment, across the Atlantic Ocean to a foreign and hostile land. In Roberts's case, it was likely his father, among other relatives, who had experienced this.[4]

The 1750s, when Roberts's father was a young man, was boomtime for African and European slave traders. In that decade, more than 600,000 boys and girls, men and women, who had survived a forced march to the coast, were bullied and beaten onto ships off the shores of western Africa. On average, it was a twelve-week passage across the Atlantic to slave plantations in the Americas. In that decade, out of every twenty enslaved people on board, records suggest about seventeen survived the sickness and heat, the torture and terror of the journey. That decade saw the largest numbers of people making that journey up to that point in time. In each of the next eight decades, the numbers of people transported across the Atlantic would be even bigger. In addition to these victims of the slave trade, a less-well-counted number were shipped from Caribbean ports to mainland North America.[5]

Rhode Island merchants were betting more of their money on the slave trade in the 1750s. From 1751 until the Revolutionary War broke out, they sent 383 ships to Africa, carrying more than 40,000 captured people to the Americas. This was almost three times as many ships as sent by the rest of the British North American colonies combined. At the same time, it was only a small fraction of the slavetrading ships sent to Africa from ports outside North America, whether under a British, Portuguese, French, Dutch, or some other flag. Altogether, this meant that larger and larger numbers of Africans—whether prisoners of war or, increasingly, kidnapped youths—found themselves working for masters in rural Rhode Island.[6]

It is likely that Roberts's father arrived in Rhode Island in the 1750s from the "Gold Coast," where most Akan speakers lived. Alternatively, he may have been born in Rhode Island or been sent to the colony by slave traders in Jamaica or Barbados. It is not certain that Roberts's father *was* Akan, since other west Africans sometimes learned the Akan language or adopted Akan day names after the middle passage. It is also possible that Cuff was named after a friend of his parents. The 1774 census of Rhode Island shows a Cuffy Brown living in Coventry, head of a household of nine "Black" people. Perhaps Cuffy Brown was a friend of Cuff Roberts's father; the elder Roberts was enslaved in that small town.[7]

By law, young Cuff would be free since his mother was free. By long-standing custom, though, town officials would not let him stay with his mother for long. Both because his father could not live with him and because they were people "of color," town officials were inclined to order Cuff to be raised in another household, a "White" household, from a young age. For young Cuff that would be the household of Joseph Nichols in West Greenwich, a town just to the east of Coventry. The town clerk did not write down how old he was when he was separated from his mother. For other boys of color, this could happen as young as age three, but on average happened around age ten. Nichols would have made this deal, probably with the Town Council of Coventry, because he would get a young field worker out of it, who would be bound to him until age twenty-one.[8]

The town fathers' practice of binding out children from African or Native families to European-descended families was yet another power they exercised under cover of the poor law. Intended to give children in poor families a prosperous home and a trade, it is probably the power that seems most heartbreaking to readers in the twenty-first century. Town officials could separate children from any parents they decided were too poor, or unfit as parents. In practice, town officials in this period seemed to think *any* parents of color were unfit. As late as the 1820s, a Providence town councilman would list "bind out the children of blacks" as one of the council's many responsibilities. This despite the fact that nowhere in state laws was that power given to town officials. Rather, they had the power to bind out poor children. But town officials had so often arrogated to themselves the power to separate any African and Native children from their parents that they treated the custom as a law.[9]

Roberts's master, Nichols, would have the responsibility to house, feed, and clothe Roberts. Roberts would have to work as Nichols directed him.

Nichols was master. Roberts was servant. Similar deals were struck for "White" boys too, but they usually included teaching the boy a particular trade, not just farm labor, and teaching him reading, writing, and arithmetic. Cuff Roberts would sign documents with an "x" his whole life, so it appears that Nichols was not tasked with teaching him to write. It was a work-toughened Cuff Roberts, then, who seized an opportunity for a new kind of life as war came to Rhode Island in the 1770s. Though he was probably contracted to work for Nichols until he was twenty-one, he was only seventeen when he stepped up to a recruiting officer for the Continental Army.[10]

A BLACK SOLDIER IN RHODE ISLAND, NEW YORK, AND YORKTOWN

The Continental Army was preparing for another spring of campaigns against the British armed forces. Roberts was seventeen; the Army was not yet three years old. Roberts was healthy and hearty; rarely would muster rolls find him sick in five years of soldiering. The Continental Army was sick, sore, and suffering. Two Rhode Island regiments were among the 11,000 Continental soldiers who had wintered at Valley Forge, Pennsylvania without enough food, enough clothing, or enough housing. Officers were resigning in alarming numbers. Enlisted men were deserting at a steady pace. Rhode Island was unable to fill its quotas for soldiers.[11]

There was hope on the horizon, however. Rumor had it that France was preparing to ally with the insurgent United States government. Not only that, but a Prussian officer, Baron von Steuben, had arrived at Valley Forge in early 1778. There, he taught close-order drill, in French, through translators, to the hungry, cold, bored soldiers. At the same time, a new commissary general reorganized the army's food supply, incentivizing men like William Larned to join the war effort with a small cut of the commissary business. And in Rhode Island, one general hit upon a solution to the state's recruitment shortfalls: a "Black regiment." The plan was to recruit enslaved men to fill a whole regiment, with the state reimbursing the men's masters in exchange for their freedom. General Washington, who had earlier been reluctant to command any Black soldiers, enslaved or free, relented. The plan went forward. Recruiters fanned out across Rhode Island.[12]

That is how officers from a newly reorganized First Rhode Island regiment met Cuff Roberts in West Greenwich one day. It was mid-March, 1778. Roberts was ready to join. The Continental Congress had told recruiters to look for "able-bodied men, not under sixteen years of age." At seventeen, Roberts was an ideal recruit. He was described in enlistment papers as a "laborer," five-foot-eight-inches tall, with "black hair, black complexion."[13]

Cuff Roberts's experience of the American Revolution was a microcosm of how Washington's armies won the war: He survived. In the face of a well-equipped, well-trained British enemy, Roberts, like the rebel armies, would not go away. In other regiments, soldiers signed up for a term that could be as little as a few months, with different increments possible up to three years. But Roberts, and many who joined the First Rhode Island in 1778, were in the army "for the duration of the war": until victory or defeat. Few soldiers had a term as long as this. Designed to stem the hemorrhaging of soldiers from Washington's armies, "duration of war" enlistments were something that could be foisted on enslaved recruits, and free men like Roberts, who had few other options. Like the signers of the Declaration of Independence and many officers of the Continental Army, these "duration of war" recruits staked their lives on winning independence.

For the next two and a half years, the First Rhode Island regiment stayed in its home state. British troops had occupied its largest town, Newport, since December, 1776. Roberts and his comrades played cat and mouse with the Crown's raiders—regular British, Hessian, and Loyalist—at least until the British evacuation of Newport in October, 1779. The biggest confrontation came during the Battle of Rhode Island, in August 1778. Rumors of a French alliance with the United States had proven true by then, and one result was a combined attack on Newport by French naval forces and American soldiers. After a storm, the French withdrew, and American ground forces quietly lifted their siege. Then they found themselves facing a British counterattack.

What Cuff Roberts witnessed at the end of August, as the First Rhode Island made a fighting withdrawal from a British and Hessian advance, was probably unlike anything he had seen yet. The First, led by Colonel Christopher Green, included 181 privates in five companies in that month, a small regiment by the standards of the Continental Army. During the most intense fighting of the Battle of Rhode Island, its soldiers came under heavy fire. Private Reuben Gulliver remembered "a bloody engagement with the enemy, Col. Green's regiment of blacks being literally cut to pieces." Private Winthrop Robinson recalled that "Col. Green had a regiment of negroes who were in the same engagement, fought bravely, but were unfortunate." A Hessian account reported: "The Hessians now rushed up the hill under a heavy fire in order to take the redoubt. Here they experienced a more obstinate resistance than they had expected. They found large bodies of troops behind the work and at its sides, chiefly wild looking men in their shirt sleeves, and among them many negroes." Muster rolls suggest that casualties in the First Rhode Island were low and historians argue about how important the regiment was to this battle. What is clear, though, is that it was bloody, and the first big battle that the teenage Cuff Roberts had yet seen.[14]

In the year after surviving the Battle of Rhode Island, hunger and cold were usually Roberts's worst enemies. While the scarcities at Valley Forge are particularly well-documented, lack of food, shoes, clothing, and pay, were constants for Continental soldiers throughout the war. Some of the hungry soldiers in Roberts's company were court martialed for stealing lambs to eat at the end of July, 1779. A year after that, Lieutenant Colonel Samuel Ward would complain to a Rhode Island member of Congress that "our soldiers are almost entirely naked." Perhaps that complaint was how Cuff Roberts got a new batch of clothes a month later: hat, coat, waistcoat, overalls, shoes, two shirts, and two pairs of stockings.[15]

The new clothes would have to see Roberts through his first big move, and big changes in his regiment. The initial idea behind recruiting enslaved men had been to meet Rhode Island's recruiting targets. It never met those. Even after the expansion of its scope to include free men of African and Native ancestry, the First Rhode Island had trouble finding enough recruits, just like its sister regiment, the "White" Second Rhode Island. In the winter of 1780–1781, then, the two Rhode Island regiments would be integrated into one, simply called the "Rhode Island Regiment." Moreover, an officer recruiting for the Rhode Island Regiment, Jeremiah Olney, advertised that "It has been found, from long and fatal Experience, that Indians, Negroes and Mulattoes, do not (and from a total Want of Perseverance, and Fortitude to bear the various Fatigues incident to an Army) cannot answer the public Service; they will not therefore on any Account be received." Olney also pooh-poohed "Foreigners" as "Soldiers of Fortune" and deserters.[16]

Did Roberts and his comrades hear about Olney's words as they prepared to march through Connecticut to New York and join the Second Rhode Island regiment? Were they angry? Did they complain that they had persevered through various fatigues with *great* fortitude? Did they recount the late, insufficient pay? The hunger? The cold? The raids? The Battle of Rhode Island? Did they ask whether they could get out of their duration-of-war enlistments if that was what Olney thought about soldiers of color? If they did voice these complaints, I have seen no record of it. Except, maybe, it could explain what Roberts did next.

Roberts went absent without leave for twelve days in February, 1781. Desertion was rampant among the poorly supplied, harshly disciplined soldiers of the Continental Army. So was stealing food from civilians. In fact, having served almost three years without deserting, stealing food, or mutinying made Cuff Roberts exceptionally disciplined. No longer. In April, 1781, an officer in the Rhode Island Regiment noted in his journal that Roberts was court-martialed for stealing. It is possible the officer miswrote, and this was actually a court-martial for being absent without leave. At any rate, Roberts was sentenced to one hundred lashes, the legal limit in the Continental Army, and so were all the accused except for one. Nathan Gale was sentenced to death for "repeat'd Desertion," even after he "threw him Self on the Mercy of ye Court."[17]

Roberts had seen one hundred lashes laid on other soldiers many times. These punishments were supposed to be as public as possible. But this was probably Roberts's first time being whipped as a soldier. Had he seen other people of color punished in this way before enlisting? Had his father suffered at the hands of men with whips on the journey from west Africa, or while enslaved in Rhode Island? It is quite likely. Whippings in the Continental Army combined public shame with intense physical pain. They were meant to be degrading, intimidating, and something any soldier would want to avoid. They were not usually life-threatening, as the much higher lash counts of the British Army could be. But Roberts likely took weeks to heal, and bore the scars his whole life. Who knows how he responded as he felt the leather lashes slice his skin, and saw his own blood spatter onto the drummer's clothes?[18]

A few months after this whipping, Roberts would be on the move again with his regiment. This time he was going south to Maryland and Virginia. Roberts's commander, Colonel Christopher Greene, had been killed by Loyalist raiders in a surprise attack in New York. At the same time, Colonel Greene's cousin, General Nathanael Greene, had been active in the Carolinas. General Greene had repeatedly lost battles to his British counterpart, Lord Cornwallis, but always escaped and regrouped, eventually convincing Cornwallis to withdraw to Virginia. Roberts was on his way to help trap Cornwallis at a place called Yorktown. He must have noticed the warmer temperatures, and the larger number of African-descended people like himself. It was a new experience. Was it exciting? Or was it frightening to be surrounded by slavery? What surely *was* frightening was the random and sudden enslavement of Antony Griffin, another Black soldier in the regiment who knew Roberts. At Head of Elk, Maryland, someone claimed to recognize Griffin. After three and a half years on the Continental Line, Griffin was abruptly sent back to his old master. Or this was an elaborate hoax to acquire a free slave. Either way, Roberts knew he faced even more dangers here than he had from Loyalist raiders in Rhode Island and New York.[19]

Private Roberts got to Virginia by boat in September, 1781, where he was one of 16,000 allied soldiers, stretched around Yorktown. It had been a spectacular feat of logistics to bring so many American and French soldiers, together with a French navy, so rapidly to Virginia. They had moved quickly enough to trap Cornwallis and 8,000 British, Loyalist, and Hessian soldiers and sailors along with more than 4,000 formerly enslaved refugees in Yorktown. There was a buzz of excitement around the allied camp. And the Rhode Island soldiers were going to *look* good, whatever happened. They had each received a new uniform back in June, complete with a special leather cap painted with an anchor: the symbol of Rhode Island. A French officer, Jean Baptiste Antoine de Verger, painted a Rhode Island soldier in his uniform near Yorktown. The painting is reproduced in Figure 2.2. For all we know it could be a portrait of Cuff Roberts.[20]

In Verger's painting, the soldiers look sharp and the camp looks green and clean and uncomplicated. But that is not what Private Roberts saw, smelt, and felt. The large numbers of escapees from slavery, in and around Yorktown, must have caused Cuff Roberts to ponder a paradox of the American Revolution. Many enslaved people thought the *British* armies would bring them liberty, not the Continental armies who claimed to fight

Figure 2.2 This watercolor painting in the 1781 diary of French officer Jean Baptiste Antoine de Verger, made at Yorktown, Virginia, clearly shows an African-descended soldier in the distinctive uniform of the Rhode Island Regiment. For all we know it could be Cuff Roberts. Courtesy of the Anne S. K. Brown Military Manuscripts Collection, Brown University.

for liberty. Thousands of men, women, and children had fled to Cornwallis's army as he had moved through North Carolina and Virginia. Working as foragers, boatmen, nurses, servants, cooks, launderers, breastwork builders, and artisans, they made the risky choice to escape their masters and trade work for freedom with the British army. But, as the Franco-American siege wrapped around Yorktown, the promise of liberty to slaves who joined the British was starting to look hollow. Even before the battle, the sights and smells of death were all around.[21]

Did Private Roberts march past hundreds of Black smallpox victims on the road to Yorktown? Probably. A Connecticut soldier described how "During the siege, we saw in the woods herds of Negroes . . . scattered about in every direction, dead and dying, with pieces of ears of burnt Indian corn in the hands and mouths." Most soldiers in each army had been inoculated against smallpox by late 1781. But refugees from slavery had not. Cornwallis had ordered that sick refugees be left outside of Yorktown. Nevertheless, inside Yorktown they continued to contract the disease. A Continental general estimated that 2,000 Black people were forced out of Cornwallis's Yorktown in one October week, during the siege. These neglected, suffering souls, left to die after dashing for freedom, were African-descended like Roberts. What did he think when he saw them? Did he feel empathy? Did he sneak them food? Did he count his blessings that he was born free? It is hard to know, but he also had to focus on what his officers were ordering him to do.[22]

The Rhode Island Regiment took a turn digging trenches closer and closer to British defenses of the town. As each side hammered the other with artillery, Private Roberts and his comrades moved between the lines with digging tools, weapons, and the wooden defenses they had prepared back at camp to fortify their trenches. They went quietly, at night, in hopes of escaping British artillery. Then, after French and Continental light infantry stormed two redoubts, the Rhode Islanders occupied a part of the trenches they had risked their lives to dig. At least one Rhode Islander was killed and three were wounded by shells. But within days, Cornwallis asked to negotiate and his army marched out of Yorktown to surrender their weapons. Continental and French soldiers lined the road on either side to watch them. Private Roberts had never seen so many enemy soldiers this close. It was a great victory. And Cuff Roberts had played his part.[23]

The aftermath was ugly, though. Yorktown was full of corpses: victims of smallpox and French or American shells. Those refugees from slavery who had survived were now at the mercy of the Continental Army. Some Continentals were paid twenty-one shillings a head for ex-slaves they rounded up and delivered to Virginia planters, seeking to replace those who had escaped. Private Roberts's Rhode Island Regiment was quickly ordered across the river to Gloucester Point. Was that to keep one of the most African-descended regiments at Yorktown away from the scenes of reenslavement?[24]

While introductory history courses often end discussion of the Revolutionary War with Yorktown, that battle was not the end of Cuff Roberts's war. Wintering in Philadelphia, the Rhode Island Regiment marched to West Point, again, in the spring of 1782. After another summer on tense guard duty near the British lines, the regiment marched to Saratoga, where Private Roberts and comrades prepared a surprise attack on the British-held Fort Oswego. After a journey by snowshoe, in February 1782, a portion of the Rhode Island Regiment used sleighs to cross a frozen Lake Oneida at night. But the guides lost their way. Fort Oswego would not be surprised, nor captured. Some of the regiment were left behind and captured. Others escaped, but lost their toes to frostbite. After this failed expedition, Private Roberts and regiment waited. News of the peace treaty came in the spring of 1783. Finally, in June, the soldiers of the regiment who had signed up "for the duration of the war" were discharged. Cuff Roberts could go home.[25]

It took a week or two to walk back to Rhode Island. Along the way, the twenty-two-year-old veteran likely reflected on the last orders of his regiment's commander. There were lots of appreciative words: "Happy day," "very great share of merit," "long and faithful service in the righteous cause of God and our country." But there were also some words that might give the civilian Roberts some concern: "lament . . . so illy rewarded," "retire . . . without receiving any pay, or even their accounts settled and the balances due ascertained," "reason to hope," "Congress or the State." In other words, after more than five years trudging the length and breadth of the country, in the face of bullets and bombs, hunger and ice, pathogens and slavers, Cuff Roberts had not been fully paid. In fact, no one had told him how much he was owed. Or even which government was planning to settle up with him.[26]

ENDING SLAVERY, AMENDING THE POOR LAWS

Under these uncertain circumstances, he strove to make a new life for himself back in Rhode Island. Newly free of the Army, in a newly free United States of America, Roberts likely went back to work as a "laborer," doing whatever exhausting physical chores a farm-owner would pay him to do. Hopes of back pay, or land grants in New York, might have danced in the veterans' heads. But there is no sign that these promises materialized, or ever amounted to much for Roberts. In fact, by 1784, the poverty of some Rhode Island veterans was a big enough issue that the state legislature passed a law. It clarified who would support "the paupers, who heretofore were slaves, and enlisted into the Continental Battalions," but were now "sick and otherwise unable to maintain themselves." The legislature's answer was that it would not be Congress, nor the state, who would assist these needy veterans. As with almost all poor relief, it would be the responsibility of the towns where the veterans were settled. In many ways, this June law could be understood as an addendum to a much more far-reaching law passed in February, 1784: gradual emancipation for enslaved Rhode Islanders. Both laws focused on whether ex-slaves would have rights to poor relief under the poor law.[27]

The gradual emancipation law, while limited, was momentous for Rhode Island's African-descended population. The text of the law started out with an unmistakable reference to the Declaration of Independence. "Whereas all Men are entitled to Life, Liberty and the Pursuit of Happiness," it began, "yet the holding Man-kind in a State of Slavery, as private Property . . .is repugnant to this Principle . . . ." Thus, the state legislature would end slavery. Gradually. That meant all children born to enslaved mothers on or after March 1, 1784 would be free at the age of majority: twenty-one for boys and eighteen for girls. Their mothers (and fathers, if enslaved) would not be freed, unless their masters chose to free them, and the local town council agreed. The process of freeing those enslaved before 1784—called manumission—would become easier, but there was no requirement that slaveholders free those born before that year.[28]

Although it began with soaring rhetoric, the law ended with legalese, defining which emancipated people would have access to poor relief. That issue seems to have been more controversial than whether to free people in the first place. Legislators changed the poor law provisions twice between a draft in 1783 and a revision in 1785. The longest single section of the 1784 emancipation law, 205 words of 470 total, focused on poor relief. Since there was no provision that a freed person receive any fruits of their labor while enslaved, nor even the clothes on their backs when emancipated, legislators anticipated that poverty could be a problem. Legislators also wanted to defend against masters who might have benefited from a lifetime of work from an enslaved person, and then try to get the town to support that enslaved person in her old age. So they gave the town responsibility for any needy freedperson, but only if the person was above the age of majority and under the age of forty. Thirteen months later, the legislature revisited the issue and lowered the upper age limit to thirty.[29]

Thus, by 1785, formerly enslaved people only had rights to town poor relief if they had been freed to become a soldier during the war, or if they had been emancipated between the ages of eighteen (or twenty-one for men) and thirty. Every other emancipated person was still the financial responsibility of their former masters "in like Manner as Parents are by Law liable to support and maintain their poor Children." In this way, the legislature took a conservative step toward liberty and equality for freedpeople. Some would be freed. Some would have the right to poor relief. Others, quite literally, would have the rights of children. Although more limited than emancipation in Massachusetts and Pennsylvania, gradual emancipation created a period of excitement and danger for people of color in Rhode Island. The danger was that some slaveholders would not free their slaves, but instead sell the people they still legally owned to masters in other states. The excitement was that new freedoms allowed people of color to move around more, choose their own jobs, and create communities more on their own terms. [30]

Cuff Roberts helped build these communities of color, just as his parents had in their day. Unlike in his parents' generation, though, more and more people of color were free from slavery, and could move closer to family and friends. Extant records of Roberts's life at this time find him first in Warwick, his grandfather's home, and now home to a thriving community of both African-descended and Narragansett-descended people. In Warwick, Cuff Roberts and Elizabeth Grummuch visited a justice of the peace one day in late February, 1788. There they got married. Cuff's name, without Elizabeth's, next pops up years later, this time in Coventry, the town of his birth.[31]

In 1794, Roberts became a member of the Maple Root Church, a Baptist church which had been founded in 1762 and still worships together today. At the time, Rhode Island was the American heartland of Baptists, with an array of different kinds of Baptist churches. Maple Root was a "Six Principle" church which emphasized the laying on of hands. Literally placing their hands on new members after baptism, these Baptists held that every believer, including Roberts, could help others become close to God. Roberts would have been one of a few African-descended members in a church that was mostly English-descended, but which emphasized the equality of its members. While I have not yet seen sources describing why Roberts chose this church in his hometown, it seems likely that Roberts had an experience of closeness to God there, and wanted to be a part of this intensely devout community in the town of his birth.[32]

The very next year, though, found both Robertses in Providence, where another free community of color was growing. They rented a flat in India

Point, where their neighbors would have been sailors and taverns in this neighborhood built around the docks. Cuff Roberts was described as a "laborer" in his lease, but probably both Cuff *and* Elizabeth took work outside the home. Cuff Roberts would have found work loading and unloading cargo vessels at the docks. Elizabeth Roberts could have taken in washing, grown vegetables, boarded single men and women, or all of the above. They would have known many other people of color. Work was good enough to support the Robertses for years. The Roberts family grew to include four children by 1806. Probably at some point in this decade, Elizabeth died. By 1806, a new Mrs. Roberts, Jenny Roberts, was part of the family. Despite the blow of Elizabeth's death, no evidence I have seen shows them needing any poor relief.[33]

In the first generation after the revolution and emancipation, though, one town after another tried to control free people of color. Many town councils did not want Black or Native communities in their towns. Casting about for a means to regulate the movement of people, town fathers turned quickly to the poor laws. This was not a new use of the old poor law. Historian Ruth Wallis Herndon finds that towns targeted people of color and women for banishment throughout the second half of the eighteenth century. But these targeted roundups would become more frequent and explicitly about race during and after the Revolutionary War. For example, the East Greenwich town council ordered "all the Indians, mulattoes & Negroes that does not belong to this Town to depart the same immediately" in 1780, while Tiverton made a similar demand on "black people" in 1786. Historian Kunal Parker has called these uses of the poor law a kind of "immigration restriction" which was used against free African Americans all over the United States after the American Revolution. Historian Joanne Pope Melish has found that these periodic round-ups intensified between 1800 and 1820, in a general effort among "White" New Englanders to rid their communities of people of color, and to forget that New Englanders ever held slaves like Cuff Roberts's father. The Roberts family would be swept up in one of the biggest such mass banishments.[34]

WARNED OUT

The end of the Revolution and the increase in manumission had prompted a surge in Black mobility in Rhode Island. Between the censuses of 1790 and 1800, the number of "all other free persons" in Providence grew by 57%. The state as a whole saw growth in that category of 19%. Another surge in mobility coincided with the coming of age of the first freed people under the gradual emancipation law. Girls born to enslaved mothers in 1784 would be eighteen in 1802. Boys would be twenty-one in 1805. Able to move where they wanted, newly freed young men and women would have good reason to leave the small farm towns of their servitude for the larger communities of color in Providence, Warwick, and elsewhere. Overseers of the poor and their town councils would try to regulate this movement.[35]

In the cold month of January, 1804, the Providence overseers brought twelve people, all of African descent, to stand in front of the Town Council and tell their stories. In March, the town council stepped up its oversight by requiring Providence landlords to compile lists of all their black tenants. They took out advertisements in three newspapers. At first, it seemed these ads were intended to remind Providencians of the old law requiring towns-people to report *any* newcomer who stayed on their property more than a week. By the end of the ad, though, it was clear that town councilmen had race on their minds. "And . . . inhabitants are further requested," the ad concluded, "to make out a list of the names of all black people dwelling in their houses or tenements, and where they belong, and to report the same to this Council" by the end of the month. In the Fall of 1804, the town council also gave special instructions to the town watch "not to suffer any Company to remain assembled in any tenement . . . occupied by black people after ten oClock at night" and also to arrest any person of color not at home after ten. Thus, the town council began using its powers to explic-itly police African Americans.[36]

In 1806, the town went further. After a summer struggling to quar-antine smallpox victims, the town council turned its attention to Black Providencians in the Fall. Someone came up with an idea to encourage, and lend cover to, the town government's efforts to banish black residents. Whoever it was knew the poor law well, and knew how the overseers of the poor worked. This mastermind drafted language for a petition, which was then copied onto four separate petitions. Identical words were written in different handwriting on each petition and all together signed by 234 householders in town, including some of the wealthiest.

"Gentlemen," the petitions began, addressing the three overseers of the poor, "This Town is now infested with swarms of idle, thievish and vaga-bond blacks, who have no legal settlement therein, nor visible means of getting a livelihood." Packing in as much insulting language as possible, this first sentence both defamed people of African descent and also pro-vided legal justification for their banishment from Providence. Anyone fa-miliar with the poor law would know that to have no settlement and no livelihood meant an almost automatic warning out by the town council and overseers. Nevertheless, the petition went on for more excoriating language, asserting: "They are most of them an annoyance to the publick peace[,] depredations on the property of the Citizens, and dangerous to the personal safety of the Inhabitants, their Children and families." Then, demonstrating an intimate understanding of the mechanics of the poor law, the petitioners instructed the overseers exactly how to do their jobs. It concluded:

> You are therefore earnestly requested by the Subscribers that measures may be taken by Complaint from you to the Town Council of this Town or in such other way as you may think most likely to effect the object to rid the Town of this great and growing nuisance.

Though it left wiggle room to the overseers, the petition laid out the steps overseers could take to use the poor law to "rid the Town" of anyone they characterized as having no *settlement* or income.[37]

These four petitions are remarkable not only for their animus against the growing Black population in Providence, but also for how well-suited they were to their goal. The petition language hit all the right legal buttons, enabling the overseers of the poor to aim the poor law specifically at African Americans in town. The petition mastermind repurposed passages of the poor laws focused on finance to make them about controlling people of color. The power of warning out dated back to sixteenth-century England. The petitioners took this old power and gave it new meaning. Now, the warning out power could be used to break up Black communities and force dozens of people onto the roads out of Providence.

The petitions were remarkable in one other way, too, which might explain how the petitioners knew the mechanics of the poor law so well. Of the 234 petitioners, two had the same names of two of the town's overseers of the poor. The second petition was signed by a "Wm. G. Larned" as well as by a "Wm. Richmond 2d." These two signers were the adult sons of two of the overseers of the poor for that year: William Larned and William Richmond. William G. Larned was William Larned's fifth child, nineteen years old at the time of the petition and, evidence suggests, living in his father's house. William G. Larned and William Richmond, 2nd, as private citizens, were petitioning their own fathers as public officials. There can be little question that Larned and Richmond agreed with the intent of the petitions. The elder Larned or Richmond may even have been the mastermind—or masterminds—who worded the petitions so that they carefully followed the right legal formula. Moreover, it was William Larned who responded to these petitions with the greatest alacrity.[38]

Just days after the petitions, Larned presented the Town Council with a list of about eighty people he thought could be warned out: 10% of the town's Black population. Although Larned made no reference to race in the list, the town clerk gave it this title: "Wm. Larned overseer Complaint against certain Blacks." "Cuff Roberts, Wife and four Children" were the first names on William Larned's list, which is reproduced in Figure 2.3. According to Town Council minutes, Roberts was also the first on the list to show up at a town council meeting.[39]

It was a Thursday morning, about nine o'clock. Had Roberts come from a job, or had he taken the day off? Chances are he had never had to visit the second floor of the Market House before. He would have been familiar with the first floor, with its farm market stalls and stores. Upstairs, though, he crowded into a room where several men and women were gathered. Four of

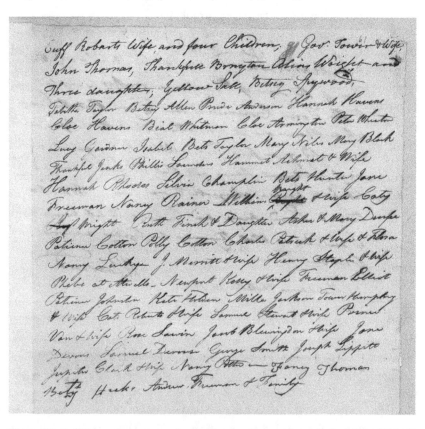

Figure 2.3 Cuff Roberts's name was the very first on Overseer Larned's list of which 'Black' residents of Providence he could bring to the Town Council for warning out, in response to the petitions asking the overseers to do just that, a few days earlier. Courtesy the Rhode Island Historical Society (RHi X17 4217, Town of Providence, "William Larned Overseer Complaint Against Certain Blacks – List of Names," 9 October 1806, ink on paper).

the men—well-dressed and seated, all of English descent—were the town council: the elected government of the whole town, who decided which business would happen in what order. The guests of the town council that day were a varied lot. Standing around were barkeeps, paying for liquor licenses. Then there was Roberts and a group of women, all of African descent. Did this make him nervous? Did he know what was coming?

The barkeeps did their business first, then it was Roberts's turn. They called him "Cuffee Roberts," and peppered him with questions, while a clerk took hasty notes, full of crossed-out words. He was born free in Coventry, Roberts affirmed, repeating what he likely had already told William Larned. He had lived in Coventry until five years ago, Roberts said. Did he not mention his war service? If he did, the clerk did not note it. He had four children, he said: Isabel, 13, was living with the Widow Cushing. No doubt Isabel was doing heavy housework already, perhaps as part of a long, indentured service. Benjamin was 11 and Henrietta was 9. They both lived with Roberts. The clerk did not write down the name of the fourth child, but he did write that Mrs. Roberts's name was Jenny. Did the clerk make an error, substituting the fourth Roberts child's name for Mrs. Roberts's? More than a decade later, Roberts would tell another clerk that his wife "Betsey" had died, and by then he was living with "Jenny," who would say her own name as "Janette." The clerk's hasty record, shown in Figure 2.4, is not perfect. It suggests, however, that Betsey Roberts had died, during

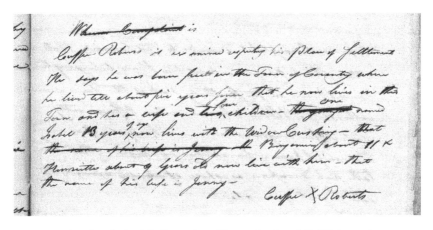

Figure 2.4 This first draft of the Town Council's examination of Cuff Roberts gives a sense of how fast the clerk had to record the interrogation, and how many mistakes he made, and tried to correct, in writing down important details. Courtesy the Rhode Island Historical Society (RHi X17 4218, Town of Providence, "Examination of Cuffee Roberts," 9 October 1806, ink on paper).

the eighteen years since 1788, and that Cuff and Janette had since made a household.[40]

Cuff Roberts had some reason to hope that he could keep that household in Providence. The four men around the table seemed indecisive about his case. He left without knowing a decision. They were far more decisive with their next few guests, though. Fanny Thomas was ordered to leave on a boat to New York. Betsey Hicks and her children were ordered to leave town in two days. James Brown was ordered to do something about his "black" tenants' "riotous" conduct. The town council adjourned without a decision in Roberts's case.

They readjourned at two o'clock the same day, though, with more African-descended families to examine. They started with Andrew Freeman, another veteran of the Revolution, with five children. They ordered him to depart before Wednesday. The clerk ran out of pages in his minutes book. The council sold some liquor licenses. Then they came back to Roberts's case. He and his family would have to leave within a week, they decided. The councilmen examined six more women from Larned's list and warned out four of them.[41]

That was it. Cuff, Jenny, Isabel, Benjamin, Henrietta, and the youngest child all had to go. The clerk recorded Cuff Roberts saying he had lived in Providence for five years, though his lease suggests more than ten. Friendships, neighbor ties, work relationships, schooling, all had to be torn asunder in the next week. Records do not describe the next week in the Roberts family life. How did the children react to the news? How fast did they pack? Did they have to leave things behind? The emotional wrenching of the move was no doubt flavored by that of all the other Black Providencians who were also being forced out. This was not just a disruptive event in a single family's life, but in a whole community's. The sorrow of leaving against their will mixed with the news of who else would have to leave. Moreover, there was the rush of packing and disposing of property. People who had been warned out had to find a way to quickly sell or store things they could not bring with them. Readers of Matthew Desmond's 2016 *Evicted*, about evictions in twenty-first-century Milwaukee, could imagine a similar dilemma two hundred years prior. If you have to leave your house in two days—or even a week—how can you possibly keep your hard-won property safe and with you? Warnings out, like evictions, could effectively make poor people poorer.

The shock was still fresh on Monday, when fourteen more people from Larned's list were examined. Half were told to leave. Another week later, those who had not left within the term set by the town council were ordered to be apprehended and locked in jail. Roberts was not on that list.

He must have known how serious the councilmen were. He and his family carried their lives to Coventry. Cuff Roberts knew Coventry well. Jenny Roberts and their children had perhaps visited before, but had probably never lived there. Just as his parents had taught him, though, Roberts would teach his own children how to knit friendships and family ties across towns, even when the powerful town fathers worked against them.

The town fathers of Providence would work against the Cuff Roberts family, and the rest of their community, for years to come. The examinations and warnings out from Larned's list would drag on, well into 1807. Into the 1830s, town fathers would repeatedly target "black" residents for expulsion under the poor law. Twice, in 1824 and 1831, "White" rioters would try to tear down Black homes. Nevertheless, the poor law would be the main instrument for these efforts at driving out Black neighbors. Although the 1806 sweep was one of the most extensive efforts, overseers of the poor and the town council would keep using the poor laws, year in, year out, to banish Black residents. Cuff Roberts, for his part, would repeatedly defy these expulsions. He would build a life in Coventry again, but he would not stay away from Providence.

CUFF ROBERTS COMES BACK

Back in Coventry, the Roberts family started to build a new life for themselves. Without the friends they had made in Providence, and with few other people of color, they thrived anyway. Perhaps Roberts reconnected with his fellow Baptists at the Maple Root Church. The census taker found Roberts head of a household in 1810, with four in the household: Roberts himself, probably his wife Jenny and their youngest child, plus a guest. From April to November of that year, Sarah Crank lived with them. Described as a "black woman then residing in said town," Crank must have been settled in Coventry, but without a place of her own. Roberts was reimbursed by the Coventry overseers for taking her in. In fact, another Coventry man was supposed to take Crank in. Thomas Whaley had agreed to house the town's paupers that year, but he refused to let Crank stay with him. Incensed at this breach of contract, the town fathers of Coventry took Whaley to court over it. Meanwhile, they depended on Roberts to make good the town's obligations to Sarah Crank.[42]

Where were the older Roberts children? Probably, they lived in other households, even in other towns, working for their keep. Roberts's children learned to work for strangers from an early age. At the same time, the Roberts children had a father who was free and kept a household of his own, to which they could come back. Cuff Roberts gave his children more security than he had from his own father, who had been constrained by slavery. It seems, too, that his youngest children were spared the workload their father had endured as a young child. Cuff Roberts was able to forge a safer haven in this hostile society than his parents had been able to. This despite town authorities who assumed the power to "bind out the children of blacks." This despite local authorities telling him where he could live, work, and build a network, and where he could not.

For a couple of years, Roberts owned his own land. Records from 1811 and 1813 show him buying land in Coventry. He would tell Providence officials that he had owned an acre and a half. That he was able to buy it speaks volumes. Unlike his neighbors, Cuff Roberts was a man who could inherit no property from his father. He would not receive a pension until 1818, so it seems that he bought land after almost three decades of scrimping and saving on laborer's wages. He sold it in 1813, then returned to Providence in 1816. Did he need the money in 1813? Was he tired of living in a small town with few Black neighbors? It is hard to know. What seems clear, though, is that Cuff Roberts was not satisfied with doing as the town authorities told him. He had a right to live in Coventry. But he wanted to live in Providence. So he went back. Cuff Roberts would make the life he wanted in defiance of the poor law.[43]

It was August, 1816, when Roberts made the move back. Nearly a decade before, the town council had made its cull of the Black population, with Cuff Roberts's name at the top of the list. Roberts had made it work in Coventry, but the aging veteran preferred a life in Rhode Island's largest town. There were opportunities for his children there, and a network of kin and old comrades. Town fathers, relying on the poor law, told him where to go, but he did not always listen. The Providence overseers would be within their authority to warn him out immediately, in 1816, but there is no evidence that William Larned or another overseer caught Roberts that year. Roberts got by. Maybe he knew how to keep away from Larned's daily peregrinations. Maybe Larned decided to accept Roberts for a while.

Roberts was still in Providence when big news came from the nation's capital. Finally, thirty-five years after he had walked home from the war, the national government was going to give pensions to some old veterans. Officers, and enlisted men with war injuries, had received pensions already. Now, enlisted men who were poor would be added to the pension rolls. Thus, in a limited way, the national government would get involved with poor relief.

In the twenty-first century, poor relief—or welfare—is often associated with the national government. The Social Security Administration, Aid to

Families with Dependent Children, food stamps, all have been funded or administered in part by the national—the federal—government. But in the nineteenth century, national government poor relief was a rare thing. Pensions amounted to a poor relief for veterans. There was also a social insurance for merchant sailors, beginning in the early nineteenth century. In the late nineteenth century, the US government would again give pensions to veterans, and provide assistance to some mothers. But overall, the marked absence of the national government from poor relief for the first century and a half of American history has led many to assume that welfare was a twentieth-century invention. As readers have seen, this assumption is very much in error. Most recipients of poor relief were cared for by local government, with local tax dollars. In this way, though, Cuff Roberts is an exception.

Cuff Roberts would not avail himself of local poor relief until the very end of his life. But he did avail himself when the *national* government decided to bestow pensions on the dying generation of Revolutionary War veterans. At the end of March 1818, Roberts called on some of the officers of the old Rhode Island regiment. They gave him documents attesting to his service. Then he visited a United States District Judge, and there he swore a "solemn oath" that the facts in his documents were true, and that he was "reduced circumstances," and he signed his "X." Roberts had lost his discharge papers, and the War Department asked for more proof. In August, Roberts got one of the old officers and a comrade-in-arms, Prince Vaughn, to appear in court and swear as to the truth of his service. Then, in October, news came. Roberts would be paid a pension of eight dollars a month, backdated to March 31, 1818. The economic historians at measuringworth.com estimate this to be a monthly salary equivalent to $2,500 at the time of this book's publication. That money would be a significant part of Robert's household income from thence forward. Moreover, it marked him as part of his world's "greatest generation." Anti-Black prejudice was still rampant, probably worsening in the 1810s. But here was a mark of respect from the national government. The country had seen two generations grow up, who respected their grandparents for their part in the Revolution. Roberts was one of the shrinking number of heroes, who had fought for independence. The national government recognized this. Would the local government?[44]

The Providence local government would not extend to Roberts the same respect the national government had. Even though Roberts had to collect his pension in Providence twice a year, local officials would continue to hassle him, question him, jail him, carry him away by wagon, and require special paperwork. He may have escaped their notice for a couple years, but in the fall of 1819, when William Larned briefly lost his post as overseer, the new overseer found him. George Olney was eager to show he could save the town's money as overseer. Part of this effort was warning out newcomers to town. Olney found Mercy Franks only days after she arrived. A "woman of colour," Franks already had work as a live-in servant with Mrs. J.C. Bucklin. Her six-year-old daughter, Hannah, had a place to live too: at Cuff Roberts's house. Roberts was again heading a household in Providence, again making a home for people of color who did not have their own. Franks's arrangements were not enough. She and six-year-old Hannah were warned out. Three weeks later, Overseer Olney had Cuff Roberts in front of the Town Council. Again.

It had been thirteen years since the roundup, and Roberts's first warning out from Providence. Then he had been a middle-aged laborer, a veteran with a still young family. Now he was a patriarch and pensioner, approaching old age: about fifty-eight. With a new overseer and a different town council, no mention was made of 1806. The council gave him a much more full examination than the hasty, pro forma questioning of 1806. He told about his parents, his household, including Jenny. Again, the council was not quite sure what to do with Cuff Roberts. They formally rejected him from being an "inhabitant," from having any rights to Providence poor relief. But they did not warn him out. A couple weeks later, Roberts was back in the Market House, answering more questions, this time about his grandparents. The council turned its attention to another resident they were trying to warn out. Sally Veney, who had refused to leave, was to be whipped in public the next morning. Though they rarely used it—and records do not show that the town sergeant actually carried it out—town fathers still had the power to whip those who did not leave and could not pay a fine. Back to Cuff Roberts they turned, this time ordering that he be removed to Coventry. It would take a while: in March, Roberts could collect his pension. Then, the town sergeant would put Roberts in jail for at least one night, and carry Roberts to Coventry on his cart, as described at the beginning of this chapter. The town sergeant's receipt for this trip is shown in Figure 2.5. This would not be the last time Roberts was ordered to leave Providence.[45]

Meanwhile, the new overseer, George Olney, resigned at the end of 1819. The town council quietly appointed William Larned back to his old post. It was Larned, then, who called Jenny Roberts and Henrietta Allen to the town council meeting in the Market House, after Cuff Roberts had already been removed. Jenny—or Janette—and Cuff Roberts had been married in Plainfield, Connecticut, not far over the state lines, she told the seated councilmen. Henrietta Allen, who shared a first name with Cuff

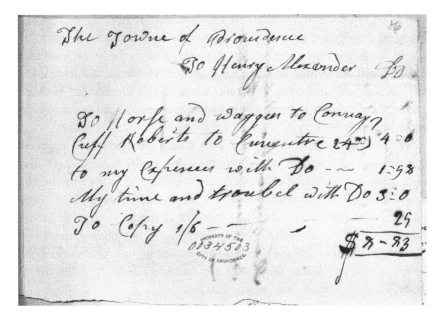

Figure 2.5 Ordered to carry Cuff Roberts back to Coventry in February, 1820, Town Sergeant Henry Alexander received a reimbursal for his time, and the use of his horse and wagon. This chapter opens by asking how Roberts might have felt as he was carried out of Providence on this wagon. Courtesy the Rhode Island Historical Society (RHi X17 3752, Town of Providence, "Receipt to Henry Alexander," 1830, ink on paper).

Roberts's daughter Henrietta, but was only thirteen years old, was visiting from Warwick, where she lived with her grandmother, Mary Caesar. This could be the same Mary Caesar who was one of the daughters of Sarah Olney, in chapter 3. Perhaps the two families were connected, as Henrietta Allen was also likely a grandchild of Cuff Roberts's. Her mother's name, she said, was Lucy Roberts. Seeing family in Providence, she was striving to keep family ties knit, just as Cuff Roberts had been doing for a lifetime. Young Henrietta was formally rejected from inhabitancy, but allowed to stay. Jenny Roberts was ordered removed to Coventry, to follow her husband. Separately, wife and husband got the same wagon ride to Coventry. The message was clear: stay out of Providence.[46]

But Cuff Roberts would not stay out of Providence. He *could* not, if he wanted to collect his pension. He would be back in August, on pension business, when he gave the United States District Court clerk an inventory of his property: a scythe, a hoe, two axes, a sickle, a rake, eight "old" chairs, two tea kettles, and a Bible. Now in his late fifties, he still depended on his "dayly labour for the support of himself, wife, and their Children, who are incapable of taking care of themselves." Still taking on casual labor.

Still using the tools of a farmer. He still described himself as "residing in the town Providence," even if he and Jenny Roberts had been removed by wagon just a few months before. No matter how many times the town told him to leave, he wanted to make his home in Providence. He lived a life in between towns, moving between Coventry and Providence, perhaps Warwick and other towns too. But in Providence, visiting did not always go smoothly for Roberts.[47]

Finally, in March 1822, he sent a note ahead. Other evidence suggests that Roberts had not learned to write his name, so the handwriting—and signature—are likely that of the Coventry Town Clerk, or one of Roberts's neighbors. The note was addressed to William Richmond. Back in 1806, Richmond had been one of three overseers of the poor involved in the roundup which banished Roberts the first time. Now William Larned was the only overseer of the poor, but Richmond had become president of the town council, the closest thing the town had to a mayor. "Mr. Richmond President of the Counsil Sir," began the note,

> I have been warned out of the town of Providence and I am an Old pensioner
> and I write a few lines to you to get liberty of the council to come into town four
> Days in a year after my pension money if you will be so kind as to Oblige your
> Obt humble Servant Cuff Robberts
>
> Coventry March 1822

Breathlessly free of punctuation, like many official documents, the note ended as any letter between citizens might end in this period: "your Ob[edien]t humble Servant." Roberts would play this game with the Providence town fathers. He would officially respect their power to control who entered the town and who did not. He would grant that even his status as a veteran and a pensioner did not entitle him to ride into Providence to collect his pension. The note worked, for a while. The town clerk briefly took notice of it in the minutes. "A Request in writing is made by Cuff Roberts that he may be permitted to come into this town four days in a year for his pension money Resolved that said request be granted." The petition and the answer, both formulaic, made the Providence town government sound quite reasonable, but their actions looked otherwise. Why was a note necessary? Why would the overseers of the poor not accept Roberts's verbal explanations?[48]

Cuff Roberts's semiannual struggle to collect his pension and maintain a life in both Providence and Coventry took place in a larger context of African American community making and hostile responses from both local government and neighbors. In the summer of 1821, the African Union

Meeting House, the town's first Black church, had been dedicated. A newspaper editorial in response complained that the African-descended population was a "transient" one and proposed "a *general Register* of all blacks in the town," a special census just to track African Americans.[49] The following summer, Overseer Larned did just what the editorial had asked for. Ostensibly walking through the city to inform "Coloured . . . Housekeepers" of the requirements of the poor law, the seventy-year-old Larned was quietly creating the *"general Register."* Larned, despite his age, probably appeared somewhat menacing to them. They no doubt knew that the notes he was making could be used to warn their families out at any moment. The existence of this handy index meant that Larned could start bringing people before the Town Council at any time, just as he had done in 1806. Evidence suggests that Larned used this list for some warnings out in July of 1822.[50]

Again, in the summer of 1824, the Town Council directed two constables to walk the streets like Larned had in 1822 and "enquire and to register the Names of all the Blacks and coloured people . . . together with their Situations and Employments." This would be an updated register like the one Larned had taken. By the Fall of that year, anti-Black sentiment in Providence was erupting in the streets. One newspaper editor repeated the complaint that the problem of transients in Providence was a race problem. "It unhappily falls to the lot of Providence," he moaned, "to receive and harbour all of the cast off and out-lawed blacks of Boston, and the adjacent cities and towns." Then, the editor focused on the overseer of the poor, who was the now seventy-two-year-old William Larned. The editor alleged about Black Providencians that "it is a fact that they are here cherished and protected, by those whose business it is to relieve us from such useless and dangerous kind of living lumber." He also asked "that measures should be adopted, and enforced, to rid the town of its superabundant share of this description of people." Like so many before him, the editor of the *Providence Beacon* looked to the town government to police African Americans. Ironically, given Larned's involvement in the 1806 roundup that had banished the Roberts family, the editor accused Larned of being too soft on Black Providencians.[51]

The *Providence Beacon*'s editor, though, professed to be shocked at what happened next. On October 17, the day after the editorial, there was a melee in the streets. As one journalist later described it, "a sort of battle royal took place between considerable parties of blacks and whites, in consequence of an attempt of the latter to maintain the inside walk in their peregrinations through the town." In other words, it was a fight over who could walk on the newly built sidewalks and who had to walk in the mucky middle of the street, where horse, pig, and dog droppings collected. One day later, a mob of European-descended men organized an attack on the African-descended population of Providence. Posting a placard to recruit rioters, forty men assembled with clubs and axes, marched to the largely Black enclaves of Hardscrabble and Olney's Lane, and methodically spent more than five hours destroying the houses of any people of color they could find. Hundreds of spectators came just to watch. A Town Watch member who was there said that he did not approve, but thought it neither "proper or prudent" to interfere. A Town Council member who was there agreed. In the end, seven houses were destroyed and a handful of others were damaged. Their owners and residents were in a state of shock. The next day, onlookers and residents surveyed the scene with astonishment and an angry fear, respectively. Records do not reveal where Cuff Roberts or William Larned were during this destructive riot. No doubt, Roberts knew some of those whose houses were destroyed. Sadly, Larned's son, Henry, the same one who was taking town council minutes at the beginning of chapter 1, had died while traveling for business, just a week before the riot, at age 33. But Larned could not have known that yet.[52]

Although there is no record of where Larned was during the riot, in the days following riot, he was quite busy. Only one day after the riot, Larned took advantage of an emergency meeting of the town council to order the examination of a sick young woman who had been widowed only two weeks before. Within a week, Larned had before the town council one of the victims of the riot, William Greene, described as a "black Man." Greene said he had been keeping a cake and fruit shop in Providence for the past four months, but that all his furniture and other possessions were lost in the riot. Without comment, the town council ordered him to leave within five days. It turned out that this was Larned's and the town council's response to the riots: warn out any of the victims that they could. A *Providence Gazette* editorial laid out this strategy. Noting that "We have frequently had occasion to deplore the increase of our coloured population" and hoping for their emigration to Haiti, the editor reminded readers of how the town council normally dealt with people of color:

> The authority vested in the Town-Council of this town has been exerted as often as complaints, made through the proper channel, the overseer of the poor, have been preferred and substantiated.

Quite explicitly, the editor said that the overseer of the poor was the official who could rid the town of unwanted newcomers, specifically African Americans. It was William Larned's role, then, to police the Black population of Providence. Though not written into state law, the town council of Providence made clear that this was part of his job description. The editors of the *Providence Gazette* knew this well: one of them was also a town councilman, named Walter R. Danforth.[53]

It was in the face of this current of popular and official hostility, then, that Cuff Roberts continued to collect his pension, and continued to make a home and knit the networks that kept his family together. He outlived William Larned, overseer of the poor, who died in office in December of 1828. Walter R. Danforth took over for Larned as overseer. It was his newspaper that had tasked the overseer of the poor with banishing people of color and had asserted the town's right to "bind out the children of blacks." By February, 1829, Danforth had Cuff Roberts back in front of the town council. What was Roberts doing back in Providence? The clerk did not write down a reason. Very likely, he was visiting family and waiting for his pension. With little comment, Roberts was ordered to "remove himself" by March 10, when his pension should have come in. Nearing seventy, Roberts still was not welcome in Providence.

Roberts had had enough of his semiannual trips to Providence, with all the hassle the town authorities gave him. In November 1829, Cuff Roberts married Nancy Ann Patterson in Massachusetts. Sixty-eight years old, this was Roberts's third marriage. In November 1830, Roberts found a justice of the peace in Boston, and had his pension transferred from Rhode Island to Massachusetts. His reasons, wrote the justice of the peace, "are that he can maintain and Support his family with more convenience and less expense." Still supporting family, still finding ways to keep them together, Roberts left behind a lifetime in Rhode Island. Just in time, as it turned out. Less than a year after his move to Boston, a violent anti-Black riot would break out in Providence, again.[54]

By then, Roberts had died, in Boston. It happened on May 22, 1831, half a year after Roberts had visited that Boston justice of the peace to get his pension moved. The next day, Roberts was buried in the city's cemetery for "Colour'd People." Cuff Roberts had outlasted the American Revolution and slavery in the North. He had worked hard to build a community for his children, so that neither their work opportunities nor town authorities could keep them apart. He had also made a point of asserting and exercising his rights, as much as he was able. Cuff Roberts is a lot like the antebellum African Americans described by historian Martha S. Jones: "people with limited access to legal authority [who] won rights by acting like rights-bearing people." Even if the overseers of the poor banished him, he would come back, claiming his right to receive his pension.[55]

Despite his efforts, Roberts did not outlast white supremacy, either in culture or in policy. In policy, he had seen his plans helped and hindered by American welfare. The national pension for Revolutionary veterans had helped support him for more than a decade, from the age of fifty-seven to seventy. In his last years, Boston's government had accepted him as a resident. His death record cited "Old age" as the cause of death and, moreover, described him as "City Poor." The phrase "City Poor" implies that the city of Boston extended some poor relief to him, without admitting him into the city's "House of Industry," then serving as a home for many of the city's poor. Letting Roberts live in Boston, unmolested, and possibly providing some relief to this veteran from out of state, Boston's poor law officials were more helpful than not, for Roberts. But poor laws had also served as the means for stifling his movement. Using the poor law, Providence officials had tried to stop him and his family from making their life there, time and time again.[56]

What do Cuff Roberts's experiences tell us about the poor laws? For Cuff Roberts, the poor laws were mostly an obstacle to be overcome. Local authorities in Providence used the poor laws to try to control his movement, to keep him out of Providence and in Coventry, the smaller town where his father had been enslaved. For decades, Roberts struggled against this control, sometimes successfully, sometimes not. The son and grandson of enslaved men, Roberts's experience was not unique. Rhode Island town record books are replete with examples of town authorities trying to keep people out in the mid-nineteenth century. So are those of the mid-Atlantic states: New York, Pennsylvania, Delaware, and Maryland. Massachusetts, unusually, had stopped banishing people from town before the American Revolution. Nevertheless, as historian Hidetaka Hirota has found, that state would pioneer the practice of deporting poor immigrants in the middle of the nineteenth century, using similar poor law provisions to those which other states used to deport people from town.[57]

Cuff Roberts struggle to live where he wanted to live, in spite of the poor law, was shared by a broad swath of Americans. Town authorities used the power of banishment to control many people's movements, and communities of color in particular. Historian Kunal Parker argues that the poor law was at the center of an effort to "make foreigners" out of African Americans. Cuff Roberts's experience shows this to be true of Providence, but not of Coventry, nor Boston. Coventry town fathers recognized Roberts as "belonging" to their town. That does not mean they were free of racial discrimination, but it complicates the picture. The poor law circumscribed Roberts's ability to move around in the newly free country, but it also gave Roberts a hometown. Legally speaking, he was not a "foreigner" there.[58]

Americans of European descent were frequently banished too. As Kristin O'Brassill-Kulfan has shown, the poor law was the main tool with which American governments controlled citizens' mobility for at least a half-century after the Revolution. While the poor laws were deployed as a tool to banish people of color, they were more than that. They were used to control the movement of the poor in general. This was "social control" of the type that historians have been describing since the 1970s. Cuff Roberts's experiences support the argument that the poor laws could be used by local governments to control where people lived and what kinds of work they could do.[59]

Even as we recognize the frustrating, controlling impact of the poor laws on Roberts's life, though, it would be a mistake to argue that was all the poor laws did, or even the single most important effect. As coercive as the Providence town authorities were, their banishments had another purpose besides social control of people of color. Warning out was also a way to make poor relief economically sustainable. Built into the Elizabethan era laws, and replicated by most American states into the twentieth century, local responsibility for poor relief required some method for ensuring no one town bore considerably more poor taxes than another. Historian Gary Nash has called warnings out a form of "economic cleansing" as practiced by eighteenth-century municipalities. For states from Rhode Island through the mid-Atlantic, this remained true well into the nineteenth century.[60]

In order to make a generous social safety net sustainable, municipalities throughout the United States worked constantly to make sure they paid the expenses of *their* needy, but not those of another town's. This was the model of welfare budgeting they had inherited, and which made sense to them. And despite its controlling effects, it worked, until transatlantic migration made it seem ineffectual in the mid-nineteenth century. Then states started to adopt something like Massachusetts's system, in which the state government picked up expenses that no single municipality did. It was under that system, in 1831, that Cuff Roberts was welcomed in Boston, perhaps even receiving poor relief there.

Dying in another state, described as "City Poor," might look like a sad ending to Cuff Roberts's long life. But his was a life of many victories, too. Born to an enslaved father, Roberts would be free. Raised in a stranger's house, Roberts would make a home so that his own children could stay with him for longer than he had been able to stay with his parents. Part of a victorious Continental Army, Roberts would make good many of the promises of freedom that army had fought for, whether his governments supported him or not. Repeatedly pushed out of Providence, Roberts would come back, again and again, building the communities he wished to, in spite of the power of the poor laws. Finally, after a life struggling against the banishment powers of the poor laws, Roberts would accept a national government veterans' pension, and then a home in Boston. The flip side of banishment from one town, was a right to support in another. Roberts would claim that right. Denied in Providence, it would be honored in Coventry, and in Boston.

Coming back to the question that opened this chapter, *was* it embarrassing for Cuff Roberts to be driven out of town on the sergeant's wagon? Reflecting on everything Roberts had done already by age fifty-nine, probably not. He had served five long years in the Continental Army, married twice, raised a family. In spite of the overseers of the poor, Roberts had protected his children from unwanted apprenticeships and had asserted his right to travel in the country he had helped make free. By 1820, he knew what he was doing when he defied the Providence town government's use of the poor laws. Chances were good that Roberts felt a great deal of pride and dignity, which no town sergeant's wagon could take away.

NOTES

1. Henry Alexander's receipt for removing Cuff Roberts to Coventry is in Providence Town Papers, MSS 214 sg 1, Volume 105, Document 0034503, RIHS. Edward Harwood's receipt for keeping Cuff Roberts in the "bridewell," or jail, is in Providence Town Papers, MSS 214 sg 1, Series 1, Volume 106, Document 0034530, RIHS.
2. There is a vast scholarship on the many ways that "unfreedom" persisted in American society, right through the Revolution. Two examples of the continuing debate over what the Revolution did and did not change are Gordon Wood, *The Radicalism of the American Revolution* (New York: Alfred A. Knopf, 1991), introduction, and Barbara Clark Smith, "The Adequate Revolution," *William and Mary Quarterly* 51:4 (October 1994), 684–692. For a description of the continuum of "unfreedom" in the eighteenth century, see Jared Ross Hardesty, *Unfreedom: Slavery and Dependence in Eighteenth-Century Boston* (New York: New York University Press, 2016), introduction. The legal term "likely to be chargeable" was widely used, referring to someone or some family who, in the estimation of the overseers of the poor and the town council, would probably need poor relief at some time in the future. It can be seen in Rhode Island law books and town records. See John D. Cushing, Ed. *The First Laws of the State of Rhode Island* (Wilmington: Michael Glazier, Inc., 1983), 352.
3. Entries for 25 November and 10 December 1819, MSS 214 sg 9, Providence Town Council Minutes Volume 9, RIHS.
4. On Akan day names, see Margaret Williamson, "Africa or old Rome? Jamaican Slave Naming Revisited," *Slavery and Abolition* 38:1 (2017), 117–134.
5. For numbers, see Slave Voyages, *The Trans-Atlantic Slave Trade Database*, online at slavevoyages.org.—as well as Gregory E. O'Malley, "Beyond the Middle

Passage: Slave Migration from the Caribbean to North America, 1619–1807," *The William and Mary Quarterly* 66:1 (January 2009), 125–172 and Gregory E. O'Malley, "Balancing the Empirical and the Humane in Slave Trade Studies," *Uncommon Sense—The Blog of the Omohundro Institute of Early American History & Culture* (14 January 2015), <https://blog.oieahc.wm.edu/balancing-the-empirical-and-the-humane-in-slave-trade-studies/>. For description of the slave trade, see Marcus Rediker, *The Slave Ship: A Human History* (New York: Penguin, 2007).

6. Christy Clark-Pujara, *Dark Work: The Business of Slavery in Rhode Island* (New York: New York University Press, 2016), 17. O'Malley, "Beyond the Middle Passage," 125–172.

7. For numbers, see Slave Voyages, *The Trans-Atlantic Slave Trade Database*. On adoption of Akan names, see Williamson, "Africa or old Rome?", 126–127. On Cuffy Brown, see 1774 Rhode Island census for Coventry, excerpted in *Rhode Island Roots* 22 (1996), 90.

8. Entry for 25 November 1819, MSS 214 sg 9, Providence Town Council Minutes Volume 9, RIHS. For larger context of binding out children, see Ruth Wallis Herndon, "'Proper' Magistrates and Masters: Binding Out Poor Children in Southern New England, 1720–1820," in Herndon and Murray, *Children Bound To Labor*.

9. For children of color in general, see, again, Herndon, "'Proper' Magistrates and Masters," 49–50. On "binding out the children of blacks," see *Providence Patriot and Columbian Phenix,* 23 July 1825.

10. For one such "X," which Roberts wrote in his late fifties, see Entry for 25 November 1819, MSS 214 sg 9, Providence Town Council Minutes Volume 9, RIHS.

11. On Valley Forge and officers resigning, see Middlekauf, *The Glorious Cause,* 412–414. On Rhode Island's quotas, see Robert A. Geake and Lorén M. Spears, *From Slaves to Soldiers: The First Rhode Island Regiment in the American Revolution* (Yardley: Westholme, 2016), 39.

12. On von Steuben, and the new commissaries, see Middlekauf, *The Glorious Cause,* 412–419.

13. Roberts's enlistment record is in the Rhode Island State Archives, reproduced in Bruce C. MacGunnigle, Ed., *Regimental Book Rhode Island Regiment for 1781 &c.* (East Greenwich: Rhode Island Society of the Sons of the American Revolution, 2011), 45. On the age of recruits, see Caroline Cox, *Boy Soldiers of the American Revolution* (Chapel Hill: University of North Carolina Press, 2016), 10–12. One source records Cuff Roberts as enslaved when he joined the Continental Army. His name is on "A list of the mens Names that were Slaves When they Inlisted," which archivists date to 1780. What was the purpose of this short list of just nine names? It is clearly not a list of all enslaved men in the regiment. No other record suggests that there were two soldiers named Cuff Roberts in the Rhode Island regiments. Given that Roberts himself repeatedly told officials he was born free, and that he also appears on "Return of Freemen Inlisted for during the War in 1st Rhode Island Battalion Commanded by Col. C. Greene," which archivists date to 1778, I believe that "list of the mens Names that were Slaves" is mistaken. See "Return of Freemen Inlisted for during the war in First Rhode Island Battalion commanded by Col. C. Greene" in MSS 673 Revolutionary War Military Records, SG 2, Series 1, Sub-series A, Box 1, Folder 19, RIHS and "A list of the mens Names that were Slaves When they Inlisted" in MSS 673 Revolutionary War Military Records, SG 2, Series 1, Sub-series A, Box 1, Folder 57, RIHS. Thanks to Jennifer

Galpern at the Rhode Island Historical Society for finding the "list of mens Names that were Slaves" among other documents.

14. For Reuben Gulliver, see "Declaration" of 15 August 1832 in Pension File Number S 29,849 (Massachusetts), Archive Publication Number M804, Archive Roll Number 1145. For Winthrop Robinson, see "Declaration" of 24 August 1832 in Pension File W. 9637 (Indiana), Archive Publication Number M804, Archive Roll Number 2068. Both pension files accessed via Ancestry.com. For details of this battle, including the size of the First Rhode Island Regiment, relevant sources, and a close tracking of the movements of the First, see Daniel M. Popek, *They " . . . fought bravely, but were unfortunate:" The True Story of Rhode Island's "Black Regiment" and the Failure of Segregation in Rhode Island's Continental Line* (Bloomington, Indiana: AuthorHouse, 2015), 213–237. The Hessian source is quoted in Popek. While I do not always agree with Popek's conclusions, his collection of sources and his narrative of the First Rhode Island regiment's movements and reorganizations are *very* helpful in reconstructing Cuff Roberts's experience of the war.

15. For Roberts's whereabouts during the Revolutionary War, I consulted forty-six documents, mostly muster rolls dated between 1778 and 1783. The majority are part of the *Revolutionary War Rolls, 1775–1783* in the War Department Collection of Revolutionary War Records, Record Group 93, microfilmed on National Archives Microfilm Public M246. I consulted a digitized version of those using Ancestry.com. The rest of the documents are in MSS 673 Revolutionary War Military Records, SG 2, Series 1, Sub-series A, Box 1, Folders 19, 55, 57, 73, and 79, as well as Box 6, Folders 22, 35, 37, 41, 42, 47, and 50, RIHS. Jennifer Galpern, Research Associate at the Rhode Island Historical Society, found many of these sources and made them digitally available to me. Also see Popek, *They " . . . fought bravely but were unfortunate,"* 267–268, 281–283, 285, 290–293, 314, 352.

16. "To the Public," *Providence Gazette*, 10 January 1781, 3. *Providence Gazette*, 9 March 1782, 3.

17. Evidence of Roberts being absent without leave is from MacGunnigle, *Regimental Book Rhode Island Regiment*, 111. Evidence of his court martial is in Robert C. Bray and Paul E. Bushnell, Eds., *Diary of a Common Soldier in the American Revolution, 1775–1783: An Annotated Edition of the Military Journal of Jeremiah Greenman* (DeKalb: North Illinois University Press, 1978), 206.

18. On whipping in the Continental Army, see Caroline Cox, *A Proper Sense of Honor: Service and Sacrifice in George Washington's Army* (Chapel Hill: University of North Carolina, 2004), 88–109.

19. Popek, *They " . . . fought bravely but were unfortunate,"* 513. I have not seen muster rolls for Roberts between January 1781, and May 1782. But in May 1782, Roberts was in the company from which Griffin had been discharged into slavery in September 1781.

20. On numbers of former slaves, see Sylvia R. Frey, *Water from the Rock: Black Resistance in a Revolutionary Age* (Princeton: Princeton University Press, 1991), 169. On numbers of soldiers and sailors, see Alan Taylor, *American Revolutions: A Continental History, 1750–1804* (New York: W.W. Norton, 2016), 294. On uniforms, see Popek, *They " . . . fought bravely but were unfortunate,"* 498–499.

21. Frey, *Water from the Rock*, 143–171.

22. Quotations from Philip Ranlet, "The British, Slaves, and Smallpox in Revolutionary Virginia," *The Journal of Negro History* 84:3 (Summer 1999), 217–226. See

also Elizabeth A. Fenn, *Pox Americana: The Great Smallpox Epidemic of 1775–82* (New York: Hill and Wang, 2001), 126–134.

23. On location of Rhode Island Regiment, see Popek, *They "... fought bravely but were unfortunate,"* 519–531.

24. On soldiers paid for escaped slaves, see Gary Nash, *The Forgotten Fifth: African Americans in the Age of Revolution* (Cambridge: Harvard University Press, 2006), 48.

25. Popek, *They "... fought bravely but were unfortunate,"* 590–604.

26. Colonel Olney's message is reprinted in Sidney S. Rider, *Rhode Island Historical Tracts No. 10. An Historical Inquiry Concerning the Attempt to Raise a Regiment of Slaves in Rhode Island* (Providence: Providence Press Company, 1880), 84–86. See also Popek, *They "... fought bravely but were unfortunate,"* 605–606.

27. On the June 1784 law, see Geake and Spears, *From Slaves to Soldiers*, 92–93.

28. For the legislation as passed, see "An Act authorizing the Manumission of Negroes, Mallattoes, & others, and for the gradual Abolition of Slavery" which is digitally reproduced on the website of Rhode Island's Secretary of State: <https://sosri.access.preservica.com/uncategorized/IO_c6fb1f13-9562-46cb-982b-3c398b1abd58/>. It is also in John Bartlett, *Records of the State of Rhode Island and Providence Plantations in New England* Vol. X, *1784 to 1792* (Providence: Providence Press Company, 1865), 8, 133.

29. For the draft legislation, see *Newport Mercury*, 10 January 1784 or *United States Chronicle* 15 January 1784. For the 1785 revision, see "An Act relative to Slaves, and to the Manumission and Support," in *The Public Laws of the State of Rhode-Island and Providence Plantations, As revised ... January, 1798*, reprinted in John D. Cushing, Ed., *The First Laws of the State of Rhode Island* (Wilmington: Michael Glazier, Inc., 1983), II: 610.

30. Rhode Island, "An Act authorizing the Manumission of Negroes, Mallattoes, & others, and for the gradual Abolition of Slavery" (1784). For further discussion of how this law was applied, see Joanne Pope Melish, "The Manumission of Nab," *Rhode Island History* 68:1 (Winter/Spring 2010), 37–43 and Gabriel Loiacono, "Poor Laws and the Construction of Race in Early Republican Providence, Rhode Island," *Journal of Policy History* 25:2 (2013), 264–287. For a longer consideration of gradual emancipation, as well as examples of masters selling their slaves out of state, see Melish, *Disowning Slavery*, chap. 3.

31. The 1774 census found Warwick to have the third largest population of "Indians," in absolute numbers, after Charlestown and South Kingstown, which abutted the Narragansett reservation; see Bartlett, *Census of the Inhabitants of the Colony of Rhode Island and Providence Plantations ... 1774*, 239. In the 1790 Federal census, the *proportion* of "All Other Free Persons" counted as neither "white" nor "slave" in Rhode Island was third largest in Warwick, after Charlestown and South Kingstown. Absolute numbers of the "All Other Free Persons" category were largest, though, in Providence and Newport, the two largest towns overall. Bureau of the Census, *Heads of Families at the First Census of the United States Taken in the Year 1790 Rhode Island* (Washington, DC: Government Printing Office, 1908), 9. Records of the Roberts-Grummuck marriage were copied into James Newell Arnold, *Rhode Island Vital Extracts, 1636–1850*, 21 volumes (Providence: Narragansett Historical Publishing Company, 1891–1912), Volume 1, "Kent County: Birth, Marriages, Deaths," 104. I consulted the digitized images from New England Historic Genealogical Society, via Ancestry.com.

32. On Roberts's membership in the Maple Root Church see Arnold, *Rhode Island Vital Extracts, 1636–1850*, Volume 10, "Town and Church Records: Births, Baptisms,

Marriages, Deaths," 270, via Ancestry.com. On the Maple Root Church and Six Principle Baptist churches in Rhode Island, see Maple Root Church, "Our Church History," <mapleroot.org/our-church-history/> and J. Stanley Lemons, *Retracing Baptists in Rhode Island: Identity, Formation, and History* (Waco: Baylor University Press, 2019), especially chaps. 2 and 10.

33. On mail, see *Providence Phoenix* for 29 September, 6 October, and 13 October 1804. On flat at India Point, see 21 September 1795 "Indenture of Lease," Document 10059 in MSS 214 sg 1, Providence Town Papers Series 1, Volume 23, RIHS.

34. Herndon, *Unwelcome Americans*, 18–20. Parker, *Making Foreigners*, 76. Melish, *Disowning Slavery*, 190–191.

35. For 1800, see *Return of the Whole Number of Persons. . . According to . . . the second Census . . . of the United States* (Washington, DC: House of Representatives, 1801), 26. For 1790 see *Return of the Whole Number of Persons. . . According to "An Act. . . " Passed March the First, One Thousand Seven Hundred and Ninety-One* (Philadelphia: N.P., 1793), 34.

36. Entries for 3, 4, 27, and 31 January 1804 in Providence Town Council Books, PCHA. *United States Chronicle* 15, 22, 29 March 1804, *Providence Gazette* 17, 24, 31 March 1804, *Providence Phoenix* 17 March 1804.

37. "Petition of Lowrey Aborn and others," "Petition of Simeon H. Olney and others to Town Council Respecting Black People Oct. 1806," "Petition of Thomas Sessions and others respecting black people Oct 1806," "Petition of Philip Allen and others respecting black people Oct 1806," Providence Town Papers (MSS 214 sg 1 Series 3, Volume 60, Nos. 008723, 008724, 008725, and 008727), RIHS.

38. For William G. Larned's age and birth order, see Eugenia Learned James, *The Learned Family in America*, 45. That he was likely still living with his father is suggested by the 1810 census, which shows four males between sixteen and twenty-five at William Larned's home. William G. Larned would have been twenty-three by the time of that census (Manuscript Census Return for Third Census of the United States, 1810, NARA microfilm publication M252, 71 rolls, Bureau of the Census, Record Group 29, National Archives, Washington, D.C., West District, Providence, Rhode Island, Roll: *58*, Page: 72, accessed online at Ancestry.com, Image 00141, Family History Library Film 0281232.

39. "Wm. Larned overseer Complaint against certain Blacks Oct 9th, 1806," in Providence Town Papers (MSS 214 sg 1, Series 3, Volume 60, No. 008728), RIHS. Providence Town Council Minutes Volume 3, 9 October 1806, MSS 214 sg 9, RIHS.

40. For the examination in 1806, see Providence Town Council Minutes Volume 3, 9 October 1806, MSS 214 sg 9, RIHS. The draft-like quality of the Town Council minutes housed at the Rhode Island Historical Society is discussed in Ruth Wallis Herndon, "On and Off the Record: Town Clerks as Interpreters of Rhode Island History," *Rhode Island History* 50:4 (1992), 103–115. For the examination more than a decade later, see Providence Town Council Minutes Volume 9, 25 November 1819, MSS 214 sg 9, RIHS.

41. Providence Town Council Minutes Volume 3, 9 October 1806, MSS 214 sg 9, RIHS. It is surprising that the Town Council did not make an exception for Isabel, leaving her in the household of Widow Cushing, but no such exception is noted in the minutes.

42. For the Manuscript U.S. Census return for 1810, I consulted the digitized version on Ancestry.com (Year: *1810*; Census Place: *Coventry, Kent, Rhode Island*; Roll: *59*; Page: *8*; Image: *00022*; Family History Library Film: *0281233*). Entries for 11

August 1810 and 5 November 1810, Coventry Town Council Minutes 1805–1818, Coventry Town Hall, Coventry, Rhode Island.

43. Manuscript Land Records: "Grantees" Volume 11, page 506 and Volume 13, page 395 and "Grantors" Volume 13, page 398, in Coventry Town Hall, Coventry, Rhode Island.

44. Cuff Robert's Revolutionary War Pension File is Number S 33,586 and includes documents dated 1818 through 1831. I consulted the digital copy made available at Ancestry.com, U.S. War Department, *Revolutionary War Pension and Bounty-Land Warrant Application Files, 1800–1900* [database online] (Provo: Ancestry.com Operations, 2010). Archive Publication Number M804, Archive Roll Number 2056. For an estimate of what eight dollars per month would be today, I used the "Unskilled Worker" formula at measuringworth.com, comparing 1818 to 2020.

45. MSS 214 sg 9, Providence Town Council Minutes, 3 November 1819, 25 November 1819, 10 December 1819, RIHS. For Henry Alexander's receipt for removing Cuff Roberts to Coventry, see Providence Town Papers, MSS 214 sg 1 Volume 105 Document 0034503, in RIHS.

46. For Henry Alexander's bill for the removal of Jenny Roberts to Coventry, see Providence Town Papers MSS 214 sg 1, Volume 105, Document 0034515, in Providence Town Papers, RIHS. For the Town Council's interview of Jenny Roberts and Henrietta Allen, see MSS 214 sg 9, Providence Town Council Minutes 16 March 1820, RIHS.

47. "Schedule of Property and Income" 1 August 1820 in Cuff Roberts Pension File Number S 33,586. The eight "old" chairs may not be chairs. The word is almost illegible and that is my best guess as to what it says.

48. The note is in Providence Town Papers MSS 214 sg 1, Volume 111, Document 0038670, RIHS. The Town Council response is in 11 March 1822, Providence Town Council Minutes Volume 11, RIHS.

49. Quoted in Jay Coughtry, *Creative Survival: The Providence Black Community in the 19th Century* (Providence: Rhode Island Black Heritage Society, n.d.), 59.

50. "A list of names of colored heads of families and the owners of their residences" in Providence Town Papers MSS 214 sg 1, Volume 112, Document 0039155, RIHS. Entry of 1 July 1822 in Providence Town Council Books, PCHA.

51. *Providence Beacon* 16 October 1824.

52. On sidewalks, see William Read Staples, *Annals of the Town of Providence from Its First Settlement to the Organization of the City Government in June 1832* (Providence: Knowles and Vose, 1843), 386. For quotations, see *Hard=Scrabble Calendar, Report of the Trials of Oliver Cummins [et al]* . . . . (Providence: Printed for the Purchaser, 1824). On the riot, see also John Crouch, *Providence Newspapers and the Racist Riots of 1824 and 1831* (Providence: Cornerstone Books, 1999), John Wood Sweet, *Bodies Politic: Negotiating Race in the American North, 1730–1830* (Philadelphia: University of Pennsylvania Press, 2003), chap. 9, William J. Brown, *The Life of William J. Brown of Providence, R.I.*, edited by Joanne Pope Melish, chapter IV; and the *Providence Beacon* 23 October 1824.

53. Entries 19 October 1824, 20 October 1824, 25 October 1824, and 2 November 1824 in Providence Town Council Books, PCHA. *Providence Gazette* 23 October 1824.

54. On Roberts's third marriage, I consulted a digitized copy of "Boston Marriage Publications, 1828–1833," Volume 11, Image 85/page 168, compiled by Jay and DeLene Holbrook as part of the collection entitled "Massachusetts, Town and Vital Records, 1620–1988," digitized at Ancestry.com. On moving pension, see

Statement before Francis Gardner, justice of the peace, 30 November 1830, in Cuff Roberts Revolutionary War Pension File, Number S 33,586. On the 1831 riot, see *History of the Providence Riots from Sept. 21 to Sept. 24, 1831* (Providence, 1831).

55. On Roberts's death and burial, I consulted a digitized copy of "Boston Deaths 1821–1832 South District" Volume 25, Image 14526/page 334, microfilmed by Jay and DeLene Holbrook, as part of *Massachusetts Vital Records Boston 1630–1849* (Oxford, Massachusetts: Holbrook Research Institute, 1985), digitized at Ancestry.com. A contributor to findagrave.com, Jacki Earp, identifies Cuff Roberts's grave in the "South Ground" of Boston's Central Burying Ground (<www.findagrave.com/memorial/113698863/cuff-roberts>).   Martha   S. Jones, *Birthright Citizens: A History of Race and Rights in Antebellum America* (Cambridge: Cambridge University Press, 2018), 10.

56. "Boston Deaths 1821–1832 South District" Volume 25, Image 14526/page 334, microfilmed by Jay and DeLene Holbrook, as part of *Massachusetts Vital Records Boston 1630–1849* (Oxford, Massachusetts: Holbrook Research Institute, 1985), digitized at Ancestry.com.

57. On New York, Pennsylvania, Delaware, and Maryland, see O'Brassil-Kulfan, *Vagrants and Vagabonds*. On Massachusetts before the American Revolution, see Dayton and Salinger, *Robert Love's Warnings*. On Massachusetts in the mid-nineteenth century, see Hidetaka Hirota, *Expelling the Poor: Atlantic Seaboard States & the 19th-Century Origins of American Immigration Policy* (New York: Oxford University Press, 2017), chap. 3.

58. Parker, *Making Foreigners*, chap. 3.

59. On mid-Atlantic officials using poor laws to control mobility, see O'Brassil-Kulfan, *Vagrants and Vagabonds*.

60. Gary Nash, "Poverty and Politics in Early American History," in Billy G. Smith, Ed., *Down and Out in Early America* (University Park, Pennsylvania: Pennsylvania State University Press, 2004), 10.

CHAPTER 3

⌒⌒

Healthcare for the Poor

How "One-Eyed" Sarah Saved Paupers' Lives

Looking up from her sick bed, the patient reflected on how she had gotten here. Fevers and chills, aches and nausea, it was hard to think of a symptom she did not have. On top of it all, she could not work and had run out of credit with every grocer in the neighborhood. Her nightmare was dying alone, too weak even to ask her neighbors for help. Fortunately, it had not come to that. Things had changed since her neighbor had discovered her, barely able to speak, and had hurried to find an overseer of the poor. Her first great relief was that Mr. Larned agreed to her whispered plea for the nurse who was now trying to bring down her fever. This nurse, Sarah, was known to be a good healer. The patient was not disappointed. Lying here, in someone else's house, in a clean bed, her senses tingled with joy at the damp cloth now being dabbed on her forehead.[1]

The patient had grown used to the face looking down at her over the last few weeks. It was a face that stood out in this town, with features that were "Indian," in a town that was mostly "Yankee" and a little bit African. The first thing one noticed about this nurse's face, though, was that one of her eyes was disfigured. Most people called the nurse "One-Eyed" Sarah. But looking up from bed, Sarah's more lucid patients saw something else: competence. Sarah knew what she was doing. This patient was not the first to request the overseers to please hire Sarah to heal them in their time of need.[2]

How Welfare Worked in the Early United States. Gabriel J. Loiacono, Oxford University Press. © Oxford University Press 2021. DOI: 10.1093/oso/9780197515433.003.0004

In the first decade of the 1800s, Sarah was one of scores of locals who helped the Providence overseers of the poor take care of the needy in their town. Nationwide, there were thousands upon thousands of people like Sarah, paid by the government to provide nursing, a home, food or clothes, a delivery of firewood, or a helping hand in some other way. Without people like Sarah, the overseers of the poor could not have done what they were elected to do: provide the necessaries of life to their poorest neighbors. Sarah was a vital part of the early United States of America's social safety net.

Despite her importance, historians know little about "One-Eyed" Sarah and others like her. There are receipts in archives around the country which record the cash that town and county treasurers paid out, a little at a time, to all these helpers of the poor. Rarely, though, do we know much beyond that: so-and-so was paid this amount of money to give room and board or nursing or groceries or firewood to some other so-and-so. This chapter will dig deeper, to try to understand how someone like Sarah came to work for the overseers of the poor, what she did, and why she did it. While investigating Sarah's life, this chapter will follow a few themes in the history of early United States poor relief: healthcare, women's labor, local government relief contractors, the expectation of "humanity" in poor relief, and the interplay of race and "respectability" with poor relief.

Sarah's story demonstrates how integral healthcare was to the poor relief of her day: it was expensive, effective healthcare, with a goal of the patient's recovery. It could include nursing, doctoring, and prescription medicines. This healthcare, though, depended heavily on the difficult, paid, but ad hoc work of women like Sarah. These women took the legal mandate of poor relief to help needy townspeople and put it into practice. Hired by the overseers of the poor, paid by the town treasurer, they were the ones who actually carried out the tasks their neighbors so desperately needed someone to do. The fact that scores of locals each decade would derive part of their income by providing for the poor was central to the success of early American poor relief. One the one hand, overseers of the poor could not provide care without this help. On the other hand, poor relief helped not only paupers but also those paupers' neighbors. Paupers got food, shelter, and medicine, while their neighbors got opportunities to earn cash, as "One-Eyed" Sarah did, or got access to cheap labor, as we shall see in chapter 4. Part of the enduring popularity of poor relief can be explained by how many Americans it helped. Some were helped directly in the form of poor relief; others were relief contractors, who earned income in the form of payments for helping the poor.

The town paid for these acts of relief not only because of their benefit to paupers and their neighbors, but also because of the prevalent assumption that poor relief was necessary and "humane." Unpacking what early Americans meant by humane is part of unpacking the story of Sarah's work. Another part of her story is race. Sarah's life teaches us a bit about how Indigenous women were and were not part of local communities. In the decades that Sarah worked, local officials were erasing the Native presence in their towns from records by describing Natives as "Black." Moreover, local officials were using the poor law to banish some "Black" inhabitants, as we saw in chapter 2. Nevertheless, local officials defended Sarah as both "Indian" and "respectable." Sarah's story is a rich one, replete with insights into how poor relief worked in the early United States of America.

But there is a problem with Sarah's story. Of the five life stories in this book, Sarah's is by far the least well-documented. It rests on two short newspaper articles. That is the only evidence I have found that describes Sarah with certainty. The two articles describe a "One-Eyed" Sarah without ever mentioning her last name. She is described by one article as having worked for the overseers of the poor until 1806 or 1807, her services having been requested by the paupers themselves, and having "restored them to health." Another article suggests that she lived in the neighboring towns of North Providence or Smithfield, not in Providence proper. Searching archives, newspapers, and other scholarship for years, I have found two other Sarahs who could be "One-Eyed" Sarah. Sarah Hill and Sarah Olney each match "One-Eyed" Sarah's story in important ways. But I have not found enough evidence to prove that either of those Sarahs is *the* "One-Eyed" Sarah. Still, stories like "One-Eyed" Sarah's are so important—and so rarely told—that it is worth telling hers with the evidence at hand. The rest of this chapter will describe what can be learned from records of Sarah Hill and Sarah Olney, as well as from the newspaper articles about "One-Eyed" Sarah. While we cannot be sure that Hill or Olney are the right Sarah, their life stories show us different ways that someone like "One-Eyed" Sarah could have become a nurse for the poor in her place and time. Learning about both of their lives, we can reconstruct some strong possibilities about "One-Eyed" Sarah. We can see how a Native woman who moved to Providence would be treated by the town, and how she might get to know the powerful overseers of the poor. We can see why the overseers would have picked her for this difficult, sensitive work. We can also see how she could make public nursing part of her household's strategy for supporting itself.[3]

AN "INDIAN" IN NEW ENGLAND

In 1811, the overseers of the poor would pointedly describe "One-Eyed" Sarah as "Indian." This is a surprisingly rare descriptive term in Providence at that time. Historians Ella Wilcox Sekatau, Ruth Wallis Herndon, and Joanne Pope Melish have all found that that Rhode Island officials described Native people as "Black," "Negro," or "of color," in the early nineteenth century. When writing about people of both Native and African ancestry, or people only of Native ancestry, government officials frequently refused to acknowledge them by nation, or even as "Indian," insisting on words like "Black" even when Native people formally objected. Ultimately, this erasure of Native people from official records allowed the Rhode Island government to claim that Narragansett people did not really exist by the late nineteenth century. This was an era in which New England government officials rarely described Native people as Native. They made an exception for "One-Eyed" Sarah, though.[4]

Town officials also made an exception for Sarah Hill, describing her as "Indian" in 1803, when she came to Providence to live. Moreover, they noted that she was "blind." Thus, in a series of coincidences, both Sarah Hill and "One-Eyed" Sarah were living in or near Providence in the middle of the first decade of the nineteenth century. Both were named Sarah, though that was a very common name in Providence at the time. Both were described as having problems of the eyes: Sarah Hill was "blind" while "One-Eyed" Sarah was, of course, "one-eyed." Both were called "Indian" in a time when few others were. The many similarities between town records of Sarah Hill and "One-Eyed" Sarah are circumstantial evidence they might be the same person. Whether they are the same person or not, Sarah Hill's life story can help us understand how a Native woman might come to the attention of the overseers of Providence and then convince them to hire her as a nurse.

Before "One-Eyed Sarah" was working for the Providence overseers of the poor, Sarah Hill was being warned out by them. Hill appeared in the Providence Town Council minutes at least three times: 1784, 1791, and 1803. Although clearly the same woman, born in Uxbridge and bound out successively to three men in Massachusetts, Hill was described differently each time she is called before the council. In 1784, the clerk called her "mustee," an English term for someone who was at least partly of Native ancestry. In 1791, she was "Negro," a term that English people had adopted from Spanish and Portuguese, more than two centuries before, to mean African. In 1803, Hill was "Indian." That third interrogation, in 1803, bucked the trend in two ways. Not only was Hill described as "Indian" this time, but she was not warned out of Providence either. She had been warned out in both 1784 and 1791. In 1803, Sarah Hill was allowed to stay in Providence at just the time that "One-Eyed" Sarah would be active as a nurse. Moreover, the 1803 interrogation described Hill as having been "blind" just in the previous four years. Could it be that an injury or illness of her eyes caused Hill to become both "blind" and "one-eyed" around age fifty?[5]

If Hill is "One-Eyed" Sarah, her life story teaches us much about how a Native woman could find nursing work paid for by poor relief funds. Hill told her life story to the Providence Town Council on more than one occasion. The most complete version was recorded by the town clerk in 1803, when Hill was fifty-four years old. The clerk's smooth copy is reproduced in Figure 3.1, and it is also worth quoting in full:

> Sarah Hill, an Indian Woman, is examined before this Council respecting her place of Settlement, Saith She was bound out at the age of Three Years to James Cooke, in Uxbridge, in the State of Massachusetts. That she was bound to said Cooke, either by the Town of Uxbridge, or her Mother cannot tell which.—That the said Cooke sold her time to Oliver Arnold, Esquire, of Gloucester, That the said Arnold sold her again to one Emerson, in said Town of Uxbridge, with whom she served out her time, being three years. That she lived in said Uxbridge about Five Years after she was free, when she came to this Town, and lived in the Family of said Oliver Arnold, Then in the Country, in divers places. That she has been blind about four Years, and is aged Fifty four Years. That she came into this Town, last Friday Week, from Warwick. That she had been living in said Warwick, at one Joseph Baileys, a black man, from whence she was removed to Ceasar Lockwoods alias Ceasar Cheese. That she has two Children, both of whom are at Sea, one sails out of this Town, the other out of Boston. That she was led to this Town by Mary Lockwood, Wife of the said Ceasar, and by his direction . . . . Sarah her X mark Hill
>
> And the said Examination being duly considered it is thereupon Resolved, that the said Sarah Hill, be, and she is hereby rejected from being an Inhabitant of this Town.

The town fathers asked specific questions, aimed at determining where the complicated laws of settlement would place Hill. Their conclusion, that Hill was "rejected from being an Inhabitant" meant that Hill had no right to

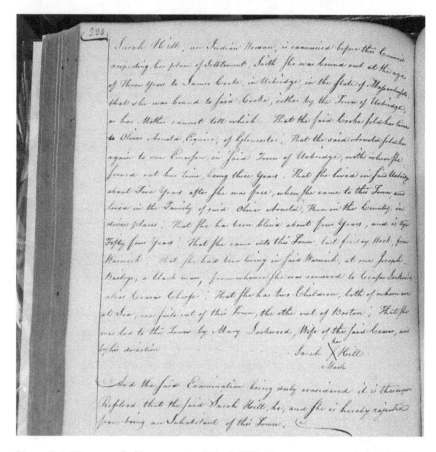

Figure 3.1 This town clerk's summary of Sarah Hill's life story was recorded in 1803, in what was at least Hill's third interrogation in front of the town council. Notice that, at the bottom, there is no order to leave town, only a formal notice that Hill is 'rejected from being an Inhabitant of this Town.' Thus, while Hill was not entitled to receive poor relief in Providence, she could live there for the time being. Entry for 7 February 1803, Providence Town Council Minutes, courtesy of the Providence City Archives.

receive poor relief from the town. They could have gone farther and warned her out, ordering her to leave or be carried out of town, but this time they did not do so. And, although this was not their goal, they brought forth a substantial short biography of Sarah Hill. The town councilmen, and the overseers of the poor, wanted to know where Hill was born, what family she had, and whether she might have acquired a settlement in any town she moved to. Hill went as far back as she could remember: three years old. That was when she was sent to work—and live in—a household headed by a James Cooke. This momentous decision was made "either by the Town of Uxbridge, or her Mother [Sarah] cannot tell which," the clerk wrote down fifty years after the decision was made.[6]

THREE YEARS OLD AND ON THE JOB MARKET

Three years old and already she was working in someone else's household. Her mother was clearly still living. Why would the adults in her life remove her from her mother? The answer, in part, is that the poor law encouraged it, arguably demanded it. Sarah Hill's life was shaped by the poor law from a very young age. The poor laws prompted overseers of the poor to remove children from the parents' household if their parents could not care for them, or were not raising them as the overseers saw fit.

Another reason Sarah Hill was taken from her mother at age three was race. British North American town officials began acting as if all Native and African parents were, *ipso facto*, unfit parents. Boston's Town Meeting, for example, had resolved in 1723 that "every free Indian, Negro, or Molatto shall bind out, all their children at or before they arrive to the age of four years to some English master, and upon neglect thereof the selectmen or overseers of the poor shall be empowered to bind out all such children till the age of twenty one years." Similarly, Providence town officials still believed in 1825 that they had a duty to "bind out the children of blacks," though that power was nowhere listed in Rhode Island poor laws. It is not clear why Uxbridge officials bound the three-year-old Sarah Hill in 1752, but it seems most likely that they believed this "Indian" child ought to be brought up in an English household. Indeed, as Ruth Wallis Herndon and Ella Wilcox Sekatau have argued, we could see Sarah Hill's indenture as a way of confiscating her labor from her family and awarding it to a wealthy, English-descended family instead.[7]

Hill's own mother or father or both, presumably, were "Indian," though Providence sources never specify which nation. Uxbridge was in traditional Nipmuc territory, and was fewer than twenty miles from both the Dudley Nipmuc reservation in present-day Webster, Massachusetts, and the Hassanamisco Nipmuc community in present-day Grafton, Massachusetts. Incidentally, one of the Providence overseers of the poor who hired "One-Eyed" Sarah, William Larned, had grown up in Thompson, Connecticut, another town in Nipmuc country, with a significant presence of Nipmucs throughout this period. This could explain why town officials decidedly described "One-Eyed" Sarah as "Indian," even as town officials did not use this word for other Native people. Perhaps Larned was more familiar with Nipmuc people than with other Natives, and more likely to acknowledge and even respect their nationality. Given their proximity, it seems likely that Hill's parents came from Dudley or Hassanamisco, but it is hard to know. Indigenous people in eighteenth-century New England moved around the region a lot, maintaining intratribal links but also forging new communities across tribal divisions. English-descended clerks were usu-ally not interested in what nation someone was beyond the category of "Indian" or "of color." New England town officials increasingly cared only about the line between "white" and not "white" in the late eighteenth and early nineteenth centuries.[8]

Whatever the motivations of the Uxbridge town officials, Sarah Hill was learning from a very young age how town government worked in New England. She knew that the Town of Uxbridge played some role in where she lived at age three, and as she grew older, she would get an even clearer concept of who made decisions about her life. She lived—as an indentured servant—in three different masters' households while a child and became free at eighteen or twenty-one years old. She stayed in Uxbridge into her twenties, and then began moving around the region. She first came to Providence before the American Revolution, and came back to the town at least three more times. On two of those occasions, town officials ordered her to be "removed," or physically brought, to Uxbridge. Despite these removals, Hill moved around quite a bit between her mid-twenties and mid-fifties. She lived in several towns in Massachusetts and Rhode Island, and by 1803 had one son who sailed out of Providence and another who sailed out of Boston.

That Hill was living with "Ceasar Lockwood alias Ceasar Cheese" suggests that Hill had found a network of friends and perhaps family as she moved from place to place. Lockwood appears in the 1790 census in Warwick as head of a household of four, in the "all other free persons" cate-gory. If the census-taker was going door-to-door, then many of Lockwood's neighbors were also in that not "white" category. Some had names, like Ceasar Lockwood's, which suggested enslaved or African backgrounds, such as Cesar Lippitt and Prime Lippitt. Others had names associated with Narragansett families, like James Profit, a surname also spelled Prophet, and the same surname as Cuff Roberts's grandfather, who had also lived in Warwick. Why would Hill leave this tight-knit community and come to Providence? Providence also had such a community of interconnected Native and African families. Also, as Hill mentions, one of her sons sailed out of Providence. Moreover, Hill came to Providence "by [Lockwood's] di-rection." They must have had a plan. They may have had a strategy to help Hill avoid being warned out or removed this time.[9]

In her many experiences moving from town to town, Hill realized the power that town officials could wield over townspeople. When she was interrogated by town officials in 1803, Hill had been through this a lot. I have seen records of two of those previous interrogations in Providence, but there were likely more, in other towns. Hill knew what town officials wanted to hear and she knew their likely reaction to her. She knew they could banish her or allow her to stay. She also knew what she could do for them. Hill's experience with town officials over the decades made her especially cognizant of the needs town officials had. Overseers of the poor needed to banish some people but needed to assist others. That assistance could include food, shelter or, frequently, healthcare. If Hill had experience providing healthcare, she could have offered that experience to the overseers of the poor in 1803.

Nowhere in her three interrogations is there evidence that Hill had healthcare skills. However, there was a widespread belief among Americans of European descent that "Indians," especially Native women, had healing skills. A cultural stereotype which was also a niche profession, "Indian" healers, or "herb doctors," were noted throughout early nineteenth-century New England. Hannah Shiner, of Medford, Massachusetts, was described as a "judge of herbs," while Hannah Dexter, of Natick, Massachusetts, was described as a "doctress, well skilled in administering medicinal roots and herbs." In Sturbridge, Massachusetts, Aunt Sarah Green "often said she was a doctor and carried herbs in her basket." Molly Ockett, a Pigwacket Abenaki healer, contemporary with "One-Eyed" Sarah and Sarah Hill, became famous for her healthcare work in Maine. The idea that Native women had unique knowledge of herbal medicine from the oral traditions of their nations was widespread in this period. This cultural stereotype of Native women as healers could explain why the overseers emphasized in the newspaper that "One-Eyed" Sarah was both "Indian" and an effective healer.[10]

In this cultural context, one could imagine Sarah Hill, so acquainted with the powers and needs of overseers of the poor, offering healthcare services to the overseers on the way to the town council meeting. Perhaps as they escorted her to the interrogation, she suggested she might be of service to them. Perhaps that is why, unlike in 1784 and 1791, the town council let her stay in Providence. After having been warned out of Providence twice, Hill knew that she was likely to be warned out again. A quid pro quo, in which she made herself valuable to the overseers, could stop that from happening again. As they were examining her, as they did most newcomers, she would have had ample opportunity to offer her skills to them. "I am not likely to be chargeable, Your Honors," she could have said, familiar with the legalese overseers used. "My son John is a sailor on one of Mr. Brown's ships," she could volunteer. "Also, I'm not so helpless as I seem, Your Honors," she might add. "I'm a nurse! Ask Mary Lockwood. Everyone sends their sick to me. I cure fevers and agues and all sorts of ailments." "Are there any sick poor here? Let me give them some of Sarah's tea," she could offer. The overseers might leap at the offer. They had many sick paupers on their hands. Arranging doctor visits was difficult enough. Finding nurses who would give full time care to some of the town's sickest and poorest people was even more difficult. And this woman, newly arrived, within their power to warn out, could be a great deal. They could save money working with her. They could offer some money and some guarantee they would not warn her out. She could offer cheap, diligent, creditable care. If she had the skills, Sarah Hill had the opportunity to make a deal with the overseers. This scenario is speculative. It would explain, though, why the town council found her to have no right to stay in Providence, yet stopped short of banishing her in 1803.

While it is not certain that Sarah Hill was "One-Eyed" Sarah, Hill's life shows how "One-Eyed" Sarah could have come to work for the overseers. As a young girl, probably Nipmuc, Hill's life had been dramatically transformed by the power of local officials. Under the broad scope of the poor laws, she had been taken from her mother's care and given to a series of English-descended families. As an adult, she learned how to cope with the power of poor law officials. A woman who had been pushed around New England by the poor law would come to know the poor law well. She learned how to migrate between towns in spite of them. She returned after they warned her out.

If Sarah Hill was "One-Eyed" Sarah, she must have drawn on her first-hand knowledge of how overseers of the poor operate to figure out how she could be of use to them. She could take advantage of the overseers' interrogation of her—as a newcomer—in order to offer a deal to them. This deal would supplement the income of her sailor son, bringing another livelihood into the family purse. It would also give the overseers a strong reason not to warn her out of town. It is quite plausible. Finally, in her fifties, with difficulty seeing well, she could have found a strategy that allowed her to stay in the town of her choice, with friends or family, and earn money from the very officials who had made her life difficult in previous years. Healthcare became a profession for her, one that paid and gave her some "respectability" in the eyes of the overseers of the poor. Not in spite of, but because of her hard life, she was well placed to offer her services to the overseers.

EARNING RESPECTABILITY AND CASH AS A LOCAL GOVERNMENT RELIEF CONTRACTOR

Sarah Hill's life experience offers one story to explain how and why "One-Eyed" Sarah could have become a nurse, working for the town. Another story about how this would be possible comes from the life of Sarah Olney. While no receipts I have seen show the overseers paying Sarah Hill directly, many of these receipts mention a Sarah Olney. The large archive of Providence Town Papers at the Rhode Island Historical Society includes thousands of slips of paper, orders on the Town Treasurer, requesting payment to individuals for services rendered to the town. The largest single category of these are treasury orders by the overseers of the poor. As we have seen in chapter 1, overseers of the poor controlled a large fraction of a municipality's budget into the 1820s. Among these thousands of slips of paper are numerous receipts to different Sarahs for services like "keeping" the "town poor" or "nursing" or "boarding and nursing" or "boarding" individuals. It has been impossible to determine for sure which, if any, of these slips of paper are for "One-Eyed" Sarah. One of the most frequently paid Sarahs was Sarah Olney. In 1782, a Sarah Olney was giving Ruth Mitchel supplies. Twenty-five years later a Sarah Olney was being reimbursed for "keeping Minerva Harvey and Jude Bowen's child." An 1804 receipt to a Sarah Olney, thirty dollars for "Keeping Town Poor," is reproduced as Figure 3.2. In that same period, Sarah Eddy, Sarah Sheaveateau, Sally Allen, and Sally Bartwell were some of the many other people also paid for "boarding" or "nursing" individuals. Sally was sometimes used as a nickname for Sarah. And these are only some of the treasury orders from that decade. There are hundreds from that decade alone. But a Sarah Olney is one of the people most commonly paid for her work for the poor. Moreover, other evidence about a Sarah Olney connect her even more to descriptions of "One-Eyed" Sarah.[11]

Both Sarah and Olney were common names in early nineteenth-century Rhode Island, but one of these Sarah Olneys also shared circumstances

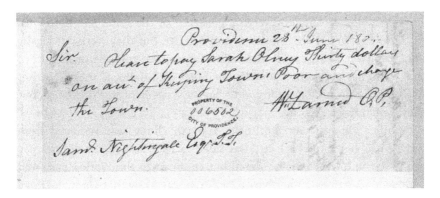

Figure 3.2 Another scrip signed by William Larned, O.P., this one reimburses a Sarah Olney. It is a relatively large sum for keeping more than one pauper an unspecified period time. Could she be 'One-Eyed' Sarah? Courtesy the Rhode Island Historical Society (RHi X17 4214, Town of Providence, "Receipt to Sarah Olney for Keeping Town Poor," 28 June 1804, ink on paper).

with "One-Eyed" Sarah: Sarah Olney, married to Aaron Olney. This Sarah is like "One-Eyed" Sarah in a couple of ways: for one, she lived in Smithfield, a town just north of Providence. One of the newspaper articles describing "One-Eyed" Sarah suggested Smithfield was Sarah's "neighborhood." Moreover, her husband Aaron Olney is a described as a "man of color" while his and Sarah's children are described in official documents as "black." I have not seen any ethnic or racial descriptors of Sarah Olney herself. The marriage patterns of late-eighteenth-century New England suggest that while European-descended people overwhelmingly married others of European descent, it was not uncommon for Native women to marry African-descended men. So, was Sarah Olney "Indian"?[12]

Local government records never make clear the ethnicity of Sarah Olney, but they do make clear that Aaron and Sarah had a number of children who lived and worked in Providence. In 1801, the Providence town council seemed to be interviewing as many people of color as it could, with the goal of warning out as many as possible, just as they would do to Cuff Roberts and family a few years later. In January 1801, they brought to their meeting chamber Celinda Olney, daughter of Aaron, a sixteen-year-old described as a "black girl." She told them she had been visiting her sister for the past two weeks and they warned her to leave town by the next morning. In May, Celinda Olney was back in Providence, this time in jail, and charged with being "a person of bad fame and reputation." This time the town council ordered her carried back to Smithfield by the town sergeant. The next month, the council ordered Mary Ceasar to appear. Mary Ceasar was probably the sister Celinda Olney had been visiting. She said she was born in Smithfield, the daughter of Sarah Olney and a man named Ceasar. She had lived in Providence for nine years, the last seven in a "tenement" belonging to Arthur Fenner, the long-serving governor of the state. She lived with Anthony Browning, a truck driver and peddler, but they were not legally married. Mary Ceasar sold cakes at her home, and told the town council that customers brought liquor to her home and drank it there. Neither Ceasar nor Browning were found to have a settlement in Providence, but they were not warned out.[13]

Another Olney from Smithfield, Hannah Olney, was removed from Providence, but came back and was fined in 1803. When she did not pay the fine, the town council ordered her confined to the Work House and whipped "15 stripes on her bare back." It seems likely that Hannah Olney was another child of Aaron's and Sarah's, sister to Celinda Olney and Mary Ceasar. This brutal effort to keep Hannah Olney out of town is in keeping with town officials' efforts to keep out people of color in the first generation after emancipation from slavery. Whipping was used as a legal means of punishing people who defied warnings out into the 1830s in Providence. State law would prohibit whipping for disobedience of removal orders in 1838. Many, but not all, of the people ordered whipped were people of color. It is not clear that these whippings were always carried out, but it is clear that Hannah Olney and family would have little love for the town council and overseers of the poor. Given this history of town officials banishing, jailing, and possibly even whipping her daughters, could Sarah Olney, wife of Aaron, be the "One-Eyed" Sarah who worked for those same overseers of the poor as a nurse?[14]

As in the case of Sarah Hill, Sarah Olney's family would know very well the powers of local government officials. Moreover, they knew the personalities of Providence's overseers of the poor, who had interrogated them and gotten them warned out on several occasions. The Olneys had been subject to the overseers' hostile attention and had learned firsthand the power the overseers wielded. Perhaps because of this hostile attention, Sarah Olney would strive to cultivate a working relationship with the overseers both as a source of income and as a way to deflect the overseers from hassling her children. Celinda and Hannah Olney, and especially Mary Caesar, all clearly wanted to live in Providence, and persisted in coming back to the town after officials warned them out. As a nurse, popular among patients, Sarah Olney could convince the overseers of her and her family's "respectability."

By the summer of 1811, overseers writing in the newspaper described "One-Eyed" Sarah as "formerly of respectable character." In a striking coincidence, Aaron Olney had just died, two months prior. Smithfield probate records describe him dying in May, and two administrators oversaw the probate of his property. An inventory found both real estate and personal property, which Sarah Olney had no doubt helped to purchase, perhaps with income from nursing Providence's paupers. Under the laws of coverture, she could not have owned any of this property herself. It was all in Aaron Olney's name. Sarah Olney had to wait until outstanding debts her husband had owed could be settled. The process found Aaron's estate insolvent, but awarded Sarah Olney the whole of Aaron's personal property, together with the widow's "Thirds" of his real estate. Other portions of the family's real estate were sold to satisfy debts. Because Aaron Olney died in May, 1811, and Sarah Olney did not receive her widow's thirds until March, 1812, she was probably in unusually straitened circumstances when newspapers described "One-Eyed" Sarah in the summer of 1811. Perhaps this is why the overseers called her "formerly respectable."[15]

Like Sarah Hill, Sarah Olney resembles "One-Eyed" Sarah in a number of ways. She lived in Smithfield and had family members who moved between towns and were not always welcomed by town officials. Her life circumstances had changed between the time she worked for the overseers and the summer of 1811, as she became a widow whose wealth was tied up in probate. If she was "One-Eyed" Sarah, we learn that, like Sarah Hill, she could find her way to nursing paupers for the town by first enduring the hostile attention of the town's officials. As she tried to figure out how to protect her young adult daughters from the town council's warnings out and whippings, she might have hit on the strategy of doing business with them. Moreover, working for the overseers of the poor could be an important economic strategy, boosting family income and helping to buy real estate in nearby Smithfield. Working for the overseers of the poor provided much-needed cash.

From Sarah Olney's or Sarah Hill's points of view, working with the overseers of the poor could be a path to respectability and income. From the overseers' points of view, working with "One-Eyed" Sarah was a way of getting vital work done. The overseers' job was to find ways to provide for the needy, cheaply and humanely. Their reliance on "One-Eyed" Sarah to do that work might have been one of the many lost stories in the history of welfare, were it not for a series of newspaper articles printed in 1811. This war of words focused on how humanely overseers were doing their job.

A WAR OF WORDS

The two newspaper articles that describe "One-Eyed Sarah" are part of a remarkable series which began in early June, 1811. That month, a writer with the pen-name "Howard" had his letter published in *The Providence Gazette and Country Journal*, a newspaper which supported the Federalist party. The letter was a searing condemnation of how inhumanely the overseers of the poor were caring for the poor of Providence. The writer chose the pen-name "Howard" in homage to a then-famous English philanthropist, John Howard.

John Howard had died in Ukraine, nearly two decades before, but had been celebrated on both sides of the Atlantic for his work visiting prisons and hospitals, urging authorities to improve conditions. American newspapers still invoked his name, which had become a byword for humane benevolence. Indeed, in New York, another writer had also taken the pen-name "Howard" earlier that same year of 1811. New York's "Howard" wrote a series of essays against imprisonment for debt, which were published in that city's *Columbian* newspaper. Providence's "Howard" was perhaps inspired by New York's "Howard" and definitely inspired by the actual John

Howard. Providence's "Howard" was part of a long reform tradition, trying to make both penal and welfare institutions more humane. This tradition spans from John Howard in the late eighteenth century through Dorothea Dix in the mid-nineteenth century to the Welfare Rights movement of the late twentieth century.[16]

Stepping into that tradition, "Howard" walked to the local workhouse one day as Spring turned to Summer. This is something that the actual John Howard would have done. Some municipal officials in the United States even invited visitors to make surprise visits to local poor relief institutions, to make sure the poor were being well cared for. There is no evidence that Providence officials made such an invitation, but New York officials had done so a few years before. Although called a "workhouse," the Providence building which "Howard" visited in 1811 in fact functioned as poorhouse, short-term homeless shelter, and insane asylum all in one. It is not clear that inmates were required to work there in 1811, as *work*houses were supposed to require them to do. As readers will see in chapter 5, there had frequently been efforts in British North America, and then in the United States, to build workhouses and poorhouses in order to more tightly control poor relief. But these efforts usually eased up after a few years, and municipalities moved back towards giving poor relief outside of poorhouses or workhouses or asylums. Providence's government had been contemplating a workhouse since the 1730s. The workhouse that "Howard" visited was probably built in 1803, but his visit came at a moment when the workhouse was not heavily used. Most paupers received "outdoor relief" in this period, in their own homes or in neighbors' homes. It would be another seventeen years before Providence had a new, specially built asylum for the poor, and another thirty-three years before the state opened an asylum for the insane. The inhabitants of the workhouse, then, were either there for a short term, or the overseers of the poor had found no other accommodations for them.[17]

"Howard" was shocked when he visited. In particular, "Howard" alleged, the workhouse was damp, cold, and dilapidated, while the workhouse keeper was not given enough supplies and the overseers of the poor rarely visited. "Howard" also noted that an insane man was kept in a filthy cage in the workhouse, and his noise did not allow other inmates to sleep. The next week, "Howard's" letter was reprinted in the *Columbian Phenix*, a newspaper that supported the Jeffersonian-Republican party, with favorable commentary from the editor. *The Providence Gazette and Country Journal*, meanwhile, printed a rebuttal, signed "A Friend to candid Investigation," which sounds very much like it was written by one of the overseers of the poor. Quickly, the letters turned into an affair of honor. The various letter writers spent nearly as much time attacking or defending their own reputations as they did describing the workhouse and other arrangements for poor relief.[18]

It was in the midst of this war of words that "Howard" brought up the work of "One-Eyed" Sarah. In response to "A Friend to candid Investigation's" angry defense, "Howard" penned a second, long letter which was published June 29. In it, "Howard" named witnesses who could confirm his original allegations and then added this new evidence:

> He ["A Friend to candid Investigation"] takes offence at my observation, that under the present system, the poor have often been "distributed amongst the vilest wretches," and intimates that "people of respectability" only are allowed to undertake the charge of them—let me then ask him whether ONE-EYED SARAH and her family are "people of respectability" or better entitled to the epithet I have given them? and whether paupers subjected to their tyranny have been treated with common humanity? And before he answers the question, let him consult "people of respectability" in their neighbourhood in North-Providence and Smithfield—*who will a tale unfold*.

Vilest wretch. Tyrant. Inhumane. "Howard's" reasons for describing Sarah were to further criticize the overseers of the poor. How could they hire this woman and her family, his letter cries out. Then, hinting that damning stories circulated in North Providence and Smithfield, two smaller, neighboring towns, "Howard" moved on to other subjects. "Howard" never did "unfold" this tale, but he did prompt some explication in an unsigned response on July 20:

> *"One-eyed Sarah,"* to whom *"Howard"* has alluded in his second letter, is an Indian woman, formerly of respectable character; none of the poor of the *town of Providence* have been under her care for four or five years past. She has had (according to the recollection of the Overseers) only two white persons, who were in a situation not fit to be mentioned, and by their own request were put to Sarah, who by her care restored them to health. Thus is the "tale unfolded."

The overseers of the poor vigorously defended their choice of Sarah to be a nurse while implying that they would not choose her now. Indian, respectable, and a competent healer, the overseers asserted, Sarah had actually been requested by the impoverished patients who depended on town poor funds for their care. It was a confident response, except with regard to race. The overseers were on the defensive about choosing an "Indian" nurse to care for "white" patients. Although "Howard" had never brought up the ethnicities of Sarah or her family or her patients, the overseers' response suggests that "Howard's" critique was largely about race. "Howard's" critique and the unsigned response are reproduced in Figures 3.3, 3.4, 3.5 and 3.6, along with the newspaper pages in which they were printed.[19]

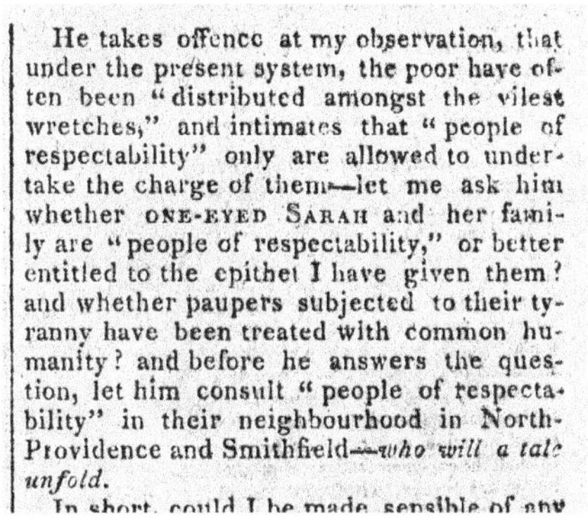

> He takes offence at my observation, that under the present system, the poor have often been "distributed amongst the vilest wretches," and intimates that "people of respectability" only are allowed to undertake the charge of them—let me ask him whether ONE-EYED SARAH and her family are "people of respectability," or better entitled to the epithet I have given them? and whether paupers subjected to their tyranny have been treated with common humanity? and before he answers the question, let him consult "people of respectability" in their neighbourhood in North-Providence and Smithfield—*who will a tale unfold.*
> In short, could I be made sensible of any

Figures 3.3 and 3.4 A small paragraph in a long, second letter, 'Howard's' description of "One-Eyed" Sarah drips with animosity toward her and her family. These images, courtesy of the American Antiquarian Society, show the entire front page and a detail of the *Providence Gazette and Country Journal* for 29 June 1811.

get hold of.—Is this the fault of the Overseers? "*One-eyed Sarah*," to whom "*Howard*" has alluded in his second letter, is an
Indian woman, formerly of respectable
character; none of the poor of the *town of
Providence* have been under her care for
four or five years past. She has had (according to the recollection of the Overseers) only two white persons, who were in
a situation not fit to be mentioned, and by
their own request were put to Sarah, who
by her care restored them to health. Thus
is the "tale unfolded." As to the "*refor-

Figures 3.5 and 3.6 Although unsigned, the response to 'Howard' of 20 July 1811 was
probably written by the overseers of the poor. Their defense of their hiring "One-eyed Sarah"
is brief, and comes in a long article accompanied by several testimonials to the overseers'
care of the poor. These images, courtesy of the American Antiquarian Society, show the entire front page and a detail of the *Providence Gazette and Country Journal* for 20 July 1811.

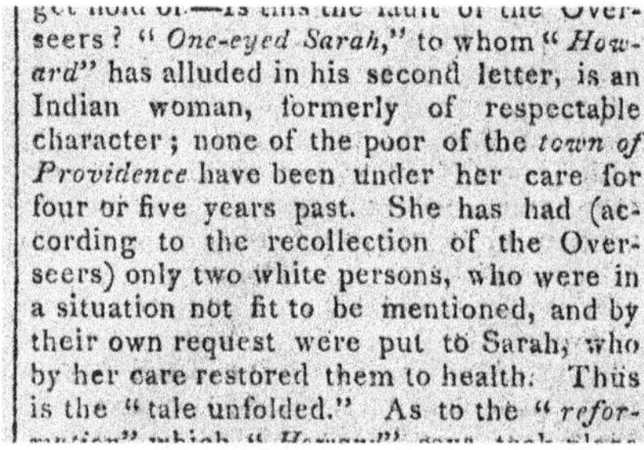

While the newspaper battle raged into August, "One-Eyed" Sarah was not
mentioned again. But these two short passages raise all sorts of questions.
Who was "One-Eyed" Sarah? Why was she "formerly" and not currently "of
respectable character"? Was she a "tyrant" or a competent healer? Or both?
Was Sarah still working as a nurse in North Providence or Smithfield?
Did Sarah care for people of color too? What is the "situation not fit to
be mentioned"? Why does "Howard" call her family "vilest wretches" and

what connotation did the term "Indian" carry for "Howard's" opponents? Before the reader despairs of too many unanswered questions, let us remember what these short passages do tell us about the themes of this chapter: healthcare, women's work, local government relief contractors, "humanity," and race.

Perhaps most significant is that the articles flesh out what women did in order to provide healthcare to their neediest neighbors, and how overseers of the poor found women to do this work. This is important. Hundreds of receipts exist for this decade of Providence's poor relief efforts, often made out to women, but none provide details like this. Nurses, paid by the government, restored patients to health. This gives an idea of the quality of care that the government provided. It was labor-intensive and effective. It went beyond providing comfort to the dying: the overseers' goal was to heal their wards, if possible. Not only that, but patients, too poor to pay for nursing themselves, could nevertheless request a particular nurse care for them. This suggests a level of agency among ill paupers and an effort from overseers of the poor which we might not otherwise believe was true.

The patients who requested Sarah, moreover, were described by the overseers as "in a situation not fit to be mentioned." It is difficult to know what that means, but one possibility is that they were suffering from a venereal disease, perhaps syphilis. A century before Sarah, Boston clergyman Cotton Mather called syphilis a "secret disease," writing that it was frequently covered up on death certificates. Officials did not want to publicly discuss it. By the early nineteenth century, some American newspapers acknowledged cases of syphilis publicly, but it still carried a great deal of stigma. It is quite likely that "A Friend" did not want to be quoted in print talking about a sexually transmitted disease.

If Sarah were treating syphilis, there were a number of possible cures she could employ. Still popular in the early 1800s among Europeans and European-Americans was mercury. Whether in ointments for topical use or pills and liquors for swallowing, doctors had some success with mercury. Its possible side effects, though, were significant: tremors, paralysis, tooth loss. Herbal treatments, including sarsaparilla-based medicines, were an alternative to mercury. These were sometimes combined with treatments of warmth, like a sauna. Sarsaparilla, long associated with Native people of the Americas, was frequently advertised for sale in American newspapers of that decade. If Sarah were curing syphilis, the cure would be up to her. It is possible she had her own homemade medicine and treatment. It must have been good if patients requested her and she "restored them to health." The overseers must have had some idea of her skill as a nurse when they hired her.[20]

Not only did the overseers hire women like Sarah, they relied on women like Sarah. Without women like Sarah, the poorest Providencians might have died untreated in their illnesses, for lack of money and attention. Providence was not unique in this way. Poor law officials around the country relied on women to do the strenuous, part-time, ad hoc work of nursing patients, devising and monitoring medical treatments, boiling water, laundering clothes and bedclothes, bathing people, sweeping, scrubbing, louse picking, clothes making, clothes mending, meal preparing, midwifing, and anything else a pauper might need done to survive. Overseers, literally, oversaw this work. Paid women like Sarah *did* the work.

Sarah was just one of many women doing this difficult work. While she and others were paid to take care of one or two paupers in their homes, other women were paid to take care of several paupers in the workhouse. In 1811, the keepers of the town's workhouse were Stephen and Betsy Shaw. Betsy Shaw's testimony was published as part of this war of words. "This may certify," she signed in July 1811, "that I have had the immediate care of all the poor at the workhouse in Providence, from September 1809, to this present time, and I solemnly declare, that the whole of said poor have had their clothes regularly washed, mended, and put on clean once every week during the said time. . . . " Stephen Shaw identified himself as the work-house "Keeper," but Betsy Shaw clearly had a lot of responsibility in the institution. Similarly, Mary Hammond signed that "I the subscriber kept the workhouse in Providence, from October, 1808 to September, 1809." She seems to have run the place by herself. This was not only true in Providence, moreover. Scholars have found that women's work was central to poor relief from Boston to rural Massachusetts to Philadelphia to Richmond. Indeed, poorhouses could sometimes be called "female space[s]." This was partly because many of the poor inmates were women, but also because many of the paid caregivers were women, like Sarah.[21]

No doubt the pay she received was important to Sarah. Her story gives just one example of a widely used economic strategy for early citizens of the United States: contracting with the local government to provide poor relief. Nurses, doctors, grocers, clothiers, firewood splitters, cart drivers, and others were paid to provide goods and services to the town's poor. Historian Elna C. Green would have us appreciate how much local economies were stimulated by local tax dollars paid out to people who supplied things for the poor in the early United States. As seen in William Larned's life, garnering income from the poor tax was a strategy that benefited a wide swath of families with a variety of goods and services to offer. One of those families was that of "One-Eyed" Sarah. While it is difficult to know how much Sarah earned all together, a June 28, 1804 receipt to Sarah Olney says she earned thirty dollars for "Keeping Town Poor," for one example. Olney may have been "One-Eyed" Sarah, as discussed above. This receipt suggests that Olney kept multiple paupers, since other receipts named individual paupers for whom the money was spent. It is also a much larger sum than other receipts note. Unfortunately, and uncharacteristically, it does not note how long a period the sum of thirty dollars covers, but it seems unlikely to have been a whole year. Other receipts suggest that the going rate for providing "board" to a single child was seventy-five cents per week, and providing "board" to a single adult earned a dollar per week.[22]

While paupers technically had no say in how they received assistance, the overseers made clear that some paupers had requested "One-Eyed" Sarah's care and the overseers had acceded to the pauper's wishes. Thus, although a pauper legally had very little independence, in reality, his or her caregiver might have a very real interest in keeping the paupers happy. After all, if getting work from the town overseer depended in part on requests from paupers themselves, then paupers were part of a patronage network that helped keep households like Sarah's afloat.

Why were municipal governments willing to pay people like Sarah? "Howard" and his opponents give us one answer: they all assume that providing free healthcare to the needy was a necessary and proper function of the local government. At least eleven letters were printed in response to "Howard's" original letter. All assumed that poor relief needed to be done and done with "humanity." As bitterly argumentative as the letters were, the argument was not about whether government should be involved in poor relief or healthcare, but about whether the government was doing a good enough job. The one letter purporting to critique poor relief was, in fact, a satire.[23]

There were others, around the United States in this period, who publicly questioned whether Americans should provide private, charitable donations. But even they assumed that government poor relief was necessary. In one example from 1818, a Pittsfield, Massachusetts Congregationalist minister argued that private charity actually increased the suffering of the poor. But this minister, Heman Humphrey, viewed public poor relief, given sparingly and preferably inside of almshouses and workhouses, as the right answer to poverty. Reverend Humphrey was a proponent of institutionalization, which would become popular again in the mid-nineteenth century: to give poor relief only inside institutions, and to treat beggars as criminals.[24]

That suspicion of the needy, however, was not a part of the 1811 argument in Providence. "Howard" closed his first letter talking about humanity and the town's reputation. After having laid out his critiques and some suggestions for improvement, he concluded that "The writer hopes, for humanity's sake and the honour of the town (which has now got to be large and populous—the number of paupers daily increasing) that this appeal will not go unattended to. . . . " While his letter would cause a local controversy, this conclusion seemed uncontroversial: All agreed that taking good care of the poor was necessary both as a good in itself and out of civic pride in Providence. They also agreed that poor relief needed to be done, in their words, with "humanity" by people of "respectability."[25]

What was it to be "humane" for "Howard" and his opponents? The word's meaning in 1811 seems quite similar to its meaning in the present day. The Oxford English Dictionary finds uses around 1800 that already include the modern definition of "characterized by sympathy with and consideration for others; feeling or showing compassion towards humans or animals; benevolent, kind." "Howard's" opponents also celebrated a meaning like this. In their first response to him, they called upon the "tender and compassionate part of the community" to visit the workhouse for themselves. Thus, humanity, compassion, even tenderness were celebrated virtues in this war of words. Too much concern about money was portrayed as a vice. The only writer who offered a dissenting view called himself "PETER QUIZ." Ostensibly, "Peter Quiz" criticized both "Howard" and the overseers for not having the courage to take more radical approaches towards poverty. These would include "*infanticide*," "killing off *old people*," and "directing that when a *poor man dies*, his wife and children should be buried with him in the same grave." "[P]*overty is to be regarded as a crime, and a Poor-House a place of punishment*," Peter Quiz thundered, with liberal use of italics.[26]

Within the next few decades, critics of poor relief would begin to make arguments that neither government nor philanthropy should give much to the poor. They would earnestly argue that poor relief only encouraged people to avoid work and led to a cycle of poverty. But "Peter Quiz" was not in earnest. Rather, like Jonathan Swift in his 1729 "A Modest Proposal," "Peter Quiz" was intentionally writing things that were so over the top he would shock his readers with extreme views. In so doing, he satirized those who did not support poor relief. While he professed to be criticizing both Howard and the overseers of the poor, "Peter Quiz" actually aimed at the overseers. After suggesting infanticide, euthanasia, and killing the widows and orphans of poor men, "Peter Quiz" then proposed a poorhouse that sounded suspiciously like the actual workhouse, the one that "Howard" had criticized. Slyly, "Peter Quiz" piled on critiques of the overseers by adopting a radically anti-poor-relief argument, clearly intended to seem out of touch with popular opinion of the day. Even his adopted name made the joke obvious: in 1811, the Oxford English Dictionary notes, "quiz" carried the meanings of "a peculiar or ridiculous thing" or "a practical joke; a hoax, a piece of mockery or banter; a witticism." The overseers got the joke and knew they were being mocked. They responded in kind in their last article, calling "Peter Quiz" a "high-headed aristocratic democrat," casting their critic as a Jeffersonian Republican "democrat" trying to cause trouble in the Federalist town.[27]

The overseers made a similar charge against "Howard," alleging that he was a Jeffersonian Republican, trying to stir up dissent in the Federalist town; this on the eve of the War of 1812, a war that would be deeply unpopular in Federalist-dominated New England. "Howard's" critics would also charge that he was not worthy of his pen-name because he was not really motivated by humanity but rather by anger over taxation. The overseers of the poor were also assessors of taxes that year, and they believed "Howard" was seeking revenge for a friend who felt his property had been assessed unfairly. "Howard" retorted that his "motives were as pure, and as disinterested, as those of the great man [John Howard], the 'assistance' of whose name I have presumed to borrow." He wrote this in the same letter in which he castigated Sarah and her family, asking "whether paupers subjected to their tyranny have been treated with common humanity?"[28]

"Howard" never spelled out exactly how he thought Sarah and family were not humane, but the accusation of some, unspecified inhumanity was serious. The overseers' defense of Sarah was that she was "formerly of re-spectable character" and that patients requested her and she healed them. A clear implication is that in order to provide humane care, the women and men who provided poor relief also needed to be "respectable." What did it mean to be "respectable" in 1810s New England? The Oxford English Dictionary finds the definition "having a good or fair standing in society, either because of status or . . . through being regarded as having a good character, a reputation for honest or decency, etc." to be in use by the early nineteenth century. But whole books have been written on the cultural connotations carried by this concept. As seen in chapter 2, racial ideologies intersected with respectability, so that Americans of European descent often disqualified Americans of African or Native descent from being considered "respectable," regardless of character, honesty, or decency. This context makes it all the more intriguing that the overseers described a Native woman, Sarah, as having possessed respectability but somehow having lost it in a few years. What is clear, though, is that all parties agreed that the providers of poor relief had to be respectable in order to provide humane care.

Ideas about respectability and race were closely intertwined in the early United States. But the war of words that described "One-Eyed" Sarah is ambiguous in what it shows about these themes. At first read, "A Friend's" letter appears to be antiracist, and to imply that racism is part of "Howard's" critique of Sarah. A bit of background, though, makes "A Friend's" defense of their "Indian" nurse more complicated. "A Friend" either was—or was allied with—a town council and overseers of the poor who were using their power to banish scores of people of color, including Cuff Roberts and family, in these years. Explicitly banishing any "Black" newcomers they could, they also tended to fold Native people into the vague categories of "Black" or "of color." Their insistence on the propriety of hiring a Native woman to do government service is especially striking in this context. One reason why the overseers might emphasize Sarah's being "Indian," even as they carried out a white supremacist policy, is because of a common stereotype. In early-nineteenth-century New England, as discussed above, many Americans believed that Native women were particularly gifted healers. It was likely no coincidence that the overseers chose a Native woman as nurse for some of their most serious cases of illness.

The overseers' defense of Sarah, prompted by Howard's critique of her work, thus reveal much about her work and its place in the larger project of poor relief. As slim as they are, these newspaper descriptions of "One-Eyed" Sarah give unusual insights into how poor relief worked, such as what poor relief included and who did the actual relief. The newspaper war of words fills out details at which we usually have to guess. "A Friend to candid Investigation" gives us an idea of what that was like: difficult, attentive, effective nursing, and winning favor with patients, all in the face of hostile attention from critics like "Howard."

"ONE-EYED" SARAH: NURSE, BUSINESSWOMAN, PROVIDER OF POOR RELIEF

As readers have seen, descriptions of "One-Eyed" Sarah reveal much about how poor relief worked. Those descriptions do not, however, make it clear what her identity was. The descriptions could fit the life stories of either Sarah Hill or Sarah Olney. Their lives, in turn, show how a Native woman might get work nursing paupers at public expense. Both Sarah Hill's and Sarah Olney's early interactions with the overseers of the poor were negative. Sarah Hill's life was shaped, against her will and probably against her parents' will, by local government officials. Separated from her parents as a three-year-old, Hill was never allowed to make a life for herself without some interference from local officials. She was warned out of Providence and probably other towns, repeatedly. Similarly, Sarah Olney's daughters were warned out and one was sentenced to whipping in Providence. Her husband's death allowed local officials to take control of—and reduce—her family's property.

Despite these negative interactions, at least one of these Sarahs seems to have turned that relationship from one of social control to one of patronage. If, as seems likely, one or both of these Sarahs worked for the overseers of the poor, it shows that Native women could find ways to earn the reputation of "respectability" and cash from powerful men who had targeted them as unrespectable and poor. Moreover, the experiences of "One-Eyed" Sarah shows how powerful elected town officials depended on the paid work of nurses of color to make good their promise to provide for the needy of their town.

The paper trail left by Providence's town fathers during the Thomas Jefferson presidential administration does not, in the end, fully acknowledge the identity and life experience of "One-Eyed" Sarah. It does, however, give us an unusual glimpse into how their government worked. Overseers of the poor controlled significant amounts of tax revenue in support of a guarantee that all Americans could find food, shelter, and healthcare in some town. In order to actually provide that lifesaving support, town fathers distributed these dollars among other townspeople who exchanged their homes or goods or skills and efforts with the double goal of helping the neediest among them and contributing to their own family's income. Many of these townspeople were women, doing the hard job of keeping the vulnerable housed, fed, clothed, and doctored. Sometimes, the needy paupers themselves could request the healthcare providers of their choice.

Among these townspeople, "One-Eyed" Sarah gained a reputation for competent, effective healthcare. A Native woman, she might have been chosen because of the reputation of Native women as skilled healers. Whether her true identity was Sarah Hill or Sarah Olney, "One-Eyed" Sarah was a savvy businesswoman, who parlayed her skills into pay. She was an independent contractor, working for local government. Sarah was able to build up a business, provide vital care for vulnerable patients, and provide herself and her family with financial stability. Once a target of the poor law, Sarah became a part of the poor law apparatus. Without Sarah, and others like her, the poor law could not be carried out. Saving lives, wheeling and dealing, overcoming the considerable powers of local officials, Sarah's story deserves to be told.

NOTES

1. This paragraph is an imaginative recreation, from the patient's point of view, of a description of "One-Eyed" Sarah and her patients in *Providence Gazette and Country Journal* 20 July 1811, 1.
2. *Providence Gazette and Country Journal,* 1.
3. For descriptions of "One-Eyed" Sarah see *Providence Gazette and Country Journal* 29 June 1811, 1 and 20 July 1811, 1.
4. For description of "One-Eyed" Sarah see *The Providence Gazette and Country Journal* 20 July 1811, 1. As readers will see below, I am confident that the writers are the overseers of the poor, though they never identify themselves in that article. Ruth Wallis Herndon and Ella Wilcox Sekatau, "The Right to a Name: The Narragansett People and Rhode Island Officials in the Revolutionary Era," *Ethnohistory* 44:3 (Summer 1997), 433–462 and Joanne Pope Melish, "The Racial Vernacular: Contesting the Black/White Binary in Nineteenth-Century Rhode Island" in James T. Campbell, Matthew Pratt Guterl, and Robert G. Lee, Eds., *Race, Nation, and Empire in American History* (Chapel Hill: University of North Carolina Press, 2007).
5. Those first two encounters of Hill with the Providence Town Council are described in Herndon and Sekatau, "The Right to a Name," 446 and Melish, "The Racial Vernacular," 21. Original entries for the three encounters are recorded in the entries dated 3 and 6 February 1784, 30 May 1791, and 7 February 1803 in MSS Providence Town Council Books, Providence City Hall Archives (PCHA). Herndon and Sekatau find that "mustee" usually denoted an "Indian" mother in Rhode Island in this period, and did not specify a father's ethnicity ("The Right to a Name," 435).
6. Entry for 7 February 1803 in MSS Providence Town Council Books, PCHA. The Rhode Island Historical Society does not have Providence Town Council minutes for this date. For other dates, the RIHS version is a "draft" version compared to the one at Providence City Hall, and the RIHS version sometimes includes more information, as described in Herndon, "On and Off the Record," 103–115.
7. On 1723 Boston Town Meeting, see Ruth Wallis Herndon, " 'Proper' Magistrates and Masters," 49 in Ruth Wallis Herndon and John E. Murray, Eds., *Children Bound to Labor: The Pauper Apprentice System in Early America* (Ithaca: Cornell University Press, 2009). On Providence Town Council in 1821, see "Probate Court" in *Providence Patriot*, 22 September 1821, 1. The article was reprinted in *Providence Patriot*, 23 July 1825, 2. On the apprenticeship of Native children in particular, see Ruth Wallis Herndon and Ella Wilcox Sekatau, "Colonizing the Children: Indian Youngsters in Servitude in Early Rhode Island," in Colin G. Calloway and Neal Salisbury, Eds., *Reinterpreting New England Indians and the Colonial Experience* (Boston: Colonial Society of Massachusetts, 2003), 137–173.
8. See Daniel Mandell, *Tribe, Race, History: Native Americans in Southern New England, 1780–1880* (Baltimore: Johns Hopkins University Press, 2008), xvii, 22–25, 151–153 for locations and statuses of Nipmuc communities.
9. For the 1790 census, see First Census of the United States, 1790 (NARA microfilm publication M637, 12 Rolls), Records of the Bureau of the Census, Record Group 29, National Archives, Washington, DC. as digitized on ancestry. com: year: 1790; census place: Warwick, Kent, Rhode Island; Series: M637; Roll: 10; Page: 48; Image: 39; Family History Library Film: 0568150. One source

describing the Prophet family is William J. Brown, *The Life of William J. Brown of Providence, Rhode Island* (Freeport, NY: Books for Libraries Press, 1971), 7–10.

10. For Hannah Shiner, see Jean M. O'Brien, "'Divorced' from the Land: Resistance and Survival of Indian Women in Eighteenth-Century New England" in Colin G. Calloway, Ed., *After King Philip's War: Presence and Persistence in Indian New England* (Hanover, NH: Dartmouth University, 1997). For Hannah Dexter and Aunt Sarah Green, see Thomas L. Doughton, "Unseen Neighbors: Native Americans of Central Massachusetts, A People Who Had 'Vanished'," in Calloway, *After King Phillip's War*. For Molly Ockett, see Bunny McBridge and Harald E. L. Prins, "Walking the Medicine Line: Molly Ockett, a Pigwacket Doctor," in Robert S. Grumet, *Northeastern Indian Lives, 1632–1816* (Amherst: University of Massachusetts Press, 1996).

11. Some of the many town treasury orders to Sarah Olney in Providence Town Papers MSS 214, sg 1, Series 3, RIHS, include the following: order dated 2 September 1782, Book 7, Document 2780 (for supplies to Ruth Mitchel), order dated 28 November 1800, Book 42, Document 001104, order dated 28 June 1804, Book 55, Document 006502, order dated 30 April 1806, Book 65, Document 0010674, and order dated 21 January 1807, Book 64, Document 0010357, this last being for "keeping Minerva Harvey and Jude Bowen's child." For Sarah Eddy, see Providence Town Council Minutes for 15 December 1800 in PCHA. For Sarah Sheaveateau, see town treasury orders to Sarah Sheaveateau 27 February and 12 April 1806, Book 62, Documents 009339 and 009340 in Providence Town Papers MSS 214, sg 1, Series 3, RIHS. On a side note, a Sarah Sheviateaux, described as "Blk," or Black, appears on a list of poor relief recipients in 1823 (Overseer of the Poor Report 1823, Book 118, Document 0043139, Providence Town Papers MSS 214, sg 1, Series 3, RIHS.) For Sally Allen, see orders dated April 1806, Book 62, Documents 009291 and 009292 and order dated 2 March 1807, Book 65, Document 0010493 in Providence Town Papers MSS 214, sg 1, Series 3, RIHS. For Sally Bartwell "boarding & attendance on Lydia Jones White for being sick," see order dated 9 March 1808, Book 67, Document 0011680, and see also in Providence Town Papers MSS 214, sg 1, Series 3, RIHS. A valuable resource which helps researchers quickly find these orders on the Providence town treasurer for publicly funded acts of charity is the Works Progress Administration index, a collection of index cards on which WPA-paid workers described each treasury order and organized cards by topic. Treasury orders signed by overseers of the poor are in boxes 27–31, in Providence Town Papers MSS 214, sg 1, RIHS.

12. Sarah Olney, married to Aaron Olney lived at the same time as Sarah Olney, married to Simeon Olney. This second couple lived in downtown Providence, where they ran a public house, including sleeping accommodations, close to the house of William Larned, the overseer of the poor. It is possible that some or all of the treasury orders cited above were to Sarah Olney, married to Simeon Olney, given in exchange for a hotel bed for those in need. After Simeon Olney died in 1808, this Sarah Olney ran the public house with her children until 1816. This Sarah Olney, however, was probably of English descent, given the available evidence, and certainly not "One-Eyed" Sarah because she continued living in downtown Providence, not Smithfield or North Providence, right through the 1811 newspaper articles. Sources for Sarah Olney, married to Simeon Olney, include: Chace, *Owners and Occupants of the Lots, Houses, and Shops in the Town of Providence, Rhode Island, in 1798*, a digitized version of the microfilmed version of the manuscript census return *West District, Providence, Rhode Island*, Roll 58, Page 72,

Image *00141*, Family History Library Film *0281232*, in *Third Census of the United States, 1810*, NARA microfilm publication M252, 71 rolls, Bureau of the Census, Record Group 29, National Archives, Washington, DC, accessed via ancestry.com database, and "Public Notice," a probate notice and advertisement in *The Columbian Phenix* 18 June 1808, 1, as well as "Noted Stand," an advertisement for sale, in *Providence Patriot* 31 August 1816, 7 September 1816, and 14 September 1816. On the subject of Native women marrying African-descended men, see Frances Harriet Whipple and Elleanor Eldridge, *Memoirs of Elleanor Eldridge*, edited by Joycelyn K. Moody (Morgantown: West Virginia University Press, 2014), chap. 2. For another example, with speculation that Native brides were looking for husbands who did farm work, see Brown, *The Life of William J. Brown*, 7–11.

13. I have not yet seen the original manuscript source of these Olney family appearances before the Providence Town Council. I found them in transcriptions of the Providence Town Council minutes in Linda L. Mathew, "Gleanings from Rhode Island Town Records: Providence Town Council Records, 1789–1801" *Rhode Island Roots: Journal of the Rhode Island Geneaological Society*, Special Bonus Issue (April 2007), 113, 116, 117, 123.

14. Entry for 12 October 1803, in MSS 214 sg 9, Providence Town Council Minutes, RIHS. On 1838 prohibition, see Creech, *Three Centuries of Poor Law Administration*, 255.

15. Entries for 25 May 1811, 17 August 1811, 7 March 1812, 4 April 1812 in "Council and Probate Journal Volume 3 1797–1822 Part 2 Smithfield" and pages 403 and 415 in "Probate Records Vol. 3 1797–1819 pages 379–745 Smithfield" in Central Falls City Hall, Central Falls, Rhode Island.

16. The Providence "Howard" letters are in *The Providence Gazette and Country Journal* issues of 8, 15, 22, and 29 June, as well as 13, 20, 27 July, and 3 August, all in 1811. Some are reprinted in *The Columbian Phenix or Providence Patriot* issues of 15 June, 6 July, and 10 August. The New York "Howard" letters are in *The Columbian* issues of 3, 6, 10, and 19 September, 3 and 16 October, 2 November, and 18 December 1810 as well as 3, 12, 14, and 24 January 1811. I am indebted to the word-search tool of Readex's *Early American Newspapers* which allowed me to find all of these articles, along with earlier tributes to John Howard such as the one in *The Providence Gazette and Country Journal* 16 February 1793, 2–3. Much has been written about John Howard since, including Neil Davie, "Feet of Marble or Feet of Clay? John Howard and the Origins of Prison Reform in Britain, 1773–1790," *XVII-XVIII: Revue de la Société d'études anglo-américaines des XVIIe et XVIIIe siècles* 76 (Dec. 2019), accessible online at <https://journals.openedition.org/1718/3446>.

17. On New York's Common Council inviting "decent and well-behaved persons" to supervise New York's almshouse, see Cray, Jr., *Paupers and Poor Relief in New York City and Its Rural Environs*, 107. On Providence's workhouse history, see Staples, *Annals of the Town of Providence from Its First Settlement to the Organization of the City Government in June 1832*, 194–195.

18. *The Providence Gazette and Country Journal* 8 and 15 June 1811. *The Columbian Phenix or Providence Patriot* 15 June 1811. By "affairs of honor," I mean the quasi-formal, public arguments about men's reputation that were so common in the early United States, and are described in Joanne B. Freeman, *Affairs of Honor: National Politics in the New Republic* (New Haven: Yale University Press, 2001).

19. *The Providence Gazette and Country Journal* 22 June 1811, 3, 29 June 1811, 1, 13 July 1811, 3, 20 July 1811, 1. Capital letters and italics in original.

20. On the "secret disease" and remedies for syphilis see John Parascandola, *Sex, Sin, and Science: A History of Syphilis in America* (Westport: Praeger, 2008), 16–18, 24–28, 80.

21. Explications of how women's work was crucial to the work of poor relief include articles from an edition of the *Journal of the Early Republic* focused on poor women, especially Ruth Wallis Herndon, "Poor Women and the Boston Almshouse in the Early Republic," *Journal of the Early Republic* 32:3 (Fall 2012) 349–382 and Monique Bourque, "Women and Work in the Philadelphia Almshouse, 1790–1840," *Journal of the Early Republic* 32:3 (Fall 2012) 383–413. Another example focused on rural Uxbridge, Massachusetts, is Daen, "'To Board & Nurse a Stranger,'" *Journal of Social History* 53:3 (Spring 2020), 1–26, which emphasizes how the work of women was typically "unrecognized and uncompensated." For Richmond, see Green, *This Business of Relief*, 37. A clear, synthetic overview is Mimi Abramovitz, *Regulating the Lives of Women*, preface.

22. On the "welfare/industrial complex," see Green, *This Business of Relief*, 1. For Sarah Olney receipt, see order dated 28 June 1804, Book 55, Document 006502, in MSS 214, sg 1 Providence Town Papers Collection, Series 3, RIHS. See for comparison Receipt to Pay Nathaniel Sivich $12 for 12 weeks board of Freelove Olney, 28 June 1804, in MSS 214, sg 1 Providence Town Papers Collection, Series 3, Book 55, Document # 006490, RIHS or Receipt to Pay Luthania Bates Six dollars for Eight weeks Board of Constant Luthers Child, 12 May 1804, in MSS 214, sg 1 Providence Town Papers Collection, Series 3, Book 55, Document # 006563, RIHS.

23. These letters are in *The Providence Gazette and Country Journal* issues of June 8, 15, 22, 29; July 13, 20; and August 3, all from 1811. Some are reprinted in *The Columbian Phenix or Providence Patriot* issues of June 15, July 6, and August 10, 1811.

24. Heman Humphrey, "On Doing Good to the Poor," a sermon preached in Pittsfield, Massachusetts, 4 April 1818, was printed multiple times. This summary relies on Heman Humphrey, *Miscellaneous Discourses and Reviews* (Amherst: J.S. and C. Adams, 1834), 56–60. The sermon was also printed on its own in 1818 and excerpted in Seth Rockman, Ed., *Welfare Reform in the Early Republic: A Brief History with Documents* (Boston: Bedford/St. Martin's, 2003), 57–63.

25. *Providence Gazette and Country Journal* 8 June 1811, 3.

26. *Providence Gazette and Country Journal* 15 June 1811, 1 and 27 July 1811, 2.

27. *Providence Gazette and Country Journal* 3 August 1811, 2.

28. *Providence Gazette and Country Journal* 15 June 1811, 2, 29 June 1811, 1, and 20 July 1811, 1.

CHAPTER 4

⚬√⌀⌐

Hard-Working Single Mother

Lydia Bates and Poor Relief in a Small Town

The last time Thomas Angell saw them together was in the summer of 1819. It was a romantic scene. Thomas T. Hill, the traveling crockery salesman, was saying goodbye to his sweetheart, Lydia Bates, the young maid in the elderly Phillips household. They were standing close together, between the wheels of Hill's wagon. It was after sunset.[1]

Two months later, much had changed. Thomas T. Hill had left, on his wagon loaded with earthenware milk pans and pitchers. Now Lydia Bates was living in William Jeffers's house, and the overseers of the poor were footing the bill for her room and board. Bates was used to moving from one house to another. She had done so many times in this rural, Rhode Island town called Scituate (pronounced SITCH-you-et). Census takers counted 2,834 people there in 1820, divided among 481 households. Most of the average six people per household were children of the householders, but not all. Households also included other family and friends, hired hands, boarders, and paupers, the latter earning their hosts' reimbursal from the overseers of the poor. In the past, Bates had moved from house to house as a temporary worker, with no need for the overseers of the poor to pay her way. But this was different. Now Lydia Bates was two months pregnant, and not finding work as usual. Perhaps morning sickness—or simply pregnancy—sapped her usual energy.

Bates had led a busy and boisterous life up to this point. For the past three years, at least, she had lived and worked in one farmhouse after

How Welfare Worked in the Early United States. Gabriel J. Loiacono, Oxford University Press. © Oxford University Press 2021. DOI: 10.1093/oso/9780197515433.003.0005

another, not only in Scituate, her hometown, but sometimes in neighboring farm towns like Johnston. At these houses she pulled flax, wove cloth, made shirts, and served as a "hired maid." In the evenings and on holidays she sought out company at parties and taverns. On at least one occasion she snuck into a party dressed as a man. On many occasions, men sought out her company. One matron, Lydia Phillips, for whom Bates worked as "maid," sniffed that Bates "sometimes had old folks after her and some time young folks." I don't know exactly how old she was. Although often described as a "girl," or "poor girl," she was legally a "Single Woman," in court documents from 1820, 1821, and 1822.[2]

Now sheltered at Jeffers's home, where she had attended a Fourth of July party two months prior, Bates no doubt wondered what the next year would bring. She had not felt like herself since the summer, when Dr. Amos Collins was called to the Phillips house to treat her. Did he figure out she was pregnant? Or did she discover this herself first? Either way, once this became public knowledge, Bates knew that the overseers of the poor would get involved. It was common practice for overseers to busy themselves overseeing the lives of unmarried mothers. Without a husband's or parents' household, Lydia Bates and her baby were considered "likely to be chargeable" to the poor relief funds of the town of Scituate. Their lives—like those of nearly every mother and child outside of wedlock—would be shaped by the poor law officials.

In Bates's case, overseers of the poor not only shaped her life, but they documented it too. Together with Thomas T. Hill, the crockery salesman, they would create files full of paper, describing Lydia Bates's life in detail for a span of about five years. These records help us look at poor relief through the experience of Lydia Bates. She was, herself, a pauper, and also helped others avoid becoming paupers. Her experiences are an example of how overseers of the poor across the United States automatically assumed responsibility for children born out of wedlock. They saw these children as almost certainly destined to need poor relief, and sought to protect the town's treasury from them. Sometimes, this meant securing a bond from the child's father, or maternal grandparents. Other times, it meant finding the child a new family, binding them to service or an apprenticeship in someone else's household. Often, it meant separating child from mother. Lydia Bates's life, and her baby Rhoda's life, would be changed forever by how overseers of the poor approached their case. Overseers of the poor would relentlessly pursue a bond from Rhoda's father, who they believed was Thomas T. Hill. In addition, they would seek a new family for Rhoda by the time she was seven years old.

Bates's experiences are also an example of how often overseers of the poor intervened in families. They separated children from parents if they thought the parents unable to raise their own children as the overseers saw fit, for financial or moral or gender or race reasons. Overseers would separate Rhoda from her mother. It is probable, too, that Lydia Bates herself had been separated from her own parents, and sent to another farmer's house, because of her parents' poverty. Although Bates's parents were most likely of English descent, they could not keep her from the overseers of the poor just as Sarah Hill's Native mother could not keep her. Social Work scholar Mimi Abramovitz calls this "social reproduction." Overseers of the poor separated Bates from her parents, and her daughter Rhoda from her, in pursuit of *their* vision of how children should be raised. Moreover, they relied on Bates's labor to care for other needy people in the town.[3]

That Lydia Bates, either as a pauper or as a hired hand, worked in other households leads to another observation: in a small town like Scituate, the line between pauper and hired hand was blurry. When arranging to help healthy children or young adults like Bates, the overseers of the poor might look more like a temp agency than a charity. Using the wide discretion available to them, Scituate's overseers of the poor could work out a cheap way to provide for their ward: they could farm her labor out, a few weeks here, a few months there, to whichever local householder would give her room and board in exchange for her work. In the case of Lydia Phillips and her husband, William, the overseers could solve two problems with one solution. The young, energetic Bates helped keep the elderly couple's household running, while they gave her a home and meals. Thus the town treasurer did not have to pay anything for either the Phillipses or Bates. Although the evidence is not clear as to whether Bates worked in the Phillipses as a hired hand or as pauper, these two situations could actually be quite similar, both involving the exchange of work for room and board. Wages might not be involved at all. The only real difference would be whether the overseers of the poor arranged the work or Bates herself did. Another similarity is that, whether as pauper or hired hand, Lydia Bates's work could help fellow townspeople, like the Phillipses. Not only was poor relief an economic engine, directed by the local government, which sent money to merchants like William Larned and nurses like "One-Eyed" Sarah, but paupers themselves could be important workers in the local economy. Like "One-Eyed" Sarah and thousands of their contemporaries around the country, Bates's hard work helped keep Scituate households afloat. Unlike "One-Eyed" Sarah, Lydia Bates might not have been paid with money, but rather with room and board for a short term. Also unlike Sarah, Bates could not have a stable home of her own.[4]

How Bates was housed leads to a final observation: she was provided for right in the bosom of her community. As Bates moved from one house to another, she lived and worked cheek by jowl with local homeowners, their children and relatives, as well as other paupers and hired hands. Bates was never isolated as a pauper. Working hard, socializing freely, she experienced camaraderie, freedom, and yet also vulnerability. Unlike William Fales, the subject of chapter 5, Bates was not supervised closely. Even while ostensibly governed by male householders, Bates went where she wanted, with whom she wanted, sometimes staying away for days and nights together. Whether as a pauper or as a hired hand, Bates made many of her own decisions. At the same time, living in other people's homes, Bates could not rely on family members to protect her from unwanted attention, especially from men. Nor could she rely on family financial resources to keep her baby, Rhoda, with her. As a pauper, Bates could not decide which household would house her, nor could she decide who would parent her child.

Because her family could not house her or persuade the overseers of the poor that she and Rhoda were not "likely to be chargeable," the town authorities would seek financial restitution for the anticipated poor relief costs for baby Rhoda. Lydia Bates repeatedly named Thomas T. Hill as Rhoda's father. Believing Bates, the overseers went to great lengths to arrest Hill and bring him to Scituate. They wanted Hill to pay for the costs of Rhoda's upbringing, so that the town treasury did not have to. Hill fought to the utmost the law allowed: all the way to the Rhode Island Supreme Judicial Court, in Providence. At least three times, the high court heard this case. The Scituate town fathers—and usually Bates herself—followed the case there each time, and the legal adversaries produced a copious amount of paperwork, mostly depositions describing Lydia Bates's life during the summer of 1819. From these sheafs of old paper, carefully kept together to this day in three case files in Pawtucket, as well as from Scituate town government records, kept in the Scituate Town Building and the Rhode Island Historical Society, we can reconstruct about ten years of the life of this hard-working, single mother with few resources.

For a brief ten years, we can see the poor relief system from Lydia Bates's point of view. Hers was not a stable life, but it was not a lonely life either. Unlike the inmates of poorhouses, Lydia Bates's life was not regimented, not isolated. She received welfare from her neighbors, and lived among her neighbors, working and socializing with them every day. She worked a lot, and her neighbors seemed to think of her more as hired help than as a pauper. She had assurance that she would not be homeless, and would not starve, and that she would receive the medical attention she needed, in the town of her birth. On the other hand, Lydia Bates's experiences are also an example of how overseers of the poor insisted on a gendered division of labor and intervened in families to ensure that children grew up as the overseers thought appropriate.

CHILDREN AND THE POOR LAWS

Lydia Bates was likely just a child when she first became a pauper, cared for by the overseers of the poor. Records, however, never explicitly name her as a young child or make clear which family she was a part of. In one court record, Thomas T. Hill offhandedly names her father as Thomas Bates. And there was a Thomas Bates living in Scituate in 1810, with two boys and two girls living in his house. Thomas Bates himself, along with an unnamed woman, were marked as forty-five or older, while the eldest girl was between ten and fifteen and the other children were nine or younger. If these ages were marked down correctly, it could mean that Thomas Bates and his wife had all their children in their thirties, or that these were their youngest children and older children were living and working in someone else's house. It is also possible that these were Lydia Bates's grandparents. Whichever is true, Thomas Bates was gone from Scituate census records by 1820.[5]

What happened to Thomas Bates or Lydia Bates in the 1810s is a mystery. Probably, Thomas Bates either died or left, and Lydia Bates was left with other relatives and eventually with the overseers of the poor. If she was taken in by some of her Bates relatives, town records suggest that they were too poor to care for her in the long run. Overseers of the poor took responsibility for two different groups of Bates children in Lydia Bates's childhood years. In neither case are the children themselves named. Instead, town records call them the "Samuel Bates" "Family" and the "William Bates Children."

It is unlikely that Lydia Bates was part of Samuel Bates's immediate family. Perhaps they were cousins. Nevertheless, their experiences with poor relief can teach us a lot about how poor relief worked in small towns like Scituate. Born in 1751, Samuel was a year older than William Larned, and like Larned and Cuff Roberts, Samuel Bates was a revolutionary war veteran. He fought in the Massachusetts line for nine months in 1779 and 1780. It is clear that he was an older father, still having children to support in the first decade of the nineteenth century, when he was over fifty. He could not make ends meet, though, so his hometown of Scituate stepped in to help. Probably something extraordinary happened, perhaps a farming accident. Years later, in 1819, a court clerk testified "that Samuel Bates is a very poor man and that he hath known him to be such for nearly twenty years." For some reason, then, Samuel became poor around 1800. In 1803, the town council voted to give Samuel at least twenty-three dollars "in part pay for keeping his family." Town governments had a great deal of choice in how to help those in need: they could give cash or goods, or take a more interventionist approach.[6]

By 1805, the overseer of the poor stepped in more decisively. He took custody of Samuel's children, moving them to Joshua Angell's house in the Fall of that year. Records then show that Samuel's children were living with Richard Rhotes in 1807, but moved to William Waterman's house that same year. At Angell's and Waterman's houses, the Bates children would have shared space with most of the town's other paupers, too. Angell and Waterman had been the lowest bidders and had been awarded a contract to feed, house, and enjoy the labor of all of the town's poor in those years. In these years, the Scituate overseer of the poor annually arranged a contract for one farmer to take in all of the town's poor for a set cost. Usually, the overseers chose the lowest bidder, so this practice was called "venduing" or "auctioning" the poor.[7]

Like William Larned in the much larger town of Providence, Scituate's overseer of the poor was tasked with caring for the town's poor, but doing it as cheaply as he could. This is probably why the town stopped giving cash to Samuel Bates. If this were going to be a long-term situation, town fathers would prefer to save money by giving one farmer the responsibility of all the town's poor, rather than paying separate amounts to each poor family. Taxpayers exerted strong pressure on the overseers to keep poor taxes as low as possible, while still providing basic care. A desire to save money often trumped the idea that children should stay with their parents.

So this group of Bates siblings would have had to move house every one to two years, as different farmers won the poor contract every one to two years. Joshua Angell got the job between 1805 and 1807, but William Waterman won it from 1807 to 1808. Another Waterman, Benjamin, got the award by 1809, and then it came back to Joshua Angell by the 1810s. To give an idea of how much money this brought in to a farmer's house, records show William Waterman receiving $159 for a year's contract in 1808, and Benjamin Waterman receiving $220 for a year's contract in 1810. Economic historians find these sums comparable to $54,000 and $57,500, respectively, in unskilled laborer's income at the time this book was published. In return for these considerable boosts to household income, the farmer's responsibility was to keep the poor housed, with sufficient food and clothing, and to be supervised by the overseers of the poor. He also got to command the labor of everyone in his household. As a strategy for bringing extra money and labor into the house, contracting for the poor could be an important contribution to a farmer's household economy. So important was this job to the town, that town records referred to the farmhouse that contained most of the town's paupers as the "poorhouse," decades before Scituate actually had a town-owned poorhouse. Without farmers bidding to do this work, the town would have no place to send its homeless inhabitants.[8]

In the small town of Scituate, it is remarkable that two Bates families needed town relief in this period. Twelve years after Samuel Bates's children were first folded into the moving "poorhouse" population, a second group of Bates children was taken into town custody. This was the family of William Bates. In March, 1817, the Scituate overseer of the poor was reimbursed $1.50 for "moving William Bates Children to the Poor house." The sparse records that track William Bates suggest a man who moved from town to town, never going far from Scituate, but never able to stay in one place for long. The 1810 census found a William Bates in Scituate. He was recorded as between sixteen and twenty-five, with a woman in the same age range and a girl under ten in the house. While the 1820 census found no Willliam Bates heading a household in Rhode Island, the 1830 census found a William Bates, in his forties, back in Scituate, sharing his home with six more people. If William Bates had a settlement in Scituate, then that town would have to take responsibility for his children even if he were living in another town at the time. Most likely, since he did not show up in the 1820 census, William Bates himself was part of someone else's household in 1817, and had to give his children up to the town. There is no mention in town records of his wife.[9]

Despite Thomas T. Hill naming Lydia Bates's father as Thomas Bates, there are two reasons to believe she was among the "William Bates Children" and moved to the temporary poorhouse in 1817. For one thing, the timing is right. Depositions taken in 1821 describe Lydia Bates as being in one farmer's house after another beginning in 1816 or 1817. A common strategy for overseers of the poor in charge of children would be to arrange for them to live and work in some other household, for the short term or the long term. It is also possible that William Bates might have arranged these work stints for Lydia Bates once he judged her old enough. Lydia would perhaps bring income to his house and at least eat at someone else's expense. Another clue that Lydia Bates lived with William Bates is a deposition given by Sarah Kent. By 1821, the date of the deposition, Kent lived in the same house with her son, William Kent, in whose house Lydia also lived for a while. Sarah Kent testified that Lydia Bates "was Bred and Born about three quarters of a mile from where I live." The 1810 census showed

William Kent's house listed just four names away from William Bates's. Thomas Bates's house is not listed nearby, but a few pages away. If the census taker was going door to door, it seems that the William Bates and William Kent families were quite close to each other. Even if Sarah Kent was not living in her son's house yet, she would have been familiar with the William Bates family before they were moved to the "poorhouse." That is likely why she would later say she had known Lydia Bates from infancy.[10]

By 1817, then, Bates's children were being watched over by the overseers of the poor of Scituate. Overseers of the poor brought the children to the local "poorhouse," the house of the farmer who had won the contract for the poor that year. As new farmers won the poorhouse contract in different years, the Bates children would have had to move to new farms, taking what few belongings they had with them. For many paupers their belongings would be only the clothes they had on their backs and maybe a change of clothes. They would have had to obey the master and mistress of the house with the obedience due to parents, including doing the chores and farm work asked of them. In return, they would receive food, clothing, housing, and medical attention, paid for by the farmer. They also would be subject to any discipline doled out by the master and mistress of the farm, including physical discipline. The overseers of the poor were supposed to check in on how the town paupers were being treated, and would consider physical discipline of children to be reasonable and humane. The master and mistress, for their part, would make a calculation that they could provide food, housing, clothing, and medical care for their charges, and still be benefiting from the money the town provided, together with the work the paupers provided.

Separating poor children from their parents was common throughout the United States in the first few decades after independence, as it had been in British North America. The most common way that municipalities did this was through individual pauper apprenticeships. As historians Ruth Wallis Herndon, John E. Murray, and others have shown, this practice was especially common before 1820 from Savannah to Maryland, from Pennsylvania to New England, and from Montreal to England. It could be formal, and legally binding, in a paper contract. Or it could be less formal and more temporary. There was a logic to it, as historian Gloria Main explains: it "relieved impoverished or otherwise incapacitated parents . . . while reducing the rolls of those on poor relief. In return for accepting the costs of maintaining and educating their apprentice helpers, craftsmen, farmers, and housekeepers benefited from cheap compulsory labor." Sometimes the arrangement had the consent of parents; sometimes it did not. Usually, the children of unmarried parents were more likely to be separated from their parents than others. Gradually, during the early nineteenth century, municipalities moved towards the principle of keeping parents and children together. Later, institutions for children without parents, such as orphanages, began to replace pauper apprenticeships. But in the 1810s, Scituate officials would have had little concern about separating Lydia Bates from her parents and had no institution for children in which to put her.[11]

As one of the children living in one poorhouse after another, Bates would be expected to work for her keep. In some ways, her childhood would be similar to a child today who lived in a series of foster homes. Her childhood was one that required a lot of adaptation on her part: new custodians, new living quarters, different personalities all the time. Bates would rarely have had her own space, or new clothes. She likely never had her own bed. Nor could she have her own way. How did she cope? What kind of life was this for her? Extant records give us little idea what the child Lydia thought about this, but it is useful to exercise historical imagination in this case. Imagine being a teenage girl, living temporarily with a neighboring farmer and his wife. They know your family, and perhaps disapprove of your family. They did not ask for you in particular, but for the whole bunch of you, perhaps a dozen or more people. In the legalese that the town clerk writes, you are "one of the poor," "on the town" treasury. You are young. You must listen. You must obey. You must work. You must conform to how they do things. You must eat what they serve. You must not cost them too much money. You must wear your clothes out, perhaps beyond a hole-filled state. It is not always easy, but you must get along, not ruffling feathers, not asking for much.

There was a light at the end of this tunnel for Bates, though: an adulthood of sorts. In 1818, the town stopped auctioning off the poor as a group and started arranging for them individually. It is difficult to know how old Bates was when the overseers separated her out. They could do it with children as young as three, but Bates was probably at least a teenager when she got to live with a family and just her, with no other paupers in the house. Depositions suggest that she was being put out to work individually as early as 1816 or 1817. It was not independence. But it was a step in that direction.[12]

A TOWN-RUN TEMP AGENCY?

Now Lydia Bates was out on her own, with a job. Depositions make it clear that Bates worked for many farmers, doing several different jobs from general housework to weaving to shirt-making to agricultural work like pulling flax. What is not clear from the records available is whether she did this work as a hired hand, making her own deals with farmers, or whether the overseers of the poor made arrangements for her. It is also possible that her working life began as a child, with her jobs arranged by overseers of the poor, but that she then began arranging her own jobs, which looked very similar to those arranged by the overseers of the poor.

If she was still technically a pauper, under the oversight of the overseers of the poor, then her bosses had to house her, feed her, and foot her doctor bills, but they did not have to *pay* her. The fact that there are extant receipts of the town paying the householders who kept her while she was pregnant and then recovering from childbirth, but not from before she became pregnant, suggest an arrangement like this: the town temporarily transferred its responsibility for Bates's well-being and its claim on her work to a farmer. The farmer got Bates's work for no money, as long as he fed and housed her. New clothes and medical care were big expenses but irregular expenses, and Lydia Bates was a healthy young woman. How much did it feel like a job? Bates probably had little say in choosing her "employer." Nor did she get cash. Still, it was more like a job than living in the "poorhouses." She worked in exchange for her sustenance, and enjoyed a lot of freedom. Many of her bosses thought of her more as an employee than as a pauper, more as hired help than as a ward of the town.

This is clear from legal depositions, which were taken at the behest of Thomas T. Hill or Scituate's overseers of the poor. The testimony makes clear that Lydia Bates moved from house to house as a worker more than as a charity case. Her primary purpose there, for the householder, was to do some specific job for him, before she moved on. The overseers of the poor could be seen here as doing the work of a temporary employment agency. Deftly, they avoided having to pay for Bates's upkeep by sending her to whichever local farmer could use her labor in return for their food and home. It was a fiscal sleight of hand, perhaps, but it seemed to serve everyone well: the farmers who took Bates in got work done. The town taxpayers got the care of a pauper for free. Bates herself got room and board and, it seems, some respect and independence. Thomas Angell testified that Lydia Bates came to his house two years prior to "work at weaving" for a number of weeks. William B. Harris said he had known her since about 1810 and she had worked for him a number of times. Oliver Leach described Bates's role in the Phillips house as being Mrs. Phillips's "maid." Clearly, Bates's work was important, even vital, to the householders she lived with. In return, these householders were either providing her poor relief at the overseers' request or at least providing a home for a woman who had no home of her own.[13]

This is an aspect of poor relief that is rarely touched upon: the pauper as worker, as vital cog in the local economy. For decades, a common theme among historians of poor relief has been "social control": the idea that poor relief and social welfare have been tools used by the elite to control the poor, whether for economic reasons, moral reasons, race reasons, gender reasons, or class reasons. One classic interpretation, Piven's and Cloward's *Regulating the Poor*, makes a case that "relief-giving is partly designed to enforce work" and that poor relief is key in "defining and enforcing the terms on which different classes of people are made to do different kinds of work." They argue that Americans shrank poor relief in economically stable times in order to pressure the poor into low wage work for private employers. If Lydia Bates's work was arranged by the overseers of the poor, then her experience supports the social control interpretation, in its economic sense, but with a twist. The overseers of the poor quite literally gave Bates specific kinds of work and laid out the terms of service, without any apparent negotiation on Bates's part. Indeed, Lydia Bates's case is a far more *direct* instance of using poor relief to shape the labor market than Piven and Cloward sketched out. They describe governments shaping the private labor market in an indirect way by reducing poor relief. Scituate's overseers of the poor, by contrast, could directly intervene in the labor market by providing workers like Lydia Bates. They did not shrink poor relief. Instead, they could use poor relief to provide low-cost labor to farmers who wanted it. This could be described as a public-private partnership, in which the government coordinates or sponsors work in the private sector. And Scituate's overseers were by no means alone. Historians have noted the extent to which child labor shaped early American political economy. Most well-known are the kinds of long-term indentures that overseers of the poor would make for children in their custody. In Lydia Bates's case, by contrast, the overseers could have made frequent temporary arrangements. Not really an apprentice, Lydia Bates was a "temp."[14]

Was she temporary because no one wanted her in his house for long? Not according to the six men who testified on 17 March, 1821. They would welcome her back repeatedly. Clearly, she worked for them at their convenience, and they did not just hire her out of an obligation to help the town's poor. Rather, they benefited from the availability of a hard-working poor girl. They were not put upon and had no objections to her and said, repeatedly, that her character was as good as any "poor girl." Indeed, during one deposition, the overseer of the poor pointedly asked Wait Burlingame "Did you turn away Lydia Bates on account of her Bad Conduct"? Burlingame answered "no I did not turn her away. . . . "

In the absence of clear, written evidence that the overseers were arranging her jobs, this overseer's question is revealing. It is as close as the extant evidence I have seen comes to showing how involved the overseers were in Bates's life between their oversight of the Bates children around 1817 and the Fall of 1819, when Bates was pregnant and they were paying for her care. The overseer, Thomas Henry, asked only two questions during this deposition. All of the other questions were asked by Thomas T. Hill, who was trying to make a case that Rhoda's father could be somebody else. Henry asked questions to undermine Hill's case. Moreover, Henry seemed to know, ahead of asking, the answers to both the questions he asked. Henry's first question was "at the time you mention of seeing the married man and Lydia Bates Walking and talking together did Lydia Bates and one or more of your Children go into the pasture to drive up your Cow?" Burlingame answered yes. Henry could not have asked such a specific question without already knowing the answer. His second question was whether Burlingame had "turn[ed] away" Bates. Both questions suggest Henry knew a great deal about Burlingame's interactions with Bates. Of course Scituate was a small town, and Henry had no doubt prepared for this deposition. Nevertheless, his knowledge of Bates's working relationship with Burlingame gives the impression that he had been overseeing her, and that he knew Burlingame had never "turn[ed her] away." That phrase also raises the question: turned her away from what? Did Burlingame have the option of turning away a request from the overseers to take Bates in? Or a request from Bates herself? That phrase implies that someone, probably the overseers, was asking Burlingame to take Bates on, on a temporary basis. Finally, the detail that Bates was doing a chore with Burlingame's children in his field shows how well integrated she was into his family. The charcoal sketch in Figure 4.1 captures how this chore might have looked. Even if she was in a farmer's house at his discretion—and for no more than months at a time—Bates was intimately bound up with her neighbors and their families.

Whether as pauper or hired hand, Bates lived and worked in these farm families for years, leaving no paper trail. The paper trail would only begin after an eventful summer during which Bates was staying with the elderly couple: William and Lydia Phillips. While it seems quite likely that Lydia Bates was a pauper as a child, and possible that she was still a pauper as a working teenager and young woman, the evidence is crystal clear that she was a pauper after staying with the Phillipses in 1819.

Figure 4.1 This undated charcoal by Edward Mitchell Bannister, *Landscape with Cows and Figures Moving through Pasture* was likely made after Bates's lifetime, but it evokes both the rural and the social aspects of Bates's life. This could be a scene of her driving cows with Wait Burlingame's children. Courtesy of Smithsonian American Art Museum website.

A PREGNANCY OUT OF WEDLOCK: THE "TOWN FATHERS" INVESTIGATE

Likely as a pauper "temp," or possibly as a hired hand, Lydia Bates lived in the house of William and Lydia Phillips from March to September of 1819. She had been temping for a few years already. William and Lydia Phillips were an aged couple of moderate means, keeping a home together however they could. Census records of 1800, 1810, and 1820 all record a household headed by a William Phillips in Scituate, and each year the census taker tallied a man and a woman over forty-five years old in the house. This means that by 1819, each of them was at least sixty-four years old. The 1800 and 1810 censuses record only the couple in their household, but the 1820 census, taken about a year after Lydia Bates became pregnant and left the Phillips household, notes that three additional women over the age of forty-five were living in there. Depositions do not mention these three women as being present while Lydia Bates was. It seems likely, though, that these are three paupers of the town whom William and Lydia Phillips had taken in for additional income. Perhaps Lydia Bates was brought to the house to help care for these additional members of the household, to serve as a young maidservant in what was becoming a group home for the elderly.

Whether for two or for five elderly housemates, Lydia Bates worked as a "maid." The census listed William Phillips as a farmer and the Phillipses probably could not have afforded to pay a maid. Maybe even providing food for Lydia Bates was difficult, but it brought them the labor of a much younger person. They had the room, as Bates testified that one could even access a second story in their house without being seen from the first story. And her work must have satisfied the Phillipses. Instead of working a few weeks here and there as she had done so often, they kept her from March until September. By September, it was clear that Lydia Bates was expecting a baby. Perhaps morning sickness was making it hard to be a good maid. She had been pregnant since early July.[15]

What happened in early July, 1819? Town authorities made it their business to investigate how Bates became pregnant and who the father was. Poor laws required them to. Any child born out of wedlock was considered the town's official business. What was unusual in Lydia Bates's case, was how vehemently Thomas T. Hill fought the town authorities. Because he hired lawyers, took depositions, and was party to at least four cases surrounding baby Rhoda, there are a lot of records purporting to show what happened in July, 1819. The records contradict each other wildly. They are records from hotly contested court cases, after all. There are at least four different stories that could be supported by the evidence.

One story, supported by Lydia Bates's own testimony, as well as other primary- and secondary-source evidence, is the courtship story. It makes a lot of sense. Lydia Bates was a young woman, without much parental supervision, looking to find a husband, or at least a man with whom to share a household. She considered more than one man, flirting, perhaps becoming sexually intimate. In the summer of 1819, the suitor she most liked was Thomas T. Hill, a thirty-two-year-old, the youngest of eleven children, who was a successful salesman. He sold ceramic milk pans and jars and pots, much like those in Figure 4.2, to Scituate farmers. Thomas T. Hill had something Lydia Bates did not: a large and financially stable family. Indeed, one of Hill's brothers served at times as his attorney.

Hill and Bates would have met easily. As a maid, Lydia Bates would be in and out of the Phillips house a lot, while Hill would travel from farm to farm, peddling his wares. According to both Oliver Leach and Lydia Phillips, Hill left milk pans with Bates that she was to deliver to customers. According to Phillips, Hill "paid" Bates with a platter in return for her help. She added that Hill delivered the platter "through a window on a moonlit

Figure 4.2 Thomas T. Hill sold earthenware ceramics like those pictured here. Bates helped him distribute milk pans, like the one in the center of this picture, which also includes a storage jar (left) and a chamber pot (right) discovered in Salem, Massachusetts and dated 1800–1820. When working as a "maid," Bates may have had to empty chamber pots, like the one on the right. Courtesy of the Peabody Essex Museum.

night." That was as far as Phillips went in suggesting a close relationship between Hill and Bates. Leach went farther.

Leach remembered Mrs. Phillips telling him the day after he collected his milk pans from Bates that "Hill and Lydia were very intimate together and she Did not know but she should loose her maid." Mrs. Phillips never says this in her own testimony, but her opinions changed after the fact. In July, if Oliver Leach is right, Mrs. Phillips expected her young maid Lydia to be married off to Thomas T. Hill. Coming down through the centuries, secondhand, readers can still hear the tone of gossipy chatter. Mrs. Phillips's neighborly talk with Oliver Leach is a combination of complaint about losing her maid, pleasure in sharing gossip, and excitement for the young people about to start a life together. She considered Hill a suitor, and saw nothing wrong with their increasing closeness, as it would likely lead to marriage.[16]

Other testimony also put Hill and Bates in an increasingly intimate relationship. Thomas Angell frequently saw Hill and Bates together at the Phillips house in the summer of 1819 as he was traveling to and from his own land. He once saw Hill walking from the Phillips's barn to their house, and the last time he saw Hill and Bates together was the romantic scene after sunset, with which this chapter began: Bates and Hill together between the wheels of the wagon. Leach's and Angell's testimonies suggest a whirlwind romance during the summer. Hill's frequent visits look like courtship. Premarital sex during courtship was not uncommon in this period, even in this land that Puritans and Baptists had shaped. Lydia Bates might very well have expected that she and Hill were moving towards matrimony. When Bates's voice is finally recorded in more than one-word answers, that is the picture she paints.[17]

Lydia Bates was frequently interviewed about the facts of the case by justices of the peace in Rhode Island and Massachusetts, but usually she answered in one or a few words, and the transcripts are almost entirely in the voice of government officials. In only one extant deposition does her voice break through. That deposition was taken in Scituate in September, 1822. Baby Rhoda was nearly two-and-a-half by then. The voice that comes through is that of a woman who had grown up quickly since Rhoda was born. It is the voice of a jilted lover, who had allowed her head to be filled with empty promises by an older man, and who took some time to realize that none of these promises were coming true. Bates testified that Hill had frequently come to her chamber in the Phillips house during July and August of 1819, and that it was there, with Hill, that Rhoda had been conceived. She said that the Phillips house was constructed in such a way that Hill could "pass up the stairs from the out side door without being seen by the family in the house except they were in the entry." It is unclear whether Bates and Hill saw each other at all from September until Rhoda was born in April, 1820. By April, the Scituate justices of the peace had already issued a warrant for Hill's arrest, indicating that Bates had named him as the father as early as January, 1820. The town sergeant waited until after Rhoda was born, then traveled to Providence and arrested Hill. On May 1, a local court of three justices of the peace found Hill to be the father, "he showing no evidence otherwise" and ordered him to pay $8.46 for prosecution costs, $15 for the first four weeks after birth, and then fifty cents every week as long as the child relied on town poor relief. He would be kept in custody until he complied. It had taken the wheels of justice to bring Hill back to Scituate, and a court decision to squeeze what we would now call "child support" out of him.[18]

Still, even after Scituate town officials had to arrest Hill, Lydia Bates was not done believing his promises. Hill's attorney filed an appeal against the justices' of the peace decision in September, 1820 and wrestled in the courts over the matter for the better part of the year. Then Hill came up with a plan. As Bates told the story, and was recorded in the deposition shown in Figure 4.3, Hill offered to bring her and Rhoda to Massachusetts

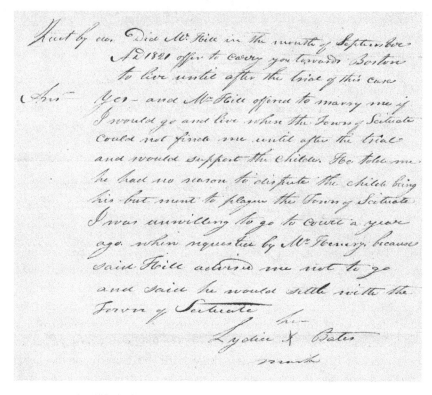

Figure 4.3 Lydia Bates frequently made her X on documents the justices of the peace put in front of her. Only one of those documents actually sounds like Lydia Bates talking, and not the legalese of the town fathers. This deposition, dated 30 September 1822, is from the March 1823 case file "Thomas T. Hill v. Overseers of the Poor of Scituate," courtesy of the Rhode Island Supreme Judicial Records Center.

in September 1821, while his attorneys appealed the case again. In what is the single longest passage of Bates's testimony in all the court documents, Lydia Bates said that

> Mr. Hill offered to marry me if I would go and live where the Town of Scituate
> could not find me until after the trial—and would support the child. He told me
> he had no reason to dispute the child being his but ment to plague the Town of
> Scituate. I was unwilling to go to court a year ago when requested by Mr. Henry
> because said Hill advised me not to go and said he would settle with the Town
> of Scituate.

Bates agreed to the plan. Hill took her to Mendon, Massachusetts, and paid for her to live there in August, September, and October 1821. He also arranged for her to give a new deposition in front of a Massachusetts justice of the peace, in which she testified that Hill was not the father, and that she had only said so under threat of punishment and imprisonment by the Scituate overseers of the poor. According to Bates's 1822 statement, she never meant to say that Hill was not the father of Rhoda, only that he did not conduct himself like a father to Rhoda.[19]

What is striking is that a year-and-a-half after Rhoda's birth, through a time when Hill had been throwing up every legal roadblock possible to his supporting the mother and child, Lydia Bates continued to take his advice, and even trusted herself and Rhoda to his care in Massachusetts, far from the neighbors and friends she had lived with all her life. Perhaps she was a lovesick fool, and it took a while to wear off. Or perhaps she thought Hill was her best shot at a more financially stable life.

Lydia Bates would have lots of reasons to believe that sexual intimacy with Thomas T. Hill was one step on the way to marriage. For one thing, lots of couples did it. As we have seen, William Larned and Sally Smith were expecting their firstborn when they were married in 1784. He was nearly thirty-two, she was fifteen or sixteen; they had about the same age difference as Thomas T. Hill and Lydia Bates. Moreover, Sally was the daughter of a John Smith, *Esquire*, so this suggests that even wealthier people could get away with it. Indeed, a commonly accepted statistic holds that in many late-eighteenth-century New England towns, one third of brides were pregnant on their wedding days. Bates may even have thought that pregnancy would help encourage Thomas T. Hill to marry her. There is evidence that she had hoped this with one other man once: Ahohab Johnson.[20]

Ahohab Johnson was a lot like Lydia Bates. He had worked for short times in many places. He could not write his name, but marked with an X. Born in Foster, like Thomas T. Hill, Johnson was in Scituate in 1819 but had moved on to Brooklyn, Connecticut in 1822 when Hill caught up with him to take his deposition. Hill traveled this far because Johnson would give him something no one in Scituate would: a statement that he had had sexual relations with Lydia Bates. Johnson testified that Bates made a shirt for him, presumably for a charge, but that then he had "carnal knowledge" of Bates twice in July of 1819. Then, Johnson testified, Bates asked him to take her with him to live.[21]

If this is true, then Lydia Bates may have fallen into a pattern. She met, flirted, and had sex with possible suitors. Then she hoped they would settle down with her, either to cohabit or to marry. And it did not work. Another deposition, Anthony Patt's in 1820, corroborates this interpretation, stating that Lydia Bates courted two men, one right after another, with a month in between, about 1815. He added that she went to bed with both suitors. Patt also testified that he knew of no bad conduct on Bates's part, suggesting that going to bed with suitors was acceptable to him, at least in the context of courtship. Similarly, Ahohab Johnson apparently had no regrets about his behavior towards Lydia Bates, nor about admitting it in a legal document. Was this acceptable behavior in Johnson's and Bates's circle of friends and acquaintances in rural New England? Was a sexual double standard so pronounced that Ahohab Johnson could announce to the world what Lydia Bates could not? Johnson's deposition could support the Courtship Story: that Lydia Bates saw sex as part of courtship, leading to a more stable relationship. His deposition could also support another story: a promiscuity story.[22]

Bursting out of these two-hundred-year-old depositions is a boisterous undercurrent of parties, visits, drinking, and horseplay among the Scituate youth in 1819. Ahohab Johnson and Lydia Bates were part of a large group of young people who saw much of each other that summer. Hired hands or householders, children of farmers or paupers, there were many young people who regularly left the oversight of their parents or masters to meet each other in the fields or at welcoming homes and taverns. Arnold Knight testified that he was at a tavern with Bates that summer. William B. Harris thought she may have been at his house on the 4th of July, but could not remember specifically because she was "frequently" there. Lydia Phillips recalled Bates telling her that she was sick because someone threw her in the river, presumably as part of horseplay at a party. Her husband William Phillips also remembered hearing two men come to his house to be with Bates. As old as he was, he got up too, and as he recalled, "we set up all Knight." Abigail Fenner testified that Bates dressed in men's clothes and tried to go to a "Cristmas" with a young man. Lydia Phillips said that she thought Bates to be "after all the men." It is clear that Bates and her friends and acquaintances frequently saw each other socially, at lots of different houses and taverns, day and night. The painting in Figure 4.4 gives an idea of how this tavern scene might have looked.[23]

Other New England sources suggest that some young people in this period saw sexual intimacy not as part of courtship but as a pastime. Additionally, it seems that virginity before marriage was less important to poor workers like Lydia Bates and Ahohab Johnson than it might have been to wealthier families. Poor relief records suggest that unwed mothers like Bates were not rare. Small towns like Scituate had at least a couple unwed new mothers to support every year. Studies of other towns, moreover, have found that sex was not always linked to courtship in this place and time. Focusing on a man's diary in Keene, New Hampshire in the 1780s, historians Laurel Thatcher Ulrich and Lois K. Stabler report that what the diarist called "Girling of It," "was a sport as well as method of

Figure 4.4 Even if painted a generation later and an ocean away, Johann Mongles Culverhouse's 1846 *Dutch Tavern Scene*, gives an idea of how Bates's night life might have looked. Generations mixed and people flirted amidst drinking, smoking, and earthenware vessels. The misgivings plainly on the face of the woman with a kerchief tied below her chin are similar to those expressed in some of the women's depositions about Lydia Bates's night life. Courtesy of the Smithsonian American Art Museum website.

courtship. It developed in a world where young persons were largely responsible for their own behavior, moving across fields and in and out of each other's households with little restraint from parents, employers, the church, or the courts." That sounds a lot like Lydia Bates's world. Ulrich and Stabler are worth quoting at length, because they paint a compelling picture of the dating scene in turn-of-the-nineteenth-century rural New England, describing how

> Young folks socialized in berry patches, across looms, and around woodpiles, developing attractions and alliances at husking bees and barnraisings that might lead to all-night encounters. Though men as well as women accepted the possibility of pregnancy and the ultimate necessity of marriage, young adulthood was characterized less by restraint than by freedom—freedom to visit, to party, to tarry, and to choose one's mate.[24]

Although a couple generations earlier, this rich description fits the sources describing Lydia Bates's social life very well. Except for one thing. It does not seem that Ahohab Johnson was prepared to marry Lydia Bates in case of pregnancy. His view of "Girling of It" implies no responsibilities for his part. If Ahohab Johnson and Thomas T. Hill *were* both sexually intimate with Lydia Bates, then one could interpret this as part of a pattern of recreational sex among Scituate youth, or as part of what Lydia Bates thought was courtship. There is also a third interpretation that could account for these sexual encounters: the prostitution story.

Thomas T. Hill wanted the court to believe either the promiscuity story or the prostitution story. He went out of his way, quite literally, to find people who would testify that Bates's "general character" was "not verry good," as Arnold Knight put it in May of 1820. Many deponents testified that Lydia Bates did not have a good character, though most of these qualified this statement by saying that "it was said." In other words, they reported that gossip about Lydia Bates was largely negative. Only a couple went further to say that Bates was a prostitute. Tracked down again in early 1821, this time in Johnston, Arnold Knight said "it has been the common report in the neighborhood that the said Lydia Bates is a common prostitute and of bad fame." Abigail Fenner of Johnston agreed that Bates was called a "common prostitute" around Johnston.[25] Few others would go this far, and it is noteworthy that these two witnesses lived in a neighboring town, not in Scituate itself.

Still, the sheer number of men, including at least one married man, that Lydia Bates is linked with in a variety of depositions raises the question: was Lydia Bates making an income by prostitution? For a young woman who worked for many households but did not have to be paid, this could be one way to earn cash, or be treated to drinks, or receive some other benefit that the overseers of the poor or her employers thought unnecessary to provide. Lydia Phillips never uses the word "prostitute" but testifies that Bates told her a married man offered Bates "a dollar for what purpose she did not say." Another witness, Wate Burlingame, testified that after he heard of Lydia Bates in bed with a married man, Bates showed Burlingame money that the married man gave her for pulling flax. Burlingame's suspicion that this was money earned by prostitution is implied—if not made explicit—in his testimony. And Thomas T. Hill and his attorneys imply the possibility of prostitution by linking Lydia Bates to a dozen different men in several depositions. They get witnesses to report that they saw, or heard about, or saw circumstantial evidence of Lydia Bates "keeping company" with Nicholas Fenner, Thomas Barns, William Tingley, Elijah Williams, Fisher Hewes, James Whiteker, Cyrus Borden, an unnamed married man, John Rogers (a married man whose wife was deceased by the time of the depositions), Edward L. Smith, Ahohab Johnson, and an unnamed stage driver. Likewise, the overseers of the poor found witnesses to connect

Bates with Thomas T. Hill. Very few men admitted to "keeping company" with Lydia Bates themselves, but Ahohab Johnson did. So did Benjamin Ingraham who said he kept company with Bates and that she told him she "had connection" with three men the night the child was conceived and could not tell which was the father. Hill did not care whether the court believed the promiscuity story or the prostitution story: he only wanted to clear himself of the likelihood of being Rhoda's father.[26]

Essentially, the court had to choose between a story presented by the overseers of the poor, a story of courtship gone wrong, or a story presented by Thomas T. Hill, one of a sexually promiscuous woman, perhaps a prostitute, who could not tell who the father of her baby was. One other possible story emerges from the many court records, though. Neither party in the case suggests it, and no deposition gives firm evidence of it, but it is worth considering alongside the three other stories. It is the rape and cover-up story. In the close-knit small town of Scituate, where kin networks wove around the neighbors, was there something that the overseers of the poor and justices of the peace were trying to hide? The overseers and justices of the peace pursued Hill with dogged determination, never seeming to question whether he was the father. Was this because they believed Lydia Bates wholeheartedly? Or was Hill a convenient, out-of-town fall guy for a responsibility that really belonged to a well-connected Scituate man? My suspicions of this story were first awakened when I read Lydia Phillips testifying that she saw some unnamed married men going away from her house as she was returning. "What was the names of those married men which you see going away from your house"? asked Thomas T. Hill. "I shall not tell," answered Lydia Phillips.[27]

Why would Mrs. Phillips not tell? One explanation is that she did not want to publicly embarrass the wives of these married men. The only married man named as having gone to bed with Lydia Bates in these depositions is a John Rogers, whose wife had since died. No other married man is named. Another explanation, though, is that Mrs. Phillips was afraid to embarrass the married men she saw. Perhaps they had ways of avenging themselves on her and her husband. After all, the Phillipses were an elderly couple, with little means, who probably depended on the overseer of the poor to help their household stay afloat. Perhaps these married men were well connected to the overseers of the poor, or the justices of the peace. Perhaps they *were* the justices of the peace or the overseers of the poor. Perhaps that is why the overseers and the justices went to such lengths, with such determination, to make Thomas T. Hill the legal father. Hill never suggested that. Given the efforts he makes to clear his name, and his own family connections in other towns, it seems likely that he would have made that accusation if he thought it would help. Still, it is a possibility that must be considered. It is a possibility because one thing that is clear from the records is this: Lydia Bates was very vulnerable.[28]

Lydia Bates, circa 1820, was a young woman without the protection of a parent-headed household. Whether still living or not, her parents did not have the means to house and feed her, to help her start her own household. Nor could they protect her from anyone who wanted to use her body, for sex or for work. Starting adulthood already a pauper, without a dowry, without a home, Bates had few resources to draw on. She was probably not paid for most of the work she did. In light of this vulnerability, the sexual history that Hill tries so hard to make public tells us something about poor relief. As a pauper, Lydia Bates had no resources with which to start a household or a marriage. As a pauper, she rarely got paid for the work that she did. As a pauper, she had few protections from sexual predators, and few alternatives to prostitution.

It seems true that Lydia Bates was sexually intimate with more than one man, probably including Thomas T. Hill. It seems true, too, that with at least two of these men, Hill and Ahohab Johnson, Bates hoped for a long-term relationship, whether marriage or making a household together. It is possible, moreover, that Bates sometimes accepted money in exchange for physical intimacy. As a pauper, there were even fewer opportunities to earn money open to her than to other poor young women. She showed herself quite willing to work hard as, for example, a maid, seamstress, or agricultural laborer. But this was likely unpaid work. A "temp" working for the overseers of the poor in exchange for her room and board, she knew that few of Scituate's farmers needed to pay her outright for her work, when they could exchange room and board for her work. Even as a hired hand, she could expect low wages if she had no home of her own, and needed to stay with her employer. She was a young woman, left to fend for herself, with no benefactor, advisor, or supporter stepping forward on her behalf, apart from the overseers of the poor and justices of the peace. The overseers, thanks to the poor laws, were obliged to provide for her and her daughter. They were also obliged to find a father to Rhoda to support her, if at all possible. Beyond this, though, none of them seemed to serve as a protector to Bates in any way beyond the legal requirements.

Despite all these odds, Bates strove to make the best life she could. With little education—she signed all documents with an X—and no financial resources, she used what she had to earn her keep and find a mate. She worked hard, and socialized abundantly. She did general house chores, she wove, she pulled flax, she sewed shirts, she delivered crockery, she charmed, she wooed, she tried to find a husband. That her efforts did not find a stable home for herself and Rhoda, at least not before 1828, ought not to distract us from all the efforts she made for herself and her daughter. That she followed Thomas T. Hill's advice in 1821 and moved to Massachusetts, refusing to testify in the case that revolved around her, seems foolish in retrospect. But for a woman with few prospects, it probably seemed like a way to finally find stability, with a financially successful man, who could provide a home for herself and her daughter, so that they would not have to move every couple months. It did not work, but not for a lack of Bates's trying. Bates did what she could, with the knowledge she had, in the context of a patriarchal culture. It is quite possible, in fact, that she was not informed about all of the legal actions taken, between 1820 and 1824, to establish who her daughter's father was.[29]

WHO WILL PAY CHILD SUPPORT?

As Lydia Bates experienced her pregnancy, gave birth in April 1820, then learned how to mother an infant, all while moving from one neighbor's home to the next, the legal battle unfolded. The town authorities of Scituate went to great lengths to find Rhoda's father and make him pay. Hill went to even greater lengths to avoid being held responsible for Rhoda's upbringing. As a result, the court records in the question of who Rhoda's father was fill three separate case files. Packed with depositions and court decisions, still sitting in the Rhode Island Supreme Judicial Court Records Center today, they are a measure of how seriously overseers of the poor took their responsibility to find child support for Rhoda. Readers in the present day will be familiar with the concept of child support, but may be surprised to find it was an element of American poor laws two hundred years ago. It was. Overseers of the poor paid particular attention to those children whom they called "bastards," then the legal term any child born out of wedlock. As readers have learned from William Larned's story, the overseers were supposed to do whatever they could, humanely, to keep poor relief costs down. So, they usually moved quickly to find someone to hold financially responsible for any child "likely to be chargeable." Depending on the circumstances, they might focus on the child's father, or the child's maternal grandparents.

In some cases, town officials would be satisfied with a bond from the baby's maternal grandparent or grandmother. Often in amounts of $500, these bonds would hold the grandparent responsible for any costs the town treasury had to pay for support until the child became an adult. If the father was unknown, or too poor, or long gone, this was a way that the overseers could protect the town treasury from additional expenses.

The arrangement could also protect the single mother and child from being separated, put in a poorhouse, or having their care auctioned off to the lowest bidder. These arrangements could be complicated. For example, when Betsey Fenner became a single mother in 1807, Fenner's mother, Susannah Barton, sold her real estate to the town for $100, with a stipulation that she could regain her house and land with a payment of $100 or some surety that she would protect the town from any expense for her granddaughter's "Maintenance education or bringing up." In effect, Barton put a lien on her house to guarantee that the town would not have to take care of her granddaughter.[30]

Lydia Bates, however, did not have a father or mother with property that could be used for baby Rhoda's support. So town officials pursued Rhoda's father instead. Indeed, the law assumed that town officials would pursue the father first and gave them wide authority to arrest, jail, sue, or even bind out in indentured servitude any father who did not agree to pay his child's upkeep. The law assumed that single mothers could not support children themselves, but did allow town officials to jail an unwed mother who refused to tell them the father's name. It did not come to that with Lydia Bates. Before and after she gave birth, Bates named Thomas T. Hill as baby Rhoda's father. The law assumed that mothers told the truth about who the father was, and only men who could prove they were not the father could escape a judgment based on a single mother's testimony.[31]

The overseers began their case in January, 1820, when Bates was still pregnant with Rhoda. They had all their paperwork lined up, then, to send the town sergeant after Hill when baby Rhoda was just a few weeks old. The town sergeant moved quickly: arresting Hill in Providence and delivering him to the Scituate justices of the peace by May 1. Hill said he was "not guilty." But, following the law, the justices of the peace believed Bates over Hill, arguing that Hill "could Shoe no proof nor Satisfactory reason that he was inocent." They ordered Hill to pay $15 to cover the first four weeks after Rhoda's birth, when Bates was allowed to recover, and then fifty cents every week as long as the child was being supported by the town. Economic historians might estimate these figures as equivalent to $5,000 and $168 per week when compared to wages for an unskilled laborer today.[32]

Hill immediately appealed, which meant that the case would go to the state Supreme Judicial Court. In one form or another, this case would visit the Supreme Court every time they sat in Providence from September 1820 until September 1824. For five Septembers and four Marches in a row, the overseers and justices of the peace of Scituate, together with Thomas T. Hill, all their lawyers, and assorted witnesses, usually including Lydia Bates herself, would all descend on Providence to argue the case again. In the first case, Hill won a reversal. But in the second case, during which Hill and his brother-in-law posted bonds for $500 for Rhoda's care, a jury found Hill to be responsible for Rhoda. Hill pursued the case a third time but lost again in 1824. The town of Scituate was still trying to force Hill and his brother-in-law to pay the money promised in the bond as late as 1827.[33]

In addition to the cases deciding whether Thomas T. Hill was Rhoda's father, Hill also started a related suit in March 1821: for assault and battery against Scituate's justices of the peace and the Providence County deputy sheriff who had helped Scituate's town sergeant arrest him. Hill accused the four men of trespass in his home and "a violent assault" during which they caused him to be "beat, bruised + otherwise evil intreated + emprisoned + deprived of his person liberty against his consent for the space of three days, to wit from the 29th day of April 1820 till the 2d day of May 1820." He also accused them of "other wrongs + enormities" and asked for $3,000 in damages. This case was continued through the Supreme Court in parallel to the main case over the paternity of Rhoda. A year after that case was decided, this case was also decided, also by jury. Technically, Hill was awarded damages by the jury. But their award of fifty cents seemed a slap in the face. Not only had Hill asked for $3,000, but fifty cents was probably a mere fraction of the court costs he had incurred to start this suit.[34]

Hill spent years fighting the child support charges against him. Ultimately, he lost his cases in spite of a great deal of time, effort, money, and support from his family and friends. The overseers of the poor triumphed, in court, in their efforts to make Hill reimburse them for Rhoda's care. Hill had traveled far to collect depositions: around central Rhode Island, to southern Massachusetts, and to eastern Connecticut. Reading the extant depositions, Hill seemed to compile the stronger case. There may have been witnesses whose testimony was in front of the court, and not recorded in the files of the records center. But what remains in the records center shows a battle of depositions. I have read thirty-six depositions about Bates. More than two thirds of these were created at the behest of Hill. All together they interrogated twenty-seven different individuals, in three states, over the course of two years. The spelling and capitalization of each deposition was typically that of the justice of the peace in front of whom the deposition was taken. In these small towns, the justices of the peace acted as their own clerks. The witness, if he or she could read, was invited to read the handwritten transcript and sign his or her name, or else make his or her mark. Sixteen witnesses signed their name. Eleven made a mark: X or +.

Above these signatures and marks, the depositions record all sorts of details about an ordinary woman who received poor relief in this period. By contrast to Lydia Bates, Thomas T. Hill seemed to have a great deal of social capital, including family members who could help him post bond. Hill's own brother was his lawyer through some stages of the case, but he could also afford other lawyers, and he did not hesitate to interrupt his lawyers and question deponents himself. Lydia Bates did not have this kind of supportive network or this level of confidence around town officials. As several of her neighbors recognized, few people spoke up in defense of "poor girls."

"AS FAIR AS ANY POOR GIRL"

Only a handful of the depositions still sitting in case files speak in defense of Lydia Bates. On March 17, 1821, the overseers of the poor arranged for six depositions to be taken, all of men who had known Lydia Bates for years, and had employed her as a "temp." Two of them called into question Thomas T. Hill's star witnesses: the elderly Phillips couple with whom Bates was staying when she conceived Rhoda. Elisha Leach testified that "as to truth and veracity," the Phillipses' "character is not so good as some and I live about half a mile from them and have been acquainted with them about thirty years." Oliver Leach, in answer to the same question, begged off: "I think it a hard question between Neighbors I should Like to pronounce it good if I thought it was." Oliver Leach's deposition, together with Lydia Phillips's from the day before, show some tension between them. Mrs. Phillips testified that Leach would not be happy if Hill left Leach's milk pans with her. The main message of these March 17 depositions, though, is simple: Lydia Bates was a good worker and a good person. As Elisha Leach, William Barnes, and Abraham Salisbury all put it: her character was as good as any "poor girl."[35]

Abraham Salisbury's deposition is short, but worth quoting at length. It is the only deposition which clearly shows the deponent to be angry. It is also the most strident in defense of Lydia Bates. Hill's lawyer (who was also his brother on this day) tried to impugn Salisbury by asking another witness whether he heard Salisbury using "foul language." Clearly, Salisbury had used strong words, but the justice did not write them down. In the words that did get written down, Salisbury went out of way his way to bring up social class. In Salisbury's view, the lawyers and witnesses were picking on Lydia Bates because she was a "poor girl," with no one to stand up for her. So he would. Where other depositions on the same day seemed calm, and the justice's written versions of each interview recorded a series of questions and answers, Salisbury's testimony seems breathless, as if he had been just waiting to give the court a piece of his mind. The opening sentence, a run-on, reads like this:

I, Abraham Salisbury of Scituate in the County of Providence and State of Rhode Island of Lawfull age and engaged according to Law Do testify and say that I have been acquainted with Lydia Bates about eight years and know nothing to the contrary but what her character stands as fair as any other poor girl and I think more has been said about said Girl than would have been said about a girl in the same situation with wealthy Parents and in the course of the eight years I have lived within a stones throw or a few rods of her for three or four years and the remainder part of the time I have lived in said town but not a very near Neighbor.

After this barrage of testimony, Thomas T. Hill, the accused father himself, had the temerity to ask Salisbury whether Bates's character was good or bad. The justice recorded only the answer "I know nothing but what is good" and then the whole deposition was done, far shorter than all the rest. Probably, Salisbury had let loose his "foul language" at this point. In response to a tin-eared Hill asking a question Salisbury had already answered, Salisbury was eager vent his spleen. One can imagine the justice of the peace, Israel Manchester, putting down his pen as Salisbury yelled at Hill and stormed out of Manchester's parlor.[36]

But before *we* leave Manchester's parlor, it is worth unpacking the word "poor," as Salisbury used it. In the present day, the phrase "poor girl" sounds sympathetic, something you might say to your young daughter who had skinned her knee. It sounds different, though, as applied to Lydia Bates. For these men, Bates was one of many "poor girls." But what was a "poor girl?" In 1820, "poor" was both a legal term and a term of class pride. As a legal term, "poor" was often used in Britain and the United States to refer to people who received government poor relief. Thus, the "overseer of the *poor*" oversaw people receiving relief from the town government. The *Poor* Law legislated what the governments' responsibilities were to provide relief. Overseers would frequently refer to a pauper as "one of the *poor* of this town," meaning that this is an individual who is currently receiving town assistance.

To hear Abraham Salisbury use the word, though, is to hear a different, less legalistic, more moralistic connotation of the word "poor." Like William Manning, a Massachusetts farmer whose 1790s essays argued against the power of the moneyed elite and on behalf of the laboring many, Salisbury brandished the word "poor" as a badge of pride. For Manning, being "poor" was clearly better than the alternative. Similarly, Salisbury's strident defense of Lydia Bates's character aims to take some of the shame out being "poor." For Salisbury, it was through no fault of Lydia Bates that she was poor, and she was not the only one. Despite what all of Thomas T. Hill's witnesses said, Salisbury angrily insisted that her character was "as fair as any other poor girl." William Barnes and Elisha Leach backed him up on that point. Moreover, Salisbury accusatorily told the men across the table, no one would say these things about Bates if her parents were wealthy.

The phrase "as fair as any other poor girl," tells much and implies more. Salisbury could be implying that Bates was a recipient of poor relief. But whether he means that, precisely, or not, he clearly suggests that "poor girls" should not be held up for blame. They did not have the same protection that wealthy girls did, nor could they meet the same societal standards. Salisbury wished that the whole town would respect "poor girls" more than they were respecting Lydia Bates.

SEPARATING FAMILIES

The angry Abraham Salisbury is as close as the records come to suggesting that anyone would stick up for Lydia Bates, as the court case dragged on and was finally settled. No parent, friend, or family member stepped forward to publicly support Bates, or give her a place to stay. Rather, Scituate town officials continued to assume responsibility for the single mother and her child, just as they had done for Bates when she was younger. And, just as they had most likely done with Bates and her parents, town authorities would ultimately separate young Rhoda from her mother.

After hiding out in Massachusetts with Hill, Bates and one-and-a-half-year-old Rhoda returned to Scituate in the Fall of 1821. Overseer of the Poor Thomas Henry had visited her in Massachusetts. He did not record what he said to her, but almost as soon as she returned, the overseers of the poor gave her the significant sum of $19.80 as support for several months of caring for baby Rhoda. Scrawling on the empty fly leaves of an old law book, the town treasurer kept records of what he paid out in the years around Rhoda's birth. After the September payment, the next is a payment in April, 1822: $5.24 to Lydia Bates "for keeping her child she had by Thomas Hill to this date." Then, if the receipts are right, Rhoda was separated from her mother at age two and sent to live with Jonathan Smith, who was keeping most of the town's "poor" that year.[37]

That first separation did not last long. By September, 1822, Overseer of the Poor Thomas Henry was paying Henry Harris for "keeping Lydia Bates + Child." They were together, in yet another house. The next receipt, to Ester Colvin, suggests she was caring only for the "Lydia Bates child" from the Fall of 1823 until the Fall of 1824. If Rhoda, age three and four, was living with Ester Colvin, was Lydia Bates working again as a temp, on some local farm? Perhaps. But mother and daughter were together again by 1826. That year, Bates was paid $17 "for support by the child she had by T. T. Hill." At the usual rate of fifty cents per week, that would be a payment for thirty-four weeks. Rhoda was six-and-a-half years old.[38]

That receipt, copied into the back pages of an old legal manual, is the last record I have seen documenting Lydia Bates's life. The court cases had been over for a couple years. Bates's life with her daughter Rhoda seemed to have settled down. Then, like so many of the poorest Americans in this period, Lydia Bates stopped generating paper records. It is quite possible more evidence will turn up at some point, but I have searched in many places. And I have no idea what happened to Lydia Bates after 1826.

Rhoda continues to pop up in records for at least a few more years. In August, 1827, Rhoda's situation was part of a Town Meeting discussion. After deciding where all of the rest of the town's poor would go, they voted that "Rhoda Martha Bates" be "left in the overseers hands for them to bind out to some good" plan. Or at least I think it says plan. The clerk's handwriting becomes illegible at that word. His handwriting also makes Rhoda's name hard to read, but he clearly gives her the last name Bates. A few months later, Eliaser Phillips was paid for "Supporting Lydia Bates child." Then, in September, 1828, the Town Meeting again separated Rhoda out from the rest of the town's paupers. This time, the clerk called her "The Thomas T. Hill Child." He noted that, again, she would "Remain under the direction of the Overseers. . . ."[39]

Now, officially, Lydia Bates had no say in Rhoda's life. Were they still together? It seems unlikely. It was up to the overseers, Rhoda's legal guardians, to find a family to raise her. Rhoda was repeating a process that her mother and uncles and aunts had already been through: a child and her labor being given to some family that was not her own. In the 1820s, it was still quite common for poor law officials around the country to believe that separating families was their best option. This had happened to Sarah Hill, decades before, at age three. In her case, race—the fact that she was "Indian"—was part of why she was separated from her parents. Another factor could be whether the overseers thought a child's parents were parenting well. The Scituate Town Council received a petition in 1823, from a number of locals, asking for a girl named Cynthia Ann Patt to be separated from her father, Anthony B. Patt because he was "very unsuitable to have the care of his child." By coincidence, Anthony B. Patt had given two depositions critical of Bates. But no one made an accusation that Lydia Bates was unfit as a parent, at least not in writing that is preserved. Still, overseers of the poor usually intervened in poor families. They thought this was the best way to ensure the child would get food, clothes, housing, and maybe an education. It was also a way of keeping that child from needing poor relief.[40]

For more than two centuries, by 1828, local officials had separated children from their parents, and bound them out to other families. This was the obvious solution to overseers of the poor all over the English-speaking world. If it was still the case that Lydia Bates could not support Rhoda herself, or did not have a parent or husband who could, then the overseers were supposed to step in and separate mother and child, arranging a place for the child in a more financially stable household. That Lydia had still cared for Rhoda at age six, having been a pauper that whole time, might actually be considered unusual for that period. So, though records do not show which family, Rhoda almost certainly was taken in by another family before her ninth birthday.

With luck, the family to whom Rhoda was "bound out" would be kind. They might treat her, sort of, as a daughter, developing an affection for her. Alternatively, they might always see her as a maidservant. They would probably teach her to read some, and perhaps to write and do arithmetic. She could not help but learn numerous housekeeping skills, and perhaps additional skills, like weaving. Perhaps she learned to make shirts like her mother. At the end of her time of service, probably eighteen, she could then go on to work independently, or marry. Hopefully, she could work for pay. If not, though, the town of Scituate might arrange "temp" arrangements as they likely had for her mother.

There is evidence, though, suggesting that something else might have happened to Rhoda: that she was taken into a farmer's house as a pauper, and eventually married the farmer's son. Throughout the 1820s, John Mathewson and Simon Mathewson kept winning the bids to keep all the town's poor for the year. In just the years that Rhoda's name stops being separated out from the rest of the town's poor, those were the men who typically brought all homeless residents to their house. Moreover, census records from 1820 and 1830 show that both men had sons about five years older than Rhoda.

Census records from 1850 through 1885, meanwhile, find a "Rhoda M. Mathewson," born in 1820, living in Scituate and married to a Henry Mathewson, five years her senior. While this evidence is not airtight, it strongly suggests that Rhoda married, had seven children, and lived well into her sixties. Her oldest child, according to the 1850 census, had been born when Rhoda Mathewson was nineteen, about ten years after Lydia Bates's daughter likely went into the Mathewson "poorhouse." At least one of Rhoda Mathewson's sons, James, served in the United States Army during the Civil War. He was killed in battle in Virginia, in 1864. He was twenty-two. His mother was forty-four. Beginning in 1879, she would work hard to win a Union Army survivor's pension for the family, as her farmer husband was suffering from a debilitating disease. She worried, in her pension filings, about having to go to Scituate's poorhouse. She also recalled the last time she saw her son James in the pension filing, describing him as tall, at six-foot-two, with "dark brown" hair and "dark hazel" eyes. Did he bear any resemblance to Lydia Bates? We do not know. But it seems likely that Lydia Bates's descendants still live today. So should her story.[41]

The records that tell her story, though, say nothing after 1826. She could have continued doing the kind of "temp" work that she had done until 1819, without many written records, but surely an illness or a burial would have been accounted for among the town papers. Perhaps Bates moved. She had seen Massachusetts and Providence during her trial, having been brought there, respectively, at the insistence of Thomas T. Hill or the town of Scituate. Maybe she saw in one of these places a place to make a new life. If she had needed poor relief again, though, she would have certainly been sent back to Scituate.[42]

Our glimpse into the life of a poor young woman ends after a decade or so. That glimpse, however, is one of the best that historians have for poor young women in rural America in the early republic period. It allows us to see some things we might expect: overseers of the poor separating children from their parents, a relative powerlessness on the part of Bates, but also Bates's best efforts to do whatever she could for herself and her daughter in these constrained circumstances. We also see some things we might not expect: a lot of freedom for a woman receiving poor relief, and overseers of the poor who could behave like a modern-day temp agency. Lydia Bates did what she could with the poor laws that governed her. Without parents who could provide for her, she found provision in the town government. The overseers of the poor did not oversee her with the concern of parents. They could find her work, if not pay. They found her homes, food, medicine, and doctors, if not stability. They promised to provide for her daughter, though they would not let Bates remain with her daughter long. It is a complicated picture, but it is the picture of welfare in a rural New England town, in the 1810s and 1820s. It is also a picture that would change dramatically a generation later.

NOTES

1. Deposition of William Angell, 17 March 1821, in Case File "Thomas T. Hill v. Overseers of the Poor of Scituate," March Term 1823, RISJCRC.

2. Deposition of Lydia Phillips, 15 September 1820, in Case File "Scituate v. Thomas T. Hill" September Term 1820, RISJCRC.
3. Abramovitz, *Regulating the Lives of Women*, xiii–xiv, 70–72.
4. On the work of women in poor relief, see Abramovitz, *Regulating the Lives of Women*, 66–67; Herndon, "Poor Women and the Boston Almshouse in the Early Republic," 349–382; Bourque, "Women and Work in the Philadelphia Almshouse, 1790–1840," 383–413; Daen, "'To Board & Nurse a Stranger': Poverty, Disability, and Community in Eighteenth-Century Massachusetts," 1–26; and Green, *This Business of Relief*, 37.
5. This reference to Thomas Bates as Lydia Bates's father is the only instance I have ever seen Lydia Bates's father named, in dozens of court records and town government documents. Intriguingly, it was recorded as part of a question that Thomas T. Hill asked of William Mann, far from Scituate in Mendon, Massachusetts. Lydia Bates herself does not seem to have been present at the deposition: Deposition of William Mann, 13 March 1822 Case File "Thomas T. Hill v. Overseers of the Poor of Scituate," March Term 1823, RISJCRC. For Thomas Bates in the 1810 census, see Third Census of the United States, 1810. (NARA microfilm publication M252, 71 rolls), accessed via Ancestry.com, Roll 58, Page 89, Image 00174, Family History Library Film 0281232.
6. On Samuel Bates's war record and the "very poor man" quotation, see "Samuel Bates" File, Massachusetts file number S38526 in *Revolutionary War Pension and Bounty-Land Warrant Application Files* (NARA microfilm publication M804, 2,670 rolls), Records of the Department of Veterans Affairs, Record Group 15, National Archives, Washington, D.C., accessed via Ancestry.com, *U.S., Revolutionary War Pension and Bounty-Land Warrant Application Files, 1800–1900*. On assistance from Scituate town government, see Folder 6 "Paid Bills 1798–1805" in Box 1 "Overseer of the Poor / Scituate Asylum," MSS 216, "Scituate Town Records," RIHS.
7. Folder 6 "Paid Bills 1798–1805" and Folder 7 "Paid Bills, 1806–1811" in Box 1 "Overseer of the Poor / Scituate Asylum," MSS 216, "Scituate Town Records," RIHS. Margaret Creech focused on this period in Scituate's history in *Three Centuries of Poor Law Administration,* 165–172.
8. On the Scituate contracts for poor relief, see Folder 6 "Paid Bills 1798–1805"; Folder 7 "Paid Bills, 1806–1811"; and Folder 8, "Paid Bills, 1812–1818," in Box 1 "Overseer of the Poor / Scituate Asylum," MSS 216, "Scituate Town Records," RIHS. For estimates of today's worth, see Measuring Worth Foundation, "Purchasing Power Today of a US Dollar Transaction in the Past."
9. For records of "moving William Bates Children to the Poor house," see 1817 receipt to James Knight in Folder 8 "Paid Bills, 1812–1818, Box 1 "Overseer of the Poor / Scituate Asylum," MSS 216, "Scituate Town Records," RIHS. For census mentions of a William Bates in Scituate, see Third Census of the United States, 1810. (NARA microfilm publication M252, 71 rolls), Bureau of the Census, Record Group 29, National Archives, Washington, D.C., accessed via Ancestry.com, Roll 58, Page 83, Image 00163, Family History Library Film 0281232, as well as Fifth Census of the United States, 1830, (NARA microfilm publication M19, 201 rolls), Records of the Bureau of the Census, Record Group 29, National Archives, Washington, D.C., accessed via Ancestry.com, Series M19, Roll 168, Page 163, Family History Library Film 0022267.
10. Third Census of the United States, 1810, (NARA microfilm publication M252, 71 rolls), Bureau of the Census, Record Group 29, National Archives, Washington, D.C., accessed via Ancestry.com, Roll 58, Page 83, Image 00163, Family History

Library Film 0281232. For Sarah Kent's deposition, see 17 March 1821 Deposition of Sarah Kent in Case File "Thomas T. Hill v. Overseers of the Poor of Scituate," March Term 1823, RISJCRC. The Kent scenario is bolstered by the fact that a Sarah Kent in Scituate was widowed in 1815, after Samuel Kent died. Thus Sarah Kent might move into William Kent's home even if she was not there in during the Census of 1810. See "Executor's Notice," 22 April 1815 *Providence Patriot*, 3.

11. Gloria Main, "Reflections on the Demand and Supply of Child Labor in Early America," in Herndon and Murray, Ed., *Children Bound to Labor*, 212. See the whole edited volume for examples of pauper apprenticeship, formal and informal, around the early United States and in Montreal and England. See also Abramovitz, *Regulating the Lives of Women*, 125–131. While Main notes a movement toward keeping parents and children together in the early nineteenth century, Abramovitz sees the opposite trend in the late nineteenth century.

12. Both Cyrus Walker and Margaret Creech find that Scituate stopped auctioning the poor as a group in 1818. See Cyrus Walker and Town of Scituate Bicentennial Committee, *The History of Scituate, R.I. by Cyrus Walker*. Hedley Smith, Ed. (N.P.: Racine Printing, 1976), 17 and Creech, *Three Centuries of Poor Law Administration*, 168. Neither Creech nor Walker say why the group auctions stopped, but a likely reason is that farmers stopped bidding for the poor at a price that the town found acceptable.

13. Depositions of Thomas Angell, William B. Harris, and Oliver Leach, 17 March 1821, in Case File "Thomas T. Hill v. Overseers of the Poor of Scituate," March Term 1823, RISJCRC.

14. One classic social control interpretation is Piven and Cloward, *Regulating the Poore*, xix. For more examples of children's labor, see Barry Levy, *Town Born: The Political Economy in New England from its Founding to the Revolution* (Philadelphia: University of Pennsylvania Press, 2011) and Herndon and Murray, *Children Bound to Labor*.

15. Deposition of William Angell, 17 March 1821, in Case File "Thomas T. Hill v. Overseers of the Poor of Scituate," March Term 1823, RISJCRC.

16. Oliver Leach deposition, 17 March 1821 and Lydia Phillips deposition, 16 March 1821, in Case File "Thomas T. Hill v. Overseers of the Poor of Scituate," March Term 1823, RISJCRC.

17. Deposition of Thomas Angell, 17 March 1821, in in Rhode Island Supreme Judicial Court Case File "Thomas T. Hill v. Overseers of the Poor of Scituate," March Term 1823, RISJCRC.

18. Deposition of Lydia Bates 30 September 1822 in Case File "Thomas T. Hill v. Overseers of the Poor of Scituate," March Term 1823, RISJCRC. On events of the first case, see assorted Justice of the Peace documents in Rhode Island Supreme Judicial Court Case File "Scituate v. Thomas T. Hill" September Term 1820, RISJCRC.

19. Lydia Bates Deposition 30 September 1822 and Ahaz Allen Deposition 13 September 1822 and William Mann Deposition 13 March 1822 in Case File "Thomas T. Hill v. Overseers of the Poor of Scituate," March Term 1823, RISJCRC.

20. On the one-third-of-brides statistic see, for example, Dorothy A. Mays, *Women in Early America: Struggle, Survival, and Freedom in a New World* (Santa Barbara: ABC-CLIO, 2004), 90.

21. Ahohab Johnson (Randal) Deposition 14 March 1822 in Case File "Thomas T. Hill v. Overseers of the Poor of Scituate," March Term 1823, RISJCRC. *Nota bene*: Ahohab is given two different last names in this document. On the exterior

and first line of the deposition, he is Ahohab Randall or Randal. Where he makes his X, he is Ahohab Johnson. I have assumed that the clerk made an error and that Johnson is more likely correct because that is what Ahohab saw when he made his mark. That he could not write does not mean he could not read.

22. Anthony B. Patt deposition 15 September 1820 in Case File "Scituate v. Thomas T. Hill" September Term 1820, RISJCRC.

23. Arnold Knight deposition and William Phillips deposition 15 September 1820 in Case File "Scituate v. Thomas T. Hill" September Term 1820, RISJCRC. William B. Harris deposition 17 March 1821, Abigail Fenner deposition 16 March 1821, and Lydia Phillips deposition, 16 March 1821 in Rhode Island Supreme Judicial Court Case File "Thomas T. Hill v. Overseers of the Poor of Scituate," March Term 1823, RISJCRC.

24. Laurel Thatcher Ulrich and Lois K. Stabler, "'Girling of It' in Eighteenth-Century New Hampshire," in Peter Benes, Ed., *Families and Children. Dublin Seminar for New England Foklife, Annual Proceedings, 1985* (Boston: Boston University, 1987, 31).

25. Arnold Knight deposition, 16 March 1821 and Abigail Fenner deposition, 16 March 1821 in Rhode Island Supreme Judicial Court Case File "Thomas T. Hill v. Overseers of the Poor of Scituate," March Term 1823, RISJCRC.

26. Lydia Phillips deposition 16 March 1821, Wate Burlingame deposition 17 March 1821, Hannah Potter deposition 17 March 1821, George Burlingame deposition 17 March 1821, Arnold Parker deposition 17 March 1821, Ahohab Johnson (Randal) deposition 18 March 1822, and Benjamin Ingraham deposition 5 September 1822 in Case File "Thomas T. Hill v. Overseers of the Poor of Scituate," March Term 1823, RISJCRC. Arnold Knight deposition, William Phillips deposition 15 September 1820, and Lydia Phillips deposition 15 September 1820 in Case File "Scituate v. Thomas T. Hill" September Term 1820, RISJCRC.

27. Deposition of Lydia Phillips, 15 September 1820 in Case File "Scituate v. Thomas T. Hill" September Term 1820, RISJCRC.

28. On John Rogers's wife, see Deposition of George Burlingame, 17 March 1821 in Case File "Thomas T. Hill v. Overseers of the Poor of Scituate," March Term 1823, RISJCRC.

29. As I try to make sense of records of Bates's life, I find helpful this article: Lepore, "Historians Who Love Too Much: Reflections on Biography and Microhistory," 129–144. Records make clear that Bates was present at the March, 1821 session of the Rhode Island Supreme Judicial Court, though, and she may have been present at others. A receipt counts "paying Henry Harris for Lydia Bates Board at March Term 00=60" (Receipt to Thomas Henry dated 8 February 1822 in MSS 216 "Scituate Town Records," Box 1 "Overseer of the Poor / Scituate Asylum," Folder 9, "Paid Bills, 1819–1823," RIHS).

30. Bond of Susannah Barton 12 September 1807, in Folder "Poor Farm – Deeds of Indenture, 1795–1839," Cranston Town Records 193, RIHS. For a larger discussion of this practice, see Loiacono, "Poverty and Citizenship in Rhode Island, 1780–1870," 62–68.

31. See "An Act Regulating the Proceedings in Cases of Bastardy," (1798), reproduced in Cushing, *The First Laws of the State of Rhode Island*, especially sections 3, 6, 9.

32. See Justice of the Peace documents in Case File "Scituate v. Thomas T. Hill" September Term 1820, RISJCRC. For estimates of today's worth, see Measuring Worth Foundation, "Purchasing Power Today of a US Dollar Transaction in the Past."

33. Following the twists and turns of these cases is not easy. Thanks to Andrew Smith, archivist at the Rhode Island Supreme Judicial Court Records Center, in Pawtucket, for all of his help. One source is the record books of the Supreme Judicial Court: "Records Book Supreme Judicial Court No. 8 1815–1821" and "Records Book Supreme Judicial Court . . . Book 9 Sept. 1819," both in the RISJCRC. But Book 9 suggests that Hill won his appeal in March, 1823, which must be an error. Hill's filings for another appeal in September, 1823 make clear that he lost in March 1823 ("Petition Thomas T. Hill v. Overseers Poor Scituate September Term 1823" in Rhode Island Supreme Judicial Court Case File "Thomas T. Hill v. Overseers of the Poor of Scituate," September Term, 1823, RISJCRC). Indeed, the three case files for this case also help one reconstruct the legal process, but not entirely. On Hill and Israel Phillips being sued for their bonds, see "State vs. Israel Phillips et al" in "Superior Court Record Book No. 10" (September Term 1827), 198–201, in RISJCRC. Scituate officials were also trying to settle with Israel Phillips in 1825. See entry for 25 November 1825 in Scituate Town Meeting Book, Folder 27 "Town Meeting–Minutes, 1828–1839," MSS 216 Box 1 Overseer of the Poor/Scituate Asylum, RIHS.
34. "Records Book Supreme Judicial Court Sept. 1819" Book 9, 446–452, in RISJCRC.
35. Depositions of Elisha Leach, Oliver Leach, William Barnes, and Abraham Salisbury, 17 March 1821, and Deposition of Lydia Phillips, 16 March 1821 in Case File "Thomas T. Hill v. Overseers of the Poor of Scituate," March Term 1823, RISJCRC.
36. Depositions of Abraham Salisbury, Thomas Angell, and Elisha Leach, 17 March 1821 in Case File "Thomas T. Hill v. Overseers of the Poor of Scituate," March Term 1823, RISJCRC. While the deposition does not say they met in Manchester's parlor, that seems the most likely place. When depositions say where they took place, they are often at the home of the justice of the peace.
37. On Thomas Henry's visit, see MSS "1822 The Town of Scituate To Thomas Henry" in Folder 9 Paid Bills, 1819–1823, MSS 216 Box 1 Overseer of the Poor/Scituate Asylum, Scituate Town Records, RIHS. The receipts to Lydia Bates and Jonathan Smith are all written on the back pages of a printed book entitled *Acts and Laws of the English Colony of Rhode-Island and Providence Plantations in New-England in America* (Newport: Samuel Hall, 1767.) These manuscript sources written on the blank pages of a printed book are housed in the archives of the Scituate Town Building, Scituate, Rhode Island. A copy of the same receipt to Jonathan Smith is also in the Rhode Island Historical Society (Receipt to Jonathan Smith dated June 15, 182 in MSS 216, Box 1, Folder 9, "Overseer of the Poor / Scituate Asylum: Paid Bills, 1819–1823," Scituate Town Records, RIHS).
38. Receipts to Ester Colvin and Lydia Bates are in manuscript back pages of *Acts and Laws of the English Colony of Rhode-Island and Providence Plantations in New-England in America* in the archives of the Scituate Town Building, Scituate, Rhode Island. For Henry Harris, see MSS "1822 The Town of Scituate To Thomas Henry" in Folder 9 Paid Bills, 1819–1823, MSS 216 Box 1 Overseer of the Poor/Scituate Asylum, RIHS.
39. The town meeting entries are for 28 August 1827 and 10 September 1828, "Scituate Town Meeting Book 1825–1838" in MSS 216 "Scituate Town Records," Box 1, Folder 27, "Town Meetings: Town Meeting Minutes, 1828–1839," RIHS. (*Nota bene*: the 10 September 1828 entry is written as September 10, 1825. Given the order these papers appear in, however, and the contents of the entry, it seems obvious that a rushing clerk miswrote 1828 as 1825.) The receipt to Eliaser

Phillips is dated 9 October 1827, in back pages of *Acts and Laws of the English Colony of Rhode-Island and Providence Plantations in New-England in America*, Scituate Archives, Scituate Town Building, Scituate, Rhode Island.

40. On Cynthia Ann Patt, see Entry for 7 April 1823 in manuscript "Scituate Town Council Book" in Scituate Archives, Scituate Town Building, Scituate, Rhode Island.

41. For the Manuscript U.S. Census returns for 1820, 1830, 1840, 1850, 1860, 1870, and 1880, I consulted the digitized versions for Scituate on Ancestry.com. A fascinating article on her son James is Robert Grandchamp, "'I have never heard of him since' – The Case of Scituate's James A. Matteson" *Small State Big History: The Online Review of Rhode Island History*. Online at http://smallstatebighistory.com/never-heard-since-case-scituates-james-matteson/. Accessed 9 September 2016. The article summarizes Rhoda Matthewsons's filings in the pension file.

42. It should be noted that the receipts at the Rhode Island Historical Society do not seem as complete as those scrawled in the back of the *Acts and Laws of the English Colony of Rhode-Island and Providence Plantations* book in the Scituate archives, and the receipts in *Acts and Laws* end in 1828.

Timeline

Lydia Bates, Rhoda Bates-Hill, William Fales, and the Early American Republic

Year	National and Local Events	Lydia Bates	Rhoda Bates-Hill	William Fales
1800	Election of Thomas Jefferson.	Lydia Bates born about this year.		
1803–1807		Samuel Bates family in "poorhouses."		
1814	Textile mills hire women like Fales's mother; New England leaders protest War of 1812.			
1817–1818		William Bates's family in "poorhouses;" Lydia Bates a hired hand or pauper on several farms.		
1819	Panic of 1819.	Bates conceives baby while living and working at Phillipses.		
1820		Scituate begins legal pursuit of Thomas T. Hill for child support.	Rhoda Martha Bates-Hill. born	
1821		Bates and Rhoda go to Massachusetts with Hill.		
1825–1826		The last records showing Rhoda living with Bates are dated 1826.		Fales moves from grandparents' house in Portsmouth, to aunt's home in Somerset, Mass in 1825.

Year	National and Local Events	Lydia Bates	Rhoda Bates-Hill	William Fales
1827–1828		Although Hill had lost third case in 1824, Scituate still suing him for payment.	Rhoda in custody of overseers; Mathewsons winning bids for poor.	Fales suffers first bout of "inflammatory rheumatism."
1834–1836				Fales moves to Rutland, Pennsylvania with mother, stepfather, in two years loses ability to walk.
1840			Around 1840, Rhoda Mathewson gives birth to first child.	Fales loses ability to sit up in a chair.
1846	The United States is at war with Mexico.			Fales moves to Portsmouth, Rhode Island Asylum, soon meets "Shepherd" Tom Hazard.
1848				Fales begins writing journal, letters, spiritual tracts.
1849–1850	New Englanders join California gold rush.			Hazard arranges for Fales to leave poor farm, live in private home. There, Fales dies in 1850.
1851				Fales's memoir published in Philadelphia; Hazard's *Report on Poor and Insane* published in Providence.
1864			One of Rhoda Mathewson's sons, James, killed in battle in Virginia.	
1885			Rhoda Mathewson awarded a Civil War survivor's pension, after six years of her petitioning, and worrying about going to the Town Farm.	

CHAPTER 5

⌀⌀⌀

Stuck in the Poorhouse

William Fales and the Experience of Institutionalization

It was winter, and William Fales had long ago learned to fear the cold. He could still remember the first time it got to him. He had been only six years old back then. One day, after wearing a wet shirt all afternoon, his arms and legs had stiffened. His body had become inflamed. Most of all it had hurt. His body's sudden misery terrified the young boy. Still, he had recovered after that first attack. Nowadays, he remembered those years as the best of his life: safe, well fed, cared for by his aunt, surrounded by his hens and sheep.

Just like Rhoda, Lydia Bates's daughter, William Fales was born in 1820, in a country town in Rhode Island. Also like young Rhoda, young William was not always able to live with his parents. But while Rhoda was under the authority of the overseers of the poor, who could separate her from her mother, William had spent his childhood with his mother, grandparents, or aunt. The overseers had not taken him under their authority, yet.

Now, in the winter of 1849, it had been three and a half years since the overseers of the poor had taken William Fales in. He was twenty-nine years old. Unlike young Rhoda and her mother, William Fales would not be cared for in his neighbors' houses. Poor relief in America had changed since Rhoda and William were children. As a young adult in dire need, William Fales would go to the poorhouse. That is where he waited today, and waited

How Welfare Worked in the Early United States. Gabriel J. Loiacono, Oxford University Press. © Oxford University Press 2021. DOI: 10.1093/oso/9780197515433.003.0006

everyday. Immobilized, and unable to leave his bed without assistance, it was all he could do to stay warm and keep his mind occupied. Smart and devoutly religious, Fales did not have anyone in the poorhouse he could really talk to. He longed for visitors. He was lonely. He was expecting someone to visit, though. It had been months since the wealthy neighbor they called "Shepherd" Tom had dropped by. Fales had a sense that "Shepherd" Tom would come soon, and bring with him some life-changing news. This time, Fales would not be disappointed.[1]

This chapter will come back to that life-changing news at its end. The main aim of the chapter, however, is to understand life in a poorhouse from an inmate's point of view. These days, we think of the poorhouse as a cultural relic, a figure of speech that does not denote the reality it used to. "Don't do that or we'll end up in the poorhouse," a parent might complain to a spendthrift child. A local bar might be called "The Pour House," playing cleverly on words. Yet, government-run institutions to house the poor still exist. Public housing buildings have, in part, replaced group home settings like the poorhouse. Meanwhile, Medicaid-supported nursing homes, jails and prisons, and privately-run homeless shelters have each taken on some of the responsibilities that were once left to poorhouses. These days, governments are far more likely to offer subsidized housing or to engage in a kind of public-private enterprise, akin to Scituate's overseers relying on neighbors for Lydia Bates's and Rhoda's housing. William Fales's life, by contrast, offers a view into a poorhouse of the mid-nineteenth century.[2]

Unusually for a pauper, Fales wrote a memoir, and many letters, describing his life before, during, and after his three-and-a-half year sojourn in the Portsmouth, Rhode Island, Town Asylum. As discussed in the introduction, asylum, town farm, poor farm, and poorhouse were interchangeable terms in this period. And, though William Fales's time in the poorhouse is not interchangeable with any other inmate's, his life can help us understand some experiences of poorhouse inmates.

Throughout the eighteenth and nineteenth centuries, in one municipality after another, voters chose to make big investments in buildings and farmland in order to create municipally owned poorhouses. Often, towns and counties went into debt to buy this real estate. They did this in the hope that their town's needy could be concentrated in the poorhouse, humanely cared for, with cost savings from an economy of scale. They even hoped that paupers might do agricultural or industrial work while in the poorhouse that would not only cover their own expenses, but also be a source of revenue to local government. That was the hope. The reality was different. Paupers, like William Fales, often could not work because of their physical or mental health. Moreover, poorhouses isolated inmates from their friends and neighbors, leading to new problems. Some scholars have argued that isolation and social control were two of the main goals of those who pushed for using poorhouses. Certainly these were outcomes of the rise of poorhouses. Other scholars have pointed to the communities created within poorhouses. None of these outcomes were the goals of voters who voted for the poorhouses, though. Concerns about humane treatment and, overwhelmingly, the rising costs of poor relief were often the reasons municipalities built poorhouses. But poorhouses were never as perfect solutions as expected. Most poorhouses did not make money. Moreover, local officials always found reason to care for people outside the poorhouse. William Fales wanted to be one of those people, cared for outside the poorhouse. Inside, he was isolated and lonely.

WHILE MOTHER WAS AWAY, WORKING AT THE COTTON MILL

Fales was born the same year as Rhoda Bates-Hill, 1820, but without the messy legal controversy that surrounded her birth. William's father was more committed to his mother than Thomas T. Hill was to Lydia Bates, though barely. Nathaniel Fales *married* William's mother, but they seem never to have made a household together. William remembered living with his grandparents for his first five years, and meeting his father only once, at age eleven. While records are silent on Rhoda's impressions of her father— or idea of who he was, even—William harbored bitterness toward his. "[It] is *he* that I am doomed to call my father," Fales wrote at age twenty-eight, "alas, it is *I* who am the unfortunate offspring of that unhappy union."[3]

Toward his mother, Fales was more sympathetic. Although he did not write her name in his memoir, as he did his father's, he described her much more fully. He remembered that she was one of thirteen children, and was "obliged at an early age to leave home" and support herself. This she did through domestic work, at first. A single, young woman, she lived with more prosperous families, cleaned their houses, peeled their potatoes, tended their gardens, washed their clothes. She did some of the work that Lydia Bates did, and she got paid. It was not much, but gave her some independence.

Then she found a new line of work, no doubt exciting at first: factory hand in a cotton mill. This must have been the late 1810s, when textile factories were just a generation old in the United States. Samuel Slater had introduced textile factories to Rhode Island in 1793. The Quaker entrepreneur Rowland Hazard had a woolen mill in South Kingstown, Rhode Island from 1802 on, and his son Thomas Robinson Hazard, who would later be William Fales's greatest friend, was working in his father's business from 1813. By 1814, mills had spread throughout New England, and Boston investors began the "Waltham-Lowell" system of recruiting New England farm girls, and young women, to work in their factories. William's mother was one of those farm girls. Where she worked, William did not know, only that it was far from her home in Portsmouth, Rhode Island.

Far from home, on her own, after a series of domestic jobs, her parents with their own financial struggles, William's mother found companionship with a man. That was precisely why critics worried about the Waltham-Lowell system: It took farm girls away from their family's oversight, to new towns, and left them overly exposed to male attention. It threatened their virtue, their chastity, critics feared. It upended the hierarchy and security of patriarchal family networks. Had William's mother been closer to home, her relatives could check in on her, hear rumors about her and quickly act on them. Far from home, she was in some sense her own mistress, able to make her own decisions. It was while working at the cotton mill that the young woman became "acquainted" with Nathaniel Fales, then "mutually attached" and "subsequently married." Was it a hasty marriage? Was it forced by her pregnancy with William as critics of the Waltham-Lowell system would fear? Or were they two young sweethearts with no one to stop them? Perhaps her own parents had prized love over financial stability themselves and would choose their own lives again. Why would they stand in her way even if they could? They needed her to be independent.

What led from "mutual attachment" to an "unhappy union?" Fales does not say, but my guess would be money. Even after marriage, the young newlyweds did not have enough money to start their own household. Why else leave young William with his grandparents? Probably, continuing money worries pulled Nathaniel and his bride apart. They both traveled for work, then stayed, and the little family drifted asunder. As his parents drifted, young William stayed with his grandparents in Portsmouth, until age five, when his mother brought him to a farm in Somerset, Massachusetts, to live with an aunt. William's memoir is unclear on whether his mother lived with them too. He would stay there for ten years. Looking back, Fales saw these years as the happiest of his life. He went to school and was put in charge of the sheep and hens. He was well fed, well clothed, and "kindly received."

Kindly received. Readers of Fales's memoir get the impression that this was a rare feeling for him. Living with others—his grandparents and later a stepfather, then the keeper and inmates of the asylum—did not elicit the same warm feelings of being *wanted* as did his stay with his aunt in Somerset. His grandparents had their own many children, his father barely knew him, and his stepfather would meet him as a frail fifteen-year-old. But his aunt would welcome him with open arms, good food, a sense of belonging, and school. It was here that he learned to love reading. When, later, all else would fail him, reading and writing would help sustain him. His body would grow weak and less able, but his mind would grow, and so would his spiritual life.[4]

A HEALTH CRISIS

Young William's family life had its challenges. But the great trial of his life was something else entirely: a debilitating feeling of cold and weakness in his limbs, which began at age six as an episodic illness, and played a major role in his early death, at age twenty-nine. Fales remembered the first onset vividly. It was a nice April afternoon in Massachusetts. Fales and another boy went swimming, naked. Rushing to get dressed because a carriage was approaching, Fales dropped his shirt in the pond. It was soaked, but he put it on anyway. That night, Fales got the chills, and felt worse and worse until he could not even stand up. He would not recover from this first onset for fifteen months.[5]

A doctor who saw Fales for those fifteen months called Fales's malady "inflammatory rheumatism." He treated Fales with "bleeding, blistering, and physic." How would Fales be diagnosed today? Retroactive diagnosis is highly speculative. That said, there still exists a diagnosis of rheumatoid arthritis. One of a variety of autoimmune conditions, rheumatoid arthritis would explain the pain and weakness in Fales's limbs, as well as its worsening over Fales's lifetime. It could appear on its own or as part of another autoimmune disease, like pediatric multiple sclerosis. Another possible explanation could be polio.[6]

While a retroactive diagnosis is uncertain, it *is* certain that Fales's doctor responded by bleeding and blistering the boy, as well as giving him "physic," or medicine. The doctor was trying to decrease the amount of blood circulating in the six-year-old's body. At the time, doctors thought this the best response to any kind of inflammation. "Bleeding" meant opening up a vein to let blood out, probably with a sharp instrument, called a lancet, and a cup. While this was usually done on an arm or foot, experts advised using the jugular vein, in the neck, for children. Young William may have escaped that because doctors also bled directly from the part of the body that was most inflamed. "Blistering" meant putting an herbal powder or ointment, sometimes derived from beetles, on the skin, with the goal of causing blisters. Those blisters might also be opened up to let blood out. "Physic" could be any kind of medicine the doctor believed would be efficacious, or it could be purgative medicines in particular, such as laxatives to increase bowel movements. Fales's doctor was in the mainstream of American medical practice that year of 1827. He thought that getting the boy to empty his bowels and give blood would restore the balance of the four "humors" in his body. In a decade or two the popularity of bleeding and blistering would decline. But Europeans and Americans of European descent had been using these methods for centuries when young William first saw the doctor pull a lancet from his case. Imagine his fear at the prospect of being cut open again. Imagine waiting for the doctor to put on the ointment, with its burn and blister. Rubbing alcohol seems to lose its sting in comparison.[7]

Although always vulnerable to illness during cold seasons after this, William was largely well until age fourteen, when his mother remarried and brought him to remote Rutland, Pennsylvania. This was a period of wrenching changes for William: his mother's remarriage after many years and his own ambivalence about whether to remain in Somerset or go with his mother and his new stepfather. William's experience testifies to the psychological and physical hardship of American westward migration. No doubt the cheap plentitude of land beckoned his stepfather away from southeastern Massachusetts to north central Pennsylvania. But the arduous journey and the "vigorous" work of cultivation all took tolls on William's frail body. The decision of whether to go, meanwhile, racked his mind. In his memoir, Fales offers two versions of why he went. On one page he says that his mother and new stepfather "concluded to take me with them, hoping, by a change of climate, I might become more healthy, and assist them in working their farm." Two pages later, he recalls that "adventurously, I expressed a wish to accompany my parents to Pennsylvania," suggesting that the fourteen-year-old had the option of staying with his kind aunt, continuing in school, raising his own sheep and hens. It was a hard decision for a teenager. In hindsight, Fales was convinced he had made the wrong one. As with his incautious dip in the pond as a six-year-old, he looked back and saw "adventure" turned to disaster. Ultimately, Fales believed, the disaster would turn again, to something better than adventure: union with God. First, though, it led through a great deal of pain.[8]

In Pennsylvania, while laboring hard on the farm for his stepfather, William relapsed, remaining ill for ten months. After a brief recovery, he became ill again in February 1836. From that month, the fifteen-year-old would never walk again. A few years later, at nineteen, Fales lost the ability to sit up in a chair. Always, his declines were accompanied by exposure to cold. Fales recalls that the backcountry Pennsylvania doctor was no match for William's disease, which seemed "entirely to baffle his skill." Fales would not give up on doctors; he continued to be visited by them in every place he lived. They generally seemed resigned, though, to treat only the secondary illnesses which cropped up, to try to make William's condition a bit more bearable.[9]

At fifteen, Fales felt "so swollen and painful, that it was difficult for me to stand or go." He still commented on the pain in his late 20s: "At times, I am exercised with great pain, especially when I remain too long in one position, and it is difficult for me to lie on my right side," the twenty-eight-year-old explained to a benefactor. "I cannot continue upon it but a little while, before the pain and cramp become so severe that I am forced to cry aloud." He remembered long, hard periods, "lying sore bound in the iron grasp of this grim disease . . . so full of trouble, pain, and sorrow, that I have now but a very imperfect recollection of what passed from day to day at that time." He apologized that "therefore much of my painful experience must remain untold." Days, even weeks, blended together in his memory as one long battle to bear the pain. In addition to the pain his disease inflicted directly, it also contributed indirectly to his suffering. In December, 1848, for example, a doctor accidentally broke Fales's jaw, trying to extract a tooth. Because of his rheumatism, he had been unable to open his mouth wide enough. Now, on top of all his other pain, he had this to contend with.[10]

Each change in the disease thrust new challenges on the boy, as he became a young man. He reacted with marvelous resilience, if you think about it. The little things he used to do, he could no longer do. Having been used to running around the countryside in Massachusetts, he now had to reconcile himself to long spells in bed. Having joyously swum in ponds, he now had to avoid cold. Used to making himself useful, he had to accept reliance on whomever would help him. Eventually he could not go to the bathroom himself. At times, he could not feed himself. Sometimes, the constant pain became so intense he involuntarily yelled out loud. Ultimately, Fales came to the conclusion that only one healer, God, would do him much good. His religiosity began during his second major lapse at age fourteen, and would grow more and more developed throughout the rest of his life. In his twenties, Fales was very devout. Stuck in bed, but with an active mind, Fales turned to prayer. His prayer life deepened, so that by the time he was moved into a poorhouse, his religious devotion was remarkable to those around him.

How Fales himself found his way to the Portsmouth Asylum, in June of 1846, is a mystery. He was twenty-five, and still living with his mother and stepfather in western Pennsylvania. His memoir says this about the four-hundred-mile move: " . . . through the mysterious workings of Providence, the way opened for me to be removed to this place in June 1846." That is all he wrote on the subject. No doubt his mother and stepfather found it hard to care for him while running a farm. Perhaps he now had younger half-siblings too. Perhaps his mother still had family in Portsmouth. If so, Fales never wrote about one of them visiting him, though he did comment on other visitors in his letters. Another mystery is why Portsmouth officials let him come back. According to settlement law, the law governing who gets poor relief where, Fales's settlement should have followed his father Nathaniel Fales's, not his mother's premarriage settlement. All the evidence suggests that Nathaniel was not from Portsmouth, having met William's mother around the cotton mill that was at "a greater distance" from Portsmouth than her first domestic jobs. Perhaps Portsmouth town officials decided that Nathaniel Fales had no settlement anywhere, in which case William's settlement would follow his mother's. Somehow, William was transported to Portsmouth, accepted by the overseer of the poor, and deposited in the asylum. The Portsmouth Asylum is pictured in Figure 5.1. A small-town poorhouse, it was more humble than the grand Dexter Asylum in Providence, pictured in Figures 5.2 and 5.3.[11]

Figures 5.1, 5.2 and 5.3 This 1936 photograph of the Portsmouth Town Farm (Figure 5.1) shows, as far as I can tell, the same building Fales lived in from 1846 to 1850. Records by the 1880s used the terms "Town Asylum" and "Town Farm" interchangeably in Portsmouth. Figures 5.2 and 5.3 show the Dexter Asylum in Providence, a grand example of an urban institution, built in 1828. The drawing (Figure 5.2) shows the asylum as it was originally designed, and still appeared in 1869. The undated photograph (Figure 5.3) is clearly after the renovations of 1871, and shows how big the walls were compared to people. Courtesy of the Providence Public Library Digital Collections.

Figures 5.1, 5.2 and 5.3 Continued.

POORHOUSES: MAKING A COMEBACK IN THE
MID-NINETEENTH CENTURY

The Portsmouth Asylum, which became Fales's home in 1846, had been founded in 1832, when young William was twelve years old, living happily with his aunt in Massachusetts. Voters in Portsmouth were part of a transatlantic trend when they opted to invest in a poor farm, which they called an asylum. This was not the first time governments had looked to poorhouses to help address poverty, though. "Hospitals and Almshouses" as well as "worke houses" were described in the Elizabethan poor laws, c.1600, which were still shaping American poor relief more than two centuries later. Moreover, as described in this book's introduction, periods of intense poorhouse- or workhouse-building had swept British North America in the mid-eighteenth century and the United States just after the Revolution. Indeed, Portsmouth had invested in a workhouse in 1780, shortly after British soldiers evacuated the area.[12]

In the 1810s and 1820s, a movement in favor of poorhouses began again. This movement would continue through the Civil War era and into the late nineteenth century, when state governments would begin to build statewide institutions. Local poorhouses in Rhode Island began closing in the 1870s. The Portsmouth Asylum would be shut down in 1929. But Fales lived there when poorhouses were still growing in popularity.

Poorhouses and workhouses were also growing in popularity on the other side of the Atlantic Ocean, where British governments were making similar reforms to those of the Americans. In 1834, only two years after Portsmouth opened its asylum, the United Kingdom's Parliament passed the "New Poor Law," a sweeping reform of the Elizabethan Poor Law. Many British municipalities already had poorhouses and workhouses. The New Poor Law required these municipalities to provide nearly all poor relief inside of an institution. It banned most people from getting "outdoor" poor relief such as cash, food, or lodging in a neighbor's home. American reformers also hoped that investing in poorhouses would make it unnecessary to give cash or food outside of the poorhouse.[13]

How can we explain the rise of asylums, or poorhouses, in the 1820s and 1830s? Many scholars have offered explanations. For David J. Rothman, in *The Discovery of the Asylum: Social Order and Disorder in the New Republic* (1971), asylums for the poor and for the insane were "first and foremost a vigorous attempt to promote the stability of the society . . ." as well as to "rehabilitate inmates." For Michael B. Katz, in *In the Shadow of the Poorhouse: A Social History of Welfare in America*, first published in 1986, the intended goals of poorhouses were "to check the expense of pauperism through cheaper care and by deterring people from applying for relief" as well as "to transform the behavior and character of their inmates . . . ." Ultimately, Katz adds, this was "key to sustaining the work ethic in nineteenth-century America." For Mimi Abramovitz, in *Regulating the Lives of Women: Social Welfare Policy from Colonial Times to the Present* first published in 1988, the trends of reducing outdoor relief and increasing institutionalization were "rehabilitative but also punitive measures to enforce work and family discipline." Abramovitz highlights "growing concerns about deviant women, proper family functioning, patriarchal governance, and a deep distrust of the poor to properly carry out the family's reproductive and maintenance tasks."[14]

Both Ruth Wallis Herndon and Karin Wulf, in separate essays in *Down and Out in Early America* (2004), show that American arguments over whether to give outdoor relief or indoor relief stretch back before the Revolution. Wulf describes debates in colonial Philadelphia over whether poor relief should simply assist or try to reform the poor. Herndon finds post-Revolution Rhode Island town officials both worried about costs and about the increasing numbers of "strangers" coming to their towns. Meanwhile, David Wagner, in *The Poorhouse: America's Forgotten Institution* (2005), shows how late nineteenth-century and twentieth-century inmates used poorhouses for their own purposes, creating communities in spite of controlling overseers. In a thoughtful endnote, Wagner argues that while municipalities often built poorhouses to save money and provide humane care, these institutions still had an effect of controlling the working classes. Timothy James Lockley, in *Welfare and Charity in the Antebellum South* (2007), finds that "Overwhelmingly Wardens of the Poor justified the construction of a poorhouse on cost grounds." They hoped to save money. Meanwhile, Seth Rockman, in *Scraping By: Wage Labor, Slavery, and Survival in Early Baltimore* (2009), makes the case that poorhouses were created in service of *competing* goals: "a civic culture of benevolence" toward the poor *and* "disciplin[ing] workers in the service of capitalism." Moreover, Rockman adds, "poor people used the system just as much as it used them." [15]

There are several defensible arguments about why American taxpayers and voters started supporting poorhouses. For this historian, the competing goals of benevolence and economy are what spurred Americans to build poorhouses. Benevolence can be seen in their hope for more humane care in a poorhouse. Economy can be seen in their hope of saving money on poor relief. The explanations of Rothman, Katz, and Abramovitz could all be loosely grouped as "social control" explanations, which emphasize how reformers wanted to control the behavior of the poor. It would be hard to deny that wealthier Americans often expressed their wish to regulate how the less wealthy behaved. But the arguments that got voters to plunge their municipalities into debt in order to buy poorhouses were usually a dash of humanitarianism with a big helping of fiscal conservatism. Social control, and the accompanying isolation of a poorhouse, were minor as motivations for building poorhouses, but very significant in how inmates experienced the poorhouse.[16]

Most poorhouse inmates came to a poorhouse out of desperation: they would have been homeless, hungry, or sick without healthcare if they had not. Once inside, their lives were governed by strict rules that dictated what and when they could eat, when they had to get out of bed, and when they had to get back in bed. If they were able to work, their days would mostly be spent at some kind of labor. Most poorhouses were attached to a farm, which the inmates were supposed to work. Some overseers of the poor also found other kinds of work, such as picking the seeds out of cotton to make the cotton factory-ready, or picking old rope strands apart to be converted into oakum, a tarred fiber used to caulk ships. Usually, poorhouses did not allow inmates to leave without special permission.

Poorhouses were not meant to be lonely places. While often isolated from other townspeople, a poorhouse might house anywhere from a dozen to several dozen people. It is a paradox, then, that William Fales experienced loneliness while living in a community with others. We must be careful to avoid attributing Fales's thoughts to those countless poorhouse inmates who never left a written testimony. Nevertheless, the circumstances that made Fales feel alone even in a house of fifteen or twenty would have applied to many poorhouse inmates.

"THIS LONELY SPOT": LIFE IN A POORHOUSE

Over the three-and-a-half years Fales would spend in the Portsmouth Town Asylum, he would often be lonely. He complained about this in his letters frequently. By June 1849, Fales had been at the asylum for three years. After he received a visit from "Shepherd" Tom Hazard and a Minister Sands that month, he wrote "Thus you see how good the Lord is to send his servants to visit this lonely spot. . . ." At other times, he bemoaned that no earthly companion was around:

> I often think if I had a friend near at hand to whom I might unburden my troubled mind, it would alleviate my sorrows. But, alas! I have no such an one here (except it is the Lord). . . .

Fales's difficulties were not only physical, but emotional as well. Because he could not move without help (and pain) he could not seek out company. He had to wait until company found him. And waiting was just hard, a trial for his patience, his intelligence, and his social nature. He was at the mercy of visitors and, he wrote, ultimately of God to bring him visitors: " . . . it is that same God who now sees me and careth for me, that suggests to the minds of those who are in health and prosperity, the duty of visiting such as He sees meet to afflict." As hard as it was to wait, Fales still counted it as the work of God that anyone came at all.[17]

Reading his complaints, one might forget that there were other people living in the poorhouse with him. But the census taker found fifteen people in the asylum in August 1850. Fales had been gone from the asylum for more than seven months by then, but fifteen is probably a low number for how many housemates Fales would have had in his time. Winter usually brought more people to the poorhouse, who could find work or other places to live in the warmer seasons. Of the fifteen in the asylum that summer, nine were between fifty and eighty years old, and likely could not find work in this farm town because of their age. Two were described by the census taker as "Insane." One was a seven-year-old boy, who shared a surname with no one else in the asylum. The only one close in age to William Fales was Elizabeth Irish, who would have been limited in her interactions with him by house rules barring the commingling of the sexes. In addition, the census taker described her and two others as "Idiotic," a commonly used but vague term officials used to note any cognitive disability they perceived. The presence of so many others in his house, though, did not seem to give Fales much solace. Almost three years into his stay, he wrote:

> I have many thoughts occur to my mind, which I would gladly express to some kind person who would condescend to edify me by rendering to me the desired explanation . . . but have no confidant at hand to whom I can reveal the secrets of my heart, my trials, or whatever burdens or perplexes me. Oh, how I have longed for some true Christian friends . . . .

True Christian friends, he wanted. Despite all the people around him, and all the things they had in common—their house, their circumstances, difficult life experiences, a daily routine—Fales did not feel much in common with the other inmates. For him, few were true Christians, and therefore could not relate to him and his journey. He remarked on this again, shortly before he would leave the asylum:

There are three things which I do most fervently desire the Lord will grant me. The first is, that he will be pleased to make me meet for the kingdom of heaven. The second is, that I may retain my reason unto the end; and the third is, that my last days or hours may be spent under the care of some Christian friends. Oh, if I were only under the care of those who worship the Father in spirit and in truth, I could then pass in cheerful contentment the time, whether longer or shorter, during which my existence may be prolonged.

But almost no one, not the other paupers, not the "woman to whose care I am entrusted," met those criteria. After he left the poorhouse, Fales would refer to the poorhouse as a place of "the wrongful dealings of the ungodly." He rarely made any specific accusations, but he never found the poorhouse a home for his soul, even when it was a home for his body. Social work historian David Wagner found a very different situation in six New England poorhouses from later in the nineteenth century. In *The Poorhouse: America's Forgotten Institution*, Wagner demonstrates how "groups of people, poor as well as middle class, elderly as well as young, are adept at surviving and creating community in all sorts of places, including these stigmatized settings." Wagner's findings should caution us that William Fales's experience was not everyone's. But Fales did not find this kind of community.[18]

Fales's fellow inmates, like a woman he described as yelling all the time, provoked in him a mixture of sympathy, revulsion, and incredulousness. She was a "poor, wretched old woman," he wrote. He was "sorrowful to think . . . that, instead of spending her life in seeking salvation, she has been sinning against a holy and just God." Insisting that he was "willing to make all possible allowance for the poor woman," he nevertheless could not hide his shock: why would anyone be so blasphemous as she? Between Fales and this fellow inmate yawned a huge gulf. Very similar in needing the poorhouse and the physical assistance of nurses, they were nevertheless very different in outlook. So Fales felt lonely living with other paupers like her.[19]

One fellow inmate Fales liked was "Poor old, blind Joseph." Mentioned just twice by Fales, in the summer of 1848 and the summer of 1850, he is the only inmate that Fales talks about positively. "Poor old, blind Joseph grows feeble," Fales wrote to a benefactor in 1848, "he desires his love to you, and we both wish you to pray for us . . . . " Fales still thought of Joseph even after he had left the asylum. "I have had some news from the Asylum," Fales relayed by letter. "Poor old Joseph . . . has had fits, and was laid upon the bed in the same little room which I used to occupy . . . his privations are many and sore indeed . . . . He is forsaken in old age, and left poor, blind, and friendless in a cold and unfeeling world . . . ." Joseph and William had something in common, their faith. Joseph was much older, though. The census taker found him in the asylum in August of 1850, Joseph Brownell, age eighty, "Pauper." Despite their age difference, Brownell would still be living when the census-taker came that year. Fales, just twenty-nine, would not.[20]

Fales also enjoyed the company of some his caretakers, while in the asylum. Of the people employed to take care of him, he was grateful for a couple of the nurses. The Portsmouth Asylum hired women to work as nurses in the asylum for the very sick, much like William Larned hired "One-Eyed" Sarah, two generations earlier. Just as "One-Eyed" Sarah and Lydia Bates did, these women performed the laborious tasks of moving and washing, touching and feeding Fales. He mentioned these women after receiving delivery by post of a "wrapper," or a kind of shawl, which men or women might wear to keep warm. "The woman to whose care I am entrusted put it on me the next day," he informed the sender. Then he added: "I have long since felt desirous to make her, and one or two others, some return for their attentions." This one throwaway line gives a glimpse into Fales's everyday care. Not only the asylum keeper and his wife, but others were involved in the daily chores of keeping Fales warm and fed. They turned the "poor wretched old woman" in her bed when she was too sick to do so herself. They fed Fales when his right arm was "lame." During good weather, they carried him outside for fresh air and sunshine. Some of these attendants did so with enough kindness and good humor that Fales wanted to make some sign of gratitude. Still, he did not find them friends. Still, he was lonely. Apart from one pauper and a couple of nurses, Fales valued his visitors most. Only they, he thought, served as true, Christian friends. As for solidarity within the poorhouse, Fales found none, as far as can be told from his memoir. Instead, he wrote, "Truly I have but one friend at hand, and that is my God."[21]

A CHRISTIAN PILGRIM

For modern readers, William Fales's memoir and letters might read as overly didactic, even preachy. There is barely a page in which he does not wish to teach a moral lesson. Indeed, that quality of moral instructiveness is precisely why Lindsay & Blakiston printed his memoir and letters. According to "S.H.L.," the editor, readers of *Memoir of William R. Fales, the Portsmouth Cripple*, could "glean from the memorandums of his feeble pencil the teaching lessons of a Father's love, tracing throughout the power of faith, the need of patience, and the worth of prayer." Moreover, since

I have never seen Fales's own manuscript version, or even figured out the identity of "S.H.L.," it is hard to know if the editor changed the tone, or left some of Fales's writing out. Just reading what was published, though, shows that Fales's life was not a fable, or a neat, readymade story for the moral instruction of others. It was a hard and real life. His illness was without doubt a great trial, and he came to understand this trial as one that would strengthen his faith, make him a better person, and prepare him for heaven. Although the editor of his writings gave the subtitle "The Portsmouth Cripple," Fales would likely have been happier with "Christian Pilgrim." He was a man traveling through a world of pain to meet his God.[22]

We "should endeavour to live in the world as strangers and pilgrims," he wrote at twenty-eight, because "we have no abiding city here." Later that year, after a particularly bad several days, he was sure that he was near death, "but it hath pleased the Lord to revive me again, and prolong my pilgrimage on earth." After nearly two decades of recurrent illness, Fales had come to see these physical sufferings as way stations that God had provided for him to strengthen his soul. He prayed in the summer of 1849, for example, that "I shall be enabled to improve by my afflictions in the way which will most tend to the glory of God." He saw his sufferings as "grievous to be borne, yet" he believed they had "the effect of driving me to the bosom of . . . God." Thus, the terrible pain he suffered each day had one magnificent silver lining: a close relationship with God. Fales found great comfort in this. That is not to say, however, that he found either his disease or his faith easy.[23]

It was difficult, day in, day out, to keep the faith. In the hot days of August, 1848, Fales found himself experiencing a night of the soul. "I have felt but little of that support which I have so often experienced," he complained in a letter. Thus, "the lightest afflictions are hard to bear." On his best days, he wanted to share the great joy he felt in God's mercy with anyone who would listen. On the worst days, he just hoped for enough faith to avoid despair. Combining all these days together made his life a journey that felt difficult, long, and yet meaningful. Its meaning was in his own salvation and in that of others.[24]

How could this bed-bound youth—who barely left the poorhouse— effect the salvation of others? Astonishingly, Fales worked for the salvation of others through the American Tract Society (ATS). A national organization, created through the 1825 merger of a Boston-based tract society and a New York-based tract society, the ATS had agents all over the country by the time Fales had become an agent in 1848. Intended to provide cheap Christian literature for the masses, Fales was first a consumer of these tracts, then a distributor, with hopes of being an author. A letter of January 1, 1849 noted that "Shepherd" Tom Hazard had brought tracts to the poorhouse for Fales to both read and distribute. "I am to distribute them among my comrades," he wrote to a benefactor. "Much of the time we have religious meetings once in two weeks, at which time I generally present a few tracts to those of the neighbors who attend." Later, Fales's editor wrote that "[a]s agent for the 'American Tract Society' his accounts were satisfactorily closed" at the time of his death. This rare glimpse into Fales's evangelical activities shows both his assertiveness in his little community, as well as a break in the monotonous isolation of the Portsmouth Asylum. Neighbors coming to the asylum for religious meetings must certainly have provided a welcome social diversion to some of the inmates.[25]

At some point, Fales turned from distributor to author. He did not become a *published* author until after his death, when the *Memoir of William R. Fales* came out. As a book, the memoir was similar to other publications of the various tract societies. One best-selling tract for the American Tract Society was *The Dairyman's Daughter*, first published in both England and the United States in the 1810s. Like Fales, the subject of *The Dairyman's Daughter*, Elizabeth Wallbridge, was young, devout, and encouraged by an illness to become closer to God. Another life story in a tract, *Clarinda: A Pious Colored Woman of South Carolina* featured someone whose journey of faith went through great personal tribulations, including a debilitating illness. *Clarinda* was first published in 1837 by the Tract Association of Friends in Philadelphia, a Quaker organization which exists today. When *Memoir of William R. Fales* was published in 1851, though, it did not have a tract society's imprint, and it was described as being in Fales's own words, according to the editor. The editor also said that Fales wrote his autobiography in the fall of 1848 without any expectation that it would be published. He expected his letters, though, to reach beyond the addressee, and he wrote essays which were also intended for wide audiences.[26]

His editor included three of these essays in *Memoirs of William R. Fales*, even though the editor wondered, in print, whether Fales was the original author of these, or had merely written out favorite essays in his own handwriting. It seems clear, though, that these were original works by Fales. "What is Our Duty?" "Be Not Discouraged" and "To Publishers" are all titles that do not match any pamphlets in the WorldCat catalog. Meanwhile, internet searches of sentences from these essays turn up only references back to the *Memoir of William R. Fales*. Moreover, the essays match themes of his personal letters so well, that these essays must be Fales's own contributions to the large catalog of early republic inspirational literature. The messages were simple. "For no man is so insignificant, that he can be sure his example will do no hurt," he wrote in "What is Our Duty?," an essay that seems to come out of his own strengthening conviction that even he had a salvific mission in life. "Perform a good deed, speak a kind word, and bestow a pleasant smile," he advised, "and we shall receive an abundant reward." In contrast to people like himself, publishers were quite significant, Fales thought. As such, he warned, in "To Publishers," publishers have a responsibility to use their power of dissemination only for the good and not for the idle or sinful. This warning matched well a letter from the then twenty-seven-year-old reflecting on "the evils arising from reading novels, and other unprofitable works." He had read many as a boy, which he now regretted. Given their format—short, punchy, summarizing themes that he wrote about elsewhere—there can be little doubt that Fales had ambitions for these essays to be published and read widely, distributed by the ubiquitous agents of the American Tract Society, agents like himself.[27]

In writing essays and distributing tracts, Fales found that he could be part of the early American republic's "benevolent empire," the large and loosely connected network of organizations devoted to evangelical Christian causes, foremost among them the salvation of ordinary Americans. Despite his marginalized place in society—a disabled pauper in an isolated poorhouse—even William Fales could aspire to contribute something to one of the great social movements of his time. He was on a pilgrimage, and being a pauper in a poorhouse would not divert him from his own road to salvation or from helping others to follow him.

In addition to his work as a writer and a tract distributor, Fales found other things for which to be grateful. The most important for him was the faith in God he found through his struggle with rheumatism. The other was that there were better times, occasionally. "My bodily sufferings were greater than common for the most of last month," he wrote about the month of May, 1850, "but since the warm weather my health has been improving a little, and I feel thankful for so much relief, that I can now take considerable sleep in the night." He was also thankful that he could still use at least one of his arms. "And though both of my arms are poor, distorted, weak things at the best, yet I have found them a great deal better than none," he reasoned at twenty-nine, "and through mercy I have never been deprived of the use of both at once, which I think a wonderful favour." Despite pain so thorough and intense that it dulled his ability to differentiate between days, and despite periods when an arm was so afflicted he could not write or read himself, his letters to friends and benefactors were often a mix: complaint and gratitude, gratitude and complaint. He was grateful for less painful moments, for benefactors, and most of all for his relationship with God. He complained about the pain, about the people who lived with him in the poorhouse and, paradoxically, about loneliness.[28]

"SHEPHERD" TOM HAZARD BRINGS
LIFE-CHANGING NEWS

Then, one winter day in 1849, William Fales's friend "Shepherd" Tom brought life-changing news: Fales was invited to leave the poorhouse, and go to live with a widow nearby, who would care for him at the expense of some wealthy benefactors from Philadelphia. There the widow and her daughter would care for Fales, night and day. Like "One-Eyed" Sarah, they would be paid for nursing one of their poorest neighbors. Unlike Sarah, they would be paid by philanthropists, not by local tax revenue. This was Fales's one possible way out of the poorhouse. He took it.[29]

Or, as the keeper of the Portsmouth Asylum put it in his book of registry, Fales "Eloped." In this, the only official Portsmouth town record of William Fales that I have found, the keeper does not sound pleased. Reading his record, you would think that the near-paralyzed twenty-nine-year-old had just snuck out one day. "Elopement" was not uncommon in poorhouses. Often, when inmates had recovered their health, or were tired of the routine and the oversight, they would just leave. Poorhouse keepers usually did not like it. There were rules against this sort of thing. If paupers who eloped came back, they could be punished, by whipping, or a diet of bread and water, or time in solitary confinement. None of these things would happen to Fales, though. He was gone from the asylum for good, thanks to the Philadelphia connections of his friend "Shepherd" Tom.[30]

"Shepherd" Tom was not exactly a shepherd. His given name was Thomas Robinson Hazard and by the time he met William Fales, he was a retired factory owner. Born in 1797, Hazard had become the owner of his own factory at age twenty-four. That same year, his father had gifted him seventy acres of pasture land and the younger Hazard began raising hundreds of sheep. Presumably, these sheep provided the wool for his and other Hazard factories to spin into cloth. That is how he acquired the nickname "Shepherd" Tom. His extended Quaker family was so large and prominent, that the nickname helped differentiate him from other Thomas Hazards in his family tree, like "College" Tom and "Nailer" Tom. Like his father before him, he made a fortune as a mill owner, producing wool textiles in factories in South Kingstown, Rhode Island. His brothers Isaac and Rowland also ran woolen mills in South Kingstown. They spearheaded a part of the business which sold "negro cloth" to slave plantation owners in Louisiana, Mississippi, and Alabama in the 1820s and 1830s. This could be cotton or wool cloth, but it was marketed specially as clothing material for enslaved men, women, and children in the antebellum South. With this market and others, the Hazard family businesses thrived.[31]

By age forty-three, "Shepherd" Tom was wealthy enough to retire from business. He had recently married a New Yorker, Frances Minturn, who was sixteen years his junior, and now they moved from the town where the Hazards had made their fortune to Portsmouth, across the Narragansett Bay, a town long home to a community of Quakers, on an island long home to Hazard ancestors. There they bought a grand estate, called "Vaucluse," which also included grazing pastures for hundreds of sheep. In 1840, the Portsmouth Town Clerk assigned "Shepherd" Tom his own earmark for his sheep. Each animal would have a "half-penny" or half-circle cut out of the left ear to show they were Hazard's. A year later, "Shepherd" Tom would become legally "settled" in Portsmouth as a "freeman." Now he could vote in Portsmouth. And, as unlikely as it was, if the growing Hazard family ever needed poor relief, Portsmouth would have to give it to them.[32]

Far from needing poor relief himself, "Shepherd" Tom publicly plunged into several different political and reform causes, including Whig Party politics and treatment of the poor. It is probably not a coincidence that less than three years after "Shepherd" Tom got the right to vote in Portsmouth, the asylum for the poor became an important local political issue. Nor can it be a coincidence that Dorothea Dix, soon to be the most well-known mental healthcare reformer in American history, also happened to be in Portsmouth in 1844. For several summers Dix had visited friends in the town. In 1840, perhaps spurred by Dix, the town had appointed a committee to look into complaints about the asylum. In 1841, Dix had publicly begun a campaign to make the conditions of jails and almshouses more humane. Eventually, her focus would be on creating separate institutions for the care of the mentally ill. In 1844, she collaborated with Hazard in a newspaper article exposing the treatment of Abram Simmons, a mentally ill man confined in a poorhouse "dungeon" in nearby Little Compton, Rhode Island. Most likely, Hazard's and Dix's visits to nearby almshouses prompted the unusual town meeting in Portsmouth in March, 1844.[33]

The town's voters called this special meeting "to enquire into the condition and fare of the Poor of the town." There were reports circulating, the town clerk wrote, that "they had been poorly fed and that they had been cruelly treated by those appointed to provide for them + supply their wants. . . ." The keeper of the asylum, William J. Carter, was grilled during the meeting. Or, as the clerk phrased it, he was "closely interrogated by many of the inhabitants of the town." Given Hazard's interest in poor law reform, he was likely a leader of the interrogation. By the end of the meeting, though, the clerk reported a consensus that the reports of poor diet and cruel treatment were "generally incorrect" and the town's freemen expressed "satisfaction in the course of the keeper + little to complain of in the Commissioners." "Shepherd" Tom did not agree that the keeper was blameless, judging by his later writings. But the town meeting as a whole did. Nevertheless, they asked the clerk to record "a universal desire that the poor be kindly used and liberally and judiciously fed. . . ." As in the 1811 "Howard" argument over the treatment of Providence's poor, everyone said they wanted paupers to be treated humanely.[34]

When Fales arrived at the asylum in 1846, then, the treatment of the inmates was already a sensitive political issue in Portsmouth. "Shepherd" Tom had made a habit of visiting the asylum from time to time. Just like "Howard," "Shepherd" Tom was a well-to-do man who felt he had a responsibility to inspect how the poorest people in his town were treated. Almost two generations had passed since "Howard" walked into the Providence workhouse in 1811. "Shepherd" Tom was keeping that tradition alive. Like his fellow Rhode Island Quaker, Anna A. Jenkins, and the more well-known Dorothea Dix, Hazard felt called to visit his local poorhouse. That is how he met William Fales.

Hazard would later describe Fales as "one of the most remarkable and interesting young men with whom I was ever acquainted." Hazard's physical description of Fales gives some idea of what the forty-nine-year-old father of four young children felt when he first saw the twenty-six-year-old Fales. "His limbs were wrenched and distorted in the most shocking manner, and there was apparently scarcely a particle of flesh on them," Hazard would write five years later. Fales's pain was "almost constant" and sometimes "excruciating." And yet, Hazard thought, "his countenance retained a highly intellectual and almost heavenly expression." "His mind was of the finest mould and of the highest order," Hazard went on, "and nothing but health and education was wanting to have rendered him one of the first of men."[35]

For his part, Fales often referred to Hazard as his "kind friend." After Hazard had arranged for his move from the asylum to the widow's private house, on land adjoining Hazard's, Fales said more. "My valued friend T.R.H. calls to see me often," Fales wrote to a mutual friend of theirs. "He shows me great kindness, and I look upon him as a sort of parent." Indeed, twenty-three years Fales's senior, Hazard was old enough to be his father. With money and time, after retirement, Hazard became a benefactor to young Fales. It was from Hazard's Quaker connections in Philadelphia that Fales's move to a private home was subsidized. Those Quaker connections also wrote back and forth with Fales in 1848, 1849, and 1850.[36]

Most likely, Hazard had been the one to bring to bring Fales pencil and paper for those letters, and to introduce Fales to his pen pals. Fales's letters were full of gratitude to the ladies of Philadelphia for their generosity and even more full of his faith in God. His last letter was dated June 26, 1850. In it, he reported news he had of his one friend from the poorhouse, "Poor old Joseph," who had been taken ill. But Fales himself was also ill. He reported that he had suffered a headache for the previous four days which nearly stopped him from seeing the page on which he was writing. A few days later Hazard came and then called a doctor. But Fales's health got worse. Hazard sat up with Fales all night July 6. For another week, Fales was in and out of consciousness, praying when conscious. Hazard reported being in awe of Fales's faith: Fales talked with God as if God was sitting next to him. He died on July 14, 1850. Forty mourners came to pay respects.[37]

After his funeral, the widow and her daughter—the ones who had been Fales's full-time caregivers for half a year—wrote a letter to Fales's Philadelphia friends. Identified only as "R.C." and "E.," they must have needed to find a new income. But their letter, as printed, was about Fales's faith. Baptists, they wrote about Fales that "the great aim of his life seemed to be, *to do good,* and the salvation of souls was ever on his mind." Fales's many friends and benefactors felt that something must be done to remember this unusual young man, who impressed so many people with his example of faith. That is why one of those "excellent ladies" of Philadelphia arranged to publish Fales's memoir, his essays, and several letters he wrote them under the title *Memoirs of William R. Fales, the Portsmouth Cripple*, the title page of which is Figure 5.4 That last word in the title, "Cripple," is not one that Fales used in his own writing. While Fales lamented his physical condition, he also saw it as having spiritually transformed him. So, while others described him as a cripple, to be pitied, Fales hoped his writings could have a positive impact on others' faith. Just like the publications of the American Tract Society, Fales's memoir was intended as spiritual literature: part of an outpouring of devotional works to inspire American Christians to faith and good works. It is that, but along the way it opens a rare window into a mid-nineteenth-century poorhouse from an inmate's point of view.[38]

Indeed, it was recognized as an exposé at the time. The editor of the Philadelphia Quaker *Friends' Review* was surprised to get an angry letter in response to his publishing excerpts of the book in 1851. The editor complained in print: "We find very unexpectedly, that an article . . . respecting William R. Fales the Portsmouth cripple, has been construed by some of those connected with the Asylum for the poor at Portsmouth, as implying a charge of neglect on the part of some of the managers of that institution." Two commissioners of the Portsmouth Asylum had written that "during the short period William R. Fales was under our care, he received frequent visits from the inhabitants of Portsmouth, who were desirous of administering not only to his physical, but to his mental wants," and that

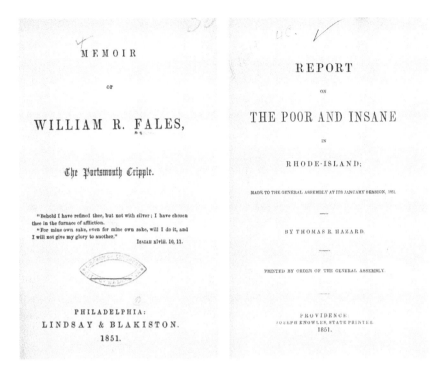

Figures 5.4 and 5.5 Books by Fales and Hazard both appeared in 1851. These title pages are reproduced at *The Internet Archives*, from Library of Congress copies at <https://archive.org/details/memoirofwilliamr00fale/page/n1/mode/2up> and https://archive.org/details/reportonpoorinsa00rhod.

"he received as much care and sympathy as he would have done, under the same circumstances, had he fallen under the care of the managers of the poor of any town or city in this or any other country." It is intriguing that the local officials of a Rhode Island town would even know what had been printed in this Philadelphia Quaker periodical, and felt the need to correct the record. When they did, they assured readers that their asylum was as humane as any in the world. Clearly, Fales's book left them feeling defensive. Moreover, they knew that more criticism was coming, from a source closer to home.[39]

"SHEPHERD" TOM: FROM VISITING WILLIAM FALES TO REFORMING POOR RELIEF

By the time Fales's memoir was published, "Shepherd" Tom had written his own book: *Report on the Poor and Insane in Rhode-Island; Made to the General Assembly at Its January Session, 1851*, the title page of which is Figure 5.5.

Hazard had been interested in the treatment of both the "insane" and the paupers in each town for several years by then. Indeed, these topics were interconnected, since people deemed insane were often put in the custody of overseers of the poor and poorhouse keepers. In 1844, the same year the Portsmouth Town Meeting held a tense, special session about their asylum for the poor, Hazard also became one of the founding trustees of the Rhode Island Asylum for the Insane, soon renamed the Butler Hospital for the Insane. Its goal, according to one early donor, was to give "our fellow beings who are . . . deprived of their reason. . . a safe retreat. . . provided with whatever may be most conducive to their comfort and to their restoration to a sound state of mind. . . ." This hospital, which still exists, was a public-private partnership, taking in both private donations and annual state subsidies for many years. The donors hoped that this hospital could rescue the mentally ill from being kept in cages inside of poorhouses, while rescuing the other inmates of the poorhouses from the violence and noise that sometimes accompanied mental illness.[40]

With his visits to William Fales in the Portsmouth Asylum, and his involvement in the Butler Hospital, "Shepherd" Tom was becoming an expert on how the state cared for the poor and mentally ill. Retired, with money, connections, and strong opinions, he became the leader of a reform movement in the state. Allied with more national figures like Dorothea Dix, Hazard became a leading voice for building more poorhouses, along with special asylums for the insane, and generally providing more humane care for the mentally ill and the needy. Around the time he arranged for William Fales to "elope" from the Portsmouth Asylum, the state legislature arranged for Hazard to become the "State Commissioner for the Poor and Insane." It was a brand new position, made up to give Hazard more leverage as he started looking into every Rhode Island towns' treatment of its neediest people.

Armed with this new title and his own sense of outrage, Hazard visited every town in the state but one. He looked around their poorhouses, if they had one, just as he done in Portsmouth's. He met many other people in Fales's situation, though he did not forge such a strong relationship with any other pauper as he had with Fales. He wrote down the name of every poorhouse inmate he discovered, along with details of their ages, birthplaces, and why they were in the poorhouse. He quizzed every town council about their treatment of the poor. How much did they spend on the poor? Did they have an asylum? How much did they pay the poorhouse keeper? How much did they watch over that keeper? Did the poor children go to school? Did the poorhouse inmates have Bibles? Could they go to church "with their wealthier brethren. . . agreeably to the usages of the different sects of Christians"? His book, more than one hundred pages long, compiled all the towns' answers to his questions, and his own opinions and recommendations.[41]

One page of this report to the state legislature focused on one pauper: William Fales. Hazard had finished the book after Fales had died in the summer of 1850. He could not resist including Fales's story, even though he knew that his friend in Philadelphia was already publishing Fales's memoir. It was here that Hazard described Fales's "highly intellectual and almost heavenly expression." He compared Fales to an eighteenth-century French archbishop, François de Salignac de La Mothe-Fénelon, remembered in Hazard's time for his spiritual searching and religious toleration. While he used Fales's story to provoke sympathy in his readers, it is also clear that Hazard felt a genuine fondness for the recently deceased Fales.

Also overrepresented in Hazard's report was the Portsmouth Asylum, but not because of Hazard's fondness for it. "The Asylum of this town is pleasantly, but inconveniently situated, being quite a distance from any open road," Hazard wrote. "The arrangements seem well calculated to promote the comfort of the poor, and, to a stranger, it appears to be well conducted." But Hazard was no stranger. He had traversed that inconvenient, isolated entrance many times over the past several years. When it came time for him to tell the legislature what he thought about the state's treatment of the poor and insane, he came back to things he had seen in Portsmouth. They were not good.[42]

After quoting the rules and regulations of the Portsmouth Asylum, Hazard focused on the arbitrary power of the poorhouse keeper to send any inmate to a "dungeon," as punishment, with only bread and water. Comparing this Portsmouth Asylum solitary confinement cell to France's famous Bastille Prison, which was destroyed at the beginning of the French Revolution, Hazard thought it was just as bad:

> The dungeon of Portsmouth has scarcely been heard of beyond the boundaries of that town, and yet its victims suffer none the less. The bread and the water of the captive in the Bastile was probably as sweet as that given to the [f]eeble old woman or the broken spirited old man in the dungeon of Portsmouth; the stone seat of the one, was no harder than that of the other; the darkness all the same.

While Hazard's comparison may seem a tad dramatic, he had seen people in this "dungeon" himself and it had clearly horrified him. This, combined with stories that elderly inmates told him of the Portsmouth asylum keeper hitting them or knocking them down, made Hazard very concerned about the suitability of poorhouse keepers for their jobs.[43]

At the same time, Hazard had seen how difficult it was for the poorhouse keeper to keep order in the poorhouse. Again, his examples came from Portsmouth and his visits to William Fales. On the day that Hazard arrived to help Fales "elope" to the widow's house in the meadow, the other inmates of the asylum were in distress. Mary Slocum, a sixty-year-old woman whom Hazard called "insane," was in chains. Another inmate, "old" Mrs. Cornell, about eighty-six-years-old, was "wild with excitement and fright," and had her arm bound up. Slocum had attacked Cornell with a broom stick. Reportedly, Mrs. Cornell died two weeks later, never having recovered from this assault. According to a third inmate, Caroline Albro, Slocum had attacked many women and young children in the asylum, using brooms, chairs, and a fire hook. Albro herself had suffered a shattered wrist bone, among other injuries. She was afraid to sleep when Slocum was free, for fear that Slocum would assault her.[44]

Hazard's solutions for these problems were several. He asked the legislature to pay for every insane pauper to go to the new Butler Hospital for the Insane. He asked for an end to corporal punishment, chains, and confinement in dark rooms. He asked the legislature to increase its spending on the education of deaf, blind, and mentally impaired students. The legislature agreed to each of these requests by the end of 1850. "Shepherd" Tom's other reforms would be much slower in coming. His main recommendation for the future of poor relief in Rhode Island was twofold. First, he wanted to end forever the practice of "auctioning" paupers to the lowest bidder. This method of finding homes for the homeless, which Scituate's overseers had used in Lydia Bates's time, was aimed at doing poor relief as cheaply as possible. For Hazard, though, it amounted to "offering a reward for the most cruel and avaricious man that can be found to abuse them." Every town, he thought, would have some homeowner who wanted to take the town's poor relief money but in return give as little food and clothing and kindness as they could get away with. Instead, Hazard wanted every town to have an asylum, but to still give poor relief of food, cash, firewood, clothes, and medical visits to some paupers in their own homes.[45]

These were moderate proposals, for Hazard's day. In the past generation, many American municipalities, along with all of Great Britain, had tried to ban any outdoor relief. Working with the assumption that giving poor relief actually encouraged people to be poor enough to need it, reformers across the Atlantic Ocean had worked to limit or totally cut off the cash, food, clothes, firewood, doctoring, and nursing, which overseers like William Larned had spent their lives arranging. Hazard had seen these poorhouse-only policies, in Portsmouth and elsewhere. He thought they had gone too far. Asylums could be run well, he thought, but they were not right for everyone. They were not right for William Fales. That is why Hazard worked so hard to get Fales out.

For Hazard, a mix of asylums and poor relief outside the asylum was the "most humane and christian-like plan that in the present state of society, can be pursued. . . . No individual or community was ever yet made poor by the practice of a liberal, discriminating charity—carried out in good faith—void of any selfish motives lurking at heart, and founded solely on love to God and his creatures," Hazard asserted. As Hazard sketched out a better future for poor relief, he saw a poorhouse in every town, with a poorhouse keeper chosen for his qualities of kindness and conscientiousness. He also urged that "Every citizen of the town should take an interest in their Asylum and occasionally visit it." For that reason, he added, thinking of Portsmouth's isolated asylum, they "should be placed on a public road." Not only would that encourage local citizens to drop by and inspect their poorhouse, Hazard thought, but "the passing and little incidents that occur on the road tend not a little to dissipate the tediousness that often connects itself with the monotonous life the old and decrepid are forced to lead."[46]

Hazard spoke from vicarious experience. He remembered the stir he would cause when he visited, how much people looked forward to visitors. He remembered, perhaps with a twinge of guilt, how much William Fales wanted Hazard to visit. If Hazard had learned anything from his friend it was that poorhouses could be lonely places. Poorhouse inmates could not always work for their upkeep. They were not right for everyone. They were not right for William Fales.

NOTES

1. The imaginative retelling of William Fales's early life in the first three paragraphs is based on William R. Fales, *Memoir of William R. Fales, The Portsmouth Cripple*, Edited by S.H.L. (Philadelphia: Lindsay & Blakiston, 1851), 20–24, 106–111.
2. On the long history of poorhouses and their successors, see Wagner, *The Poorhouse*, chapter 8.
3. Fales, *Memoir of William R. Fales*, 20.
4. Fales, *Memoir of William R. Fales*, 20, 39.
5. Fales, *Memoir of William R. Fales*, 20–21.
6. In speculating how Fales might be diagnosed today, I rely on the Mayo Clinic webpages on Rheumatoid Arthritis and Polio: https://www.mayoclinic.org/ diseases-conditions/rheumatoid-arthritis/symptoms-causes/syc-20353648, https://www.mayoclinic.org/diseases-conditions/rheumatoid-arthritis/

diagnosis-treatment/drc-20353653, https://www.mayoclinic.org/diseases-conditions/polio/symptoms-causes/syc-20376512, accessed 21 January 2020.

7. Fales, *Memoir of William R. Fales*, 21. James H. Cassedy, *Medicine in America: A Short History* (Baltimore: Johns Hopkins University Press, 1991), 25. Geri Walton, "Medical Blistering in the Georgian Era," in *Geri Walton: Unique History from the 18th and 19th Centuries* <https://www.geriwalton.com/medical-blistering-in-georgian-era/>. John Forbes, Alexander Tweedie, and John Connolly, *The Cyclopaedia of Practical Medicine*, Volume I (London: Sherwood, Gilbert, and Piper, and Baldwin and Cradock; Whitaker, Treacher, and Co., 1833), 275–281, 484–488, accessed at https://catalog.hathitrust.org/Record/009245848.

8. Fales, *Memoir of William R. Fales*, 22, 24.

9. Fales, *Memoir of William R. Fales*, 21–25, with quotation on 22.

10. Fales, *Memoir of William R. Fales*, 22, 78, 81, 60.

11. Fales, *Memoir of William R. Fales*, 23, 20. On applicable settlement laws, see "An Act ascertaining what shall constitute a legal settlement," in Rhode Island, *Public Laws of the State of Rhode Island and Providence Plantations* (Providence: Knowles and Vose, 1844), 340–341.

12. Edward Homer West, *History of Portsmouth 1638–1936* (n.p.), 30–31, accessed via *archive.org*.

13. The Raytheon Employees Wildlife Habitat Committee is a volunteer organization interested in stewardship of the real estate owned by the Raytheon Company, a producer of electronics, weapons, systems, etc. for military, civil government, and other customers. The committee did a lot of research into the Portsmouth Asylum, the site of which is now owned by Raytheon. They published their findings and excerpts of primary sources on the website: https://rewhc.org/townfarmintro.shtml. On Britain's New Poor Law, see David Englander, *Poverty and Poor Law Reform in 19th Century Britain, 1834–1914* (New York: Longman, 1998), 14–15.

14. Rothman, *The Discovery of the Asylum*, xviii-xx. Katz, *In the Shadow of the Poorhouse*, 23, 25. Abramovitz, *Regulating the Lives of Women*, 111.

15. Karin Wulf, "Gender and the Political Economy of Poor Relief in Colonial Philadelphia," in Smith, *Down and Out in Early America*, 176–177, and Herndon, "Who Died an Expence to This Town," in Smith, *Down and Out in Early America*. Wagner, *The Poorhouse*, 2, 156–157. Lockley, *Welfare and Charity in the Antebellum South*, 28. Rockman, *Scraping By*, 197.

16. For a more full version of this historian's argument about why Americans voted to build poorhouses, see Gabriel Loiacono, "Economy and Isolation in Rhode Island Poorhouses, 1820–1850," *Rhode Island History* 65:2 (Summer 2007), 31–47.

17. Fales, *Memoir of William R. Fales*, 85, 79, 46.

18. Fales, *Memoir of William R. Fales*, 79–80, 107, 85, 115. Inmates of the Portsmouth Asylum are listed in the 1850 Manuscript Census returns for Portsmouth, Rhode Island, 24–25, Seventh Census of the United States, 1850 (National Archives Microfilm Publication M432, 1009 rolls), Records of the Bureau of the Census, Record Group 29, National Archives, Washington, DC, accessed via Ancestry.com, *1850 United States Federal Census* (Provo, UT: Ancestry.com Operations, Inc., 2009), Images reproduced by FamilySearch: Year: 1850; Census Place: Portsmouth, Newport, Rhode Island; Roll: M432_842; Page: 35A; Image: 357. Wagner, *The Poorhouse*, 3.

19. Fales, *Memoir of William R. Fales*, 56–58.

20. Fales, *Memoir of William R. Fales*, 38, 144–145. 1850 Manuscript Census returns for Portsmouth, Rhode Island, 24–25.

21. Fales, *Memoir of William R. Fales*, 56–57, 84–85, 95. On the work of women in poor relief, again, see Abramovitz, *Regulating the Lives of Women*, 66–67, Herndon, "Poor Women and the Boston Almshouse in the Early Republic," 349–382, Bourque, "Women and Work in the Philadelphia Almshouse, 1790–1840," 383–413, Daen, "'To Board & Nurse a Stranger,'" 1–26, and Green, *This Business of Relief*, 37. Fales, *Memoir of William R. Fales*, 104.

22. Fales, *Memoir of William R. Fales*, xi.

23. Fales, *Memoir of William R. Fales*, 64, 94, 92, 91.

24. Fales, *Memoir of William R. Fales*, 30.

25. Fales, *Memoir of William R. Fales*, 62, 130. See also S.J. Wolfe, "Dating American Tract Society Publications Through 1876 from External Evidences: A Series of Tables," online at American Antiquarian Society website <http://www.americanantiquarian.org/node/6693>.

26. Cynthia S. Hamilton, "Spreading the Word: The American Tract Society, *The Dairyman's Daughter*, and Mass Publishing," *Book History* 14 (2011), 25–57. Susanna Ashton and Robyn E. Adams Introduction to "Clarinda: A Pious Coloured Woman of South Carolina," in Susanna Ashton, Ed., *I Belong to South Carolina: South Carolina Slave Narratives* (Columbia: University of South Carolina Press, 2010).

27. Fales, *Memoir of William R. Fales*, 130–132, 136–138, 39.

28. Fales, *Memoir of William R. Fales*, 141, 123, 95.

29. Fales, *Memoir of William R. Fales*, 110–117.

30. Entry for December 28, 1850 in "Book of Registry for the Portsmouth Asylum," in John T. Pierce, Sr., Ed., *Historical Tracts of the Town of Portsmouth, Rhode Island* (Hamilton Print Co., 1991).

31. Patrick T. Conley, *The Makers of Modern Rhode Island* (Charleston: The History Press, 2012), 45–47, 174–177. Seth Rockman, "Negro Cloth: Mastering the Market for Slave Clothing in Antebellum America," in Sven Beckert and Christine Desan, Eds., *American Capitalism: New Histories* (New York: Columbia University Press, 2018).

32. On Hazard's earmark, see *The Early Records of the Town of Portsmouth* (Providence: E.L. Freeman and Sons, 1901), 380 . On Hazard's becoming a "freeman," see manuscript entry for 21 April 1841 in Portsmouth Town Meeting Minutes, Portsmouth Town Hall, Portsmouth, Rhode Island.

33. On the 1840 meeting, see William Michael Ferraro, "Lives of Quiet Desperation: Community and Polity in New England Over Four Centuries: The Cases of Portsmouth and Foster, Rhode Island" (PhD diss., Brown University, 1991), 255–256. On the 1844 collaboration with Hazard, see Francis Tiffany, *Life of Dorothea Lynde Dix* (Boston: Houghton Mifflin Company, 1890), 96.

34. Manuscript Entry for 4 March 1844, Portsmouth Town Meeting Minutes, Portsmouth Town Hall, Portsmouth, Rhode Island.

35. Thomas R. Hazard, *Report on the Poor and Insane in Rhode-Island; Made to the General Assembly at Its January Session, 1851* (Providence: Joseph Knowles, State Printer, 1851), 103–104.

36. Fales, *Memoir of William R. Fales*, 143–144.

37. Hazard's description of Fales's last days are published in Fales, *Memoir of William R. Fales*, 144–149.

38. Details of the book's publication are in Fales, *Memoir of William R. Fales*, xi–xii, 13–19 and in Hazard, *Report on Poor and Insane in Rhode-Island*, 103–104. It is possible the original, pencil-written version of the memoir and letters exists somewhere,

but I have not yet found it. The editor, one of those unnamed Philadelphia ladies, must have changed some of the words in Fales's writings. For example, none of the names Fales names are spelled out, except for those who had died. Thus, the editor became "S.H.L.," while Hazard became "T.R.H." The widow became "R.C." and I have not been able to match those initials to 1850 census records of Portsmouth and neighboring towns. A scholar versed in disability studies could do much with the *Memoir of William R. Fales.*

39. *Friends' Review* 18 January 1851, 280. For the excerpts of Fales's memoir reprinted, with the signature "H.," likely for Hazard, see *Friends' Review* 14 December 1850, 202–203, and *Friends' Review* 21 December 1850, 211–212, accessed on *books. google.com.*

40. Henry M. Hurd, et al., *The Institutional Care of the Insane in the United States and Canada*, Volume 3 (Baltimore: Johns Hopkins Press, 1916), 554–562.

41. Hazard, *Report on Poor and Insane in Rhode-Island,* 9–10.

42. Hazard, *Report on Poor and Insane in Rhode-Island,* 13.

43. Hazard, *Report on Poor and Insane in Rhode-Island,* 91–95, 102.

44. Hazard, *Report on Poor and Insane in Rhode-Island,* 102–103.

45. Hazard, *Report on Poor and Insane in Rhode-Island,* 105–108.

46. Hazard, *Report on Poor and Insane in Rhode-Island,* 88–89.

Epilogue

What Can We Learn From These Five Lives?

It has been 170 years since William Fales died and "Shepherd" Tom Hazard wrote of his dreams for the future of "humane" poor relief. Much has happened since then in the history of American poverty and responses to poverty. This epilogue will briefly survey some major developments between 1850 and the present day, ending with a summary of what these five microhistories can tell us about our own period.

AMERICAN RESPONSES TO POVERTY, 1850–2020

Already, as Fales and Hazard were writing their books, immigrants from the German states and Ireland were reshaping American culture, politics, and poor relief. In reaction to these new immigrants, many Americans became "nativists," who believed that native-born Americans needed to defend their governments, churches, and poor relief from being overly influenced by foreigners. After 1850, it became a cliché to say that immigrants were mostly paupers and paupers were mostly immigrants. At the same time, a growing chorus of voices suggested that asking for relief was, in and of itself, a crime. As a committee of distinguished citizens in Providence put it in 1859: petty criminals included "not only the habitual drunkards of

How Welfare Worked in the Early United States. Gabriel J. Loiacono, Oxford University Press. © Oxford University Press 2021. DOI: 10.1093/oso/9780197515433.003.0007

both sexes, the common prostitute, and the idler, but beggars also . . . who, by their tales of suffering and poverty, *impose* upon the community." In their city, the asylum keeper reportedly insisted inmates do even meaning-less work, such as "carrying wood from one corner of the yard to another and piling it there, when it was all removed it was brought back again in piled in the old place." Some states, notably Massachusetts, went as far as to deport immigrants who asked for poor relief, beginning in the 1850s. In the 1890s, Massachusetts deportation policy became federal immi-gration policy. Since the mid-nineteenth century, immigration has been almost constantly intertwined with poor relief in the American public im-agination. From the American Party of the 1850s to the "Make America Great Again" campaign of the 2010s, voters have expressed concern that immigrants might strain or overwhelm taxpayers' relief efforts. The only time American poor relief *has* been overwhelmed was during the Great Depression of the 1930s. Immigration was not the cause, and the federal government ultimately stepped in to help. Nevertheless, it seems unlikely that discussions of immigration will be uncoupled from discussions poor relief any time soon.[1]

The politics of immigration dominated the middle of the 1850s but very quickly gave way to the politics of slavery and to the Civil War. The Civil War saw a spike in poor relief as local officials in the Union rushed to set up parallel poor relief systems aimed at needy families of soldiers. In the Confederacy, local, state, and even national poor relief grew prodigiously in an ultimately insufficient effort to combat food supply disruptions; naval blockade; a high rate of casualties; military defeat; and the massive impact of men, women, and children leaving slavery. To assist those who had just escaped from—or outlasted—slavery, as well as those who had fought for the Union, the federal government made two limited forays into poor relief.[2]

Apart from hospitals for sailors and veterans' pensions, the federal gov-ernment had avoided involvement in poor relief prior to the Civil War. In fact, "Shepherd Tom" Hazard's friend, Dorothea Dix, had successfully pushed the United States Congress to pass a bill which set aside federally controlled lands to fund hospitals for the mentally ill in 1854, only to see the bill vetoed by President Franklin Pierce on the grounds that it was uncon-stitutional to make "the Federal Government the great almoner of public charity throughout the United States." Less than a decade later, under the auspices of Union General O. O. Howard, a War Department Bureau of Refugees, Freedmen, and Abandoned Lands was created to provide food, clothing, firewood, and medical care both to freedpeople in need and to other refugees in the recently defeated Confederacy. Escaping slavery with "nothing but freedom," despite lifetimes of labor, freedpeople benefited, in a limited way, from U.S. Army–coordinated poor relief and schools. General Howard adamantly did not want the Bureau's poor relief to last too long, though. Moreover, the Bureau eventually refused to support land redistribution to survivors of slavery, no matter how long they had worked that land. The "Freedmen's Bureau," as it was nicknamed, closed in 1872. By contrast, federal government pensions for Union soldiers and sailors only grew. In fact, by 1900, an estimated 18 percent of American men and women over sixty-five received Union soldier pensions. Confederate veterans and their dependents also received pensions from their state governments, though that system varied from state to state.[3]

State governments also became more involved in traditional poor relief after the Civil War. After creating state-supported private institutions like Rhode Island's Butler Hospital for the Insane, states soon turned to wholly public institutions. To continue with the example of Rhode Island, the state legislated a Board of State Charities and Corrections in 1869, which was slowly built out to include a prison, an insane asylum, a workhouse, and an almshouse. In theory, the state almshouse would now give a home to needy people in the state who had no settlement in any one town. Rhode Island was typical of American state institutions in this way: the late nineteenth century was a time of professionalization and institutionalization, especially in the North. By 1879, leaders of many state-level poor relief institutions were meeting in a National Conference of Charities and Corrections. Organizations like this one would encourage more uniformity, social scientific study, coordinated government approaches to poor relief, and the growth of social work as a profession. Elected officials like William Larned, who learned to do a kind of triage social work on the job, were becoming less common than professionals, who studied for their profession by reading manuals and reports.[4]

As Americans slowly recovered from slavery and the Civil War, prewar ideas came back into vogue. Just as in William Fales's youth, some Americans argued that governments and even private charities should not give "outdoor relief," cash or food or firewood outside of the poorhouse. A huge exception was made for Civil War pensioners. Younger Americans who were unemployed and displaced, though, met with a confusing mixture of charity and principled refusal to give charity. As the writer William Dean Howells described it, "when I am in the presence of want ... I have to give, or else go away with a bad conscience. ... Of course I do not give much, for I wish to be a good citizen as well as a good Christian; and ... I hear another voice reproaching me for encouraging street beggary." Howells's internal struggle was in fact a national one: was it better to give to those who asked or to withhold?[5]

The proponents of "scientific charity" said to withhold. They argued that charity and poor relief needed to be much more tightly controlled. Private citizens should stop giving to people in the street, they insisted. Moreover, they said, governments should separate needy children from their parents, expand the capacity of asylums for the insane, and deny able-bodied men any relief, whether in poorhouses, temporary lodging in police stations, or even as boarders in private homes. Characterized as "tramps," and perceived as ever more numerous and threatening, poor men were treated as criminals just for having no place to go. Meanwhile, charity organizations gave to women only if they deemed the woman respectable, and conforming to gender roles. They discouraged women from being employed outside the home. In response to this "scientific charity" lobby, legislators increasingly criminalized begging, and tried to hold everyone in need to a "contract." No one, leaders of government and charitable organizations theorized, should get relief without giving something in return. An imaginary contract, they argued, should ensure that the poor give something, anything, in return for relief. Makework, such as moving chopped wood back and forth, was making a comeback. "Peter Quiz," the anonymous writer in chapter 2 who had satirized a harsh response to poverty in 1811, would have sounded less satirical, and closer to mainstream opinion, by 1881.[6]

But American responses to poverty were never quite as uniform as "scientific charity" reports pretended. Individual, private charity never went away. If it had, "scientific charity" organizations would not have kept warning against it. Poorhouses, meanwhile, were not always tightly controlled. Moreover, after 1900, "Progressive Era" reformers began to see flaws in the practice of "scientific charity." Led by Settlement House workers from around the country, including Jane Addams and Lillian Wald, "Progressives" continued the trend of professionalization and education for social workers. Indeed, one scholar has it that "social work was progressivism." Unlike the previous generation, though, Progressive social workers pushed back against separating poor children from their parents. They were also much more supportive of government poor relief, including outdoor relief, than the previous generation had been. One outcome of this sea change was local or state government "mother's pensions," aimed at allowing widowed and divorced mothers to stay at home with their children. Assisting mostly White, widowed women, the pensions were both a throwback to outdoor relief and an effort to bolster traditional gender roles. Still, if Lydia Bates had given birth to Rhoda in 1920 instead of 1820, their chances of staying together in their home with a pension would have been greater. State governments also passed a large number of workmen's compensation laws, providing a form of insurance for families whose breadwinner lost the ability to work. Looking across the Atlantic Ocean at Germany, these state officials were imitating, in a more patchwork way, the "social insurance" programs becoming popular in western Europe. Thus, the Progressive Era gave rise to what one scholar calls a "renaissance of public welfare," and encouraged the growth of something we now call "the welfare state."[7]

If you ask Americans today when welfare began, chances are good they will answer this: during the Great Depression. Is that true? It depends how you define welfare. If, by welfare, you mean government assistance to the poor, then no. Readers of this book will be well aware that American governments have been assisting the poor, in a big way, from before American independence. Poor relief was the welfare of its day: expensive and extensive. While it has been more generous or more limited in different periods, there has never been a moment in the history of the United States when American governments did not offer poor relief.

On the other hand, the word "welfare" was rarely used to describe government assistance to the poor before the mid-twentieth century. Moreover, most scholars use the term "welfare state" to describe something identified with the twentieth century. What that something is, exactly, depends on which scholar you ask. Historian Alice Kessler-Harris loosely defines the welfare state as a government that "provided for the well-being of its citizens so that they might more effectively participate in the polity." Sociologist David Garland calls it "a set of social protections, superimposed upon capitalist economic process, designed to modify and moralize the market economy." Social Work scholar Mimi Abramovitz offers a "socialist-feminist" view which "holds that the welfare state originated to meet the changing requirements of patriarchy *and* capitalism and to mediate their conflicts." For Garland and Kessler-Harris, the welfare state looks different in different countries. In today's United States, Garland argues, the welfare state includes not only government assistance to the poor, but also Social Security, public schools, public libraries, tariffs on imported goods, tax breaks, interest rates on borrowing, and social work. In short, the welfare state is everything the government does to make an industrialist, capitalist economy work better, and to protect people from negative effects of that economy. An important corollary to this definition is that the welfare state is *not* socialism. It is a necessary partner to capitalism.[8]

So even though American poor relief is older than the Declaration of Independence, most scholars tell a story about the welfare state that starts around the Great Depression and continues today. For David Garland it is as simple as this: "Franklin D. Roosevelt's New Deal established the American welfare state." Clearly, parts of the government responsibilities that Garland includes in the welfare state predate Roosevelt's presidency. Not only poor relief, but also public schools, tariffs on certain imported goods, even some of the things social workers do were already the norm in the 1830s, not the 1930s. Still, there is no question that Roosevelt's New Deal programs were a massive change in American poor relief and continue to shape welfare today.[9]

As of the moment I am writing, the Great Depression of 1929 to 1941 remains the biggest economic disaster ever in United States history. With an official unemployment rate of 25 percent in 1932, and unknown rates of underemployment, poor relief costs in cities, towns, and counties across the nation skyrocketed. Relying mostly on property tax revenue, and with debts of their own, almost 1,000 municipalities had defaulted by 1933. Moreover, the poor relief local governments *did* provide was small. Most state governments stepped in to help with the finances and administration of relief, more than they ever had in the past. One of the most famous of these became New York, led by Governor Franklin D. Roosevelt. Even so, states and municipalities called on the federal government for help. When Roosevelt was elected President in 1932, he immediately started implementing some of these New York programs at the federal level.[10]

American poor relief has never been the same since the Roosevelt administration enacted its "New Deal." Moving quickly, responding to unprecedented crises, the administration asked Congress to get the Federal Government directly involved in poor relief as never before. Between 1933 and 1936, a newly made Federal Emergency Relief Administration spent more than three billion dollars bolstering state and local poor relief. But it was the longer-term programs of the "Second New Deal," which would have the biggest impact on local poor relief. The 1935 Social Security Act created pensions for industrial workers and Aid to Dependent Children. Respectively, these two programs would empty local poorhouses of many their elderly inhabitants, while ensuring federal "outdoor relief" to poor families with children. The Act was neither fair nor an answer to all the challenges of poor relief. In exchange for support from White, Southern Democratic Congressmen, the Roosevelt administration tried to avoid challenging the Jim Crow social order of the early twentieth century. The Social Security Act, for example, excluded agricultural and domestic workers, who were largely African-American, Latinx, Asian-American, and female, from the pensions. Moreover, as administered, Aid to Dependent Children discouraged women from working "men's jobs," while at the same time encouraging African-American women to work in low-paid service jobs.[11]

The Social Security Act, then, reprised some of the raced and gendered applications of poor relief which readers of this book will recognize from Cuff Roberts's and Lydia Bates's stories. At the same time, the act reshaped the terrain of poor relief nationwide. Between federal pensions, unemployment compensation, and federal outdoor relief for families, local poor relief agencies found themselves administering federal programs, but shouldering less financial responsibility for the needy of their communities. Gradually, local poor relief would remake itself to fit the new terrain. Within a generation, the last poorhouses would shut down, or reinvent themselves as publicly owned long-term care facilities. The state and local shares of total poor relief expenditures would drop from a combined 97.9 percent in 1932 to 37.5 percent in 1939.[12]

As the Great Depression gave way to the US military buildup for World War II, unemployment finally subsided and the economy thrived again. Victory in World War II, in turn, was the start of what some scholars call *"les trente glorieuses,"* or three glorious decades. For Americans and western Europeans, the mid-1940s through the mid-1970s were a triumph of the welfare state. National economies, managed by national governments, supported high employment and a rising standard of living for many, though not all, citizens. Strengthened programs of social insurance and poor relief provided for many of the elderly, unemployed, or otherwise needy. Nevertheless, local officials remained important in poor relief. It was they, after all, who actually met the people who needed help and decided whether and how to provide it. They may not have had the title "overseer of the poor" anymore, but local officials retained much of the power that William Larned exercised, even as they dispensed federal money.[13]

It was in the context of these "three glorious decades" and this new relationship between federal money and local officials that President Lyndon B. Johnson spearheaded a "War on Poverty." Johnson's ambitious legislative agenda would make enduring additions to the federal programs of the New Deal: Head Start preschool grants and Work Study grants for college students, along with Medicare and Medicaid. What Johnson and his allies called the "Great Society" continues to shape Americans' lives today.

It was also in the context of those "three glorious decades" that ordinary women and men, as well as teenagers and young children, successfully used court cases, public advocacy, and civil disobedience to effect major social changes. The most well known of these movements were the civil rights movement, led by African Americans, and the women's rights movement, later known as "second-wave feminism." Both would raise questions about how fair access to the welfare state was. Moreover, they would both contribute to the less well-known welfare rights movement.

This movement was largely centered on women receiving Aid to Families with Dependent Children, which had been modified and expanded during the War on Poverty. Participants were united by the idea that they should not have to give up their individual rights in order to receive benefits. They did not want their personal details to be publicized, or to have their homes inspected at night by officials looking for evidence of a "man-in-the-home." Some wanted daycare or better benefits. Some wanted everything the law allowed them, as well as protections against "vengeful agency personnel." Organized under an umbrella group, the "National Welfare Rights Organization," this group acted like a union: organizing to improve conditions and benefits of its members.[14]

As those "three glorious decades" came to an unlooked-for end, however, criticism of welfare and welfare rights grew more popular. In a globalizing economy, underemployment in the United States crept upwards. Wages and benefits began to stagnate. Former California Governor Ronald Reagan began talking about "a woman in Chicago," in stump speeches for the Republican presidential nomination in 1976. Reagan described this woman in Chicago as having "80 names, 30 addresses, 12 Social Security cards and . . . four nonexisting deceased husbands," as well as a "tax-free cash income . . . over \$150,000." There was such a case in Chicago, but Reagan's speeches seemed to multiply her until the stock figure of the "welfare queen" became a stand-in for most welfare recipients. Running again in 1980, and this time winning, Reagan's administration reduced funds for New Deal and Great Society programs, but left them intact.[15]

It was the Democrat Bill Clinton who oversaw a major rewriting of the 1935 Social Security Act. Promising to "end welfare as we know it" in his 1992 campaign, he went far toward that goal with the 1996 Personal Responsibility and Work Opportunity Reconciliation Act. It ended the sixty-year-old program Aid to Families with Dependent Children, which had often been called "welfare" in common parlance. That aid was replaced with "Temporary Assistance to Needy Families," a set of block grants, for administration by state governments. The "Temporary" in the title meant that assistance could be stopped after sixty months of receiving federal aid, continuous or not. Clinton's "welfare reform" was ultimately endorsed by his successor, George W. Bush. Bush's campaign coined the term "compassionate conservatism," in an effort to describe poor relief that was both fiscally conservative and yet responsive to the needs of the poor. In this way, both he and Clinton hearkened back to the poor law reform of the mid-nineteenth century. As William Fales had experienced it, that nineteenth-century reform was also aimed at less expensive but more "humane" care that discouraged poor relief and encouraged employment, including low-wage, tenuous jobs.[16]

A recession, beginning in 2008, made the rising cost of food stamps an issue in the early years of Barack Obama's presidency. But the biggest argument during his presidency was whether and how to build out the welfare state to include healthcare. Ultimately the 2010 Affordable Care Act aimed to improve healthcare by making health insurance more affordable for more people, through a mixture of subsidies and Medicaid expansion. In some ways, the healthcare environment of 2010 was worlds away from the United States, circa 1810, in which "One-Eyed" Sarah could be hired to nurse the needy at town expense. One constant, though, is that in both these worlds, a health crisis could bankrupt a family. In 1810, that family could count on nursing, doctoring, and medicine in the town where they had a settlement. In 2010, while healthcare was often more effective, how it would be paid for was less clear.

As I write and rewrite these words, questions about welfare seem as unsettled as ever. By the time you are reading this page, maybe the crises of 2020 will have receded in significance. Hopefully, we will have found positive resolutions. At the moment, though, Americans and others around the world are struggling with three crises. The first two are both connected to the Covid-19 pandemic. One, of course, is the pandemic itself. Governments from one continent to another have taken dramatically different approaches to public health, some more coercive and others more voluntary, some emphasizing national efforts and others state or local. One side effect of our public health efforts, however, has been a contraction of the economy, leading to the second crisis: levels of unemployment not seen in the United States for about eighty years. How to take care of those suddenly in need, whether with unemployment insurance, food assistance, or other help is one of the big questions we face. The federal government has already offered an unusual disbursement of poor relief and stimulus; Congress and President Trump are discussing another round now, not unlike the unusual amounts of money disbursed by Overseer Larned in 1800 after an epidemic in Providence.

The other big crisis of this summer in the United States also has important precedents in early American poor laws: unequitable police attention to people of color, with sometimes tragic consequences. George Floyd, who had lost his job during the economic contraction connected to the pandemic, was killed by Minneapolis police who were investigating an alleged, minor, nonviolent crime: spending a counterfeit twenty-dollar bill. Caught on video, it is sickening to see: a policeman kneeled on Floyd's neck and Floyd was asphyxiated. Although it is only the latest in a series of unjustifiable killings by police, disproportionately of African Americans, some cases well known, others not, Floyd's case has drawn global attention to American police and people of color.

While there were no police in the United States two hundred years ago, during the life of Cuff Roberts, there was police power. As readers will have seen, it was frequently exercised by overseers of the poor, together with town councils and constables. Then, as now, people mostly of African or Native ancestry were more scrutinized, more harassed, and more likely to see their lives turned upside down, than Americans of more European ancestry, though anyone might experience this harassment. In many ways, police attention to people of color has changed less over time than poor relief as a whole. Learning Cuff Roberts's story can help Americans reflect on how the past has shaped the present, and how we might like the future of police power to change.

Even before the spread of Covid-19 or George Floyd's death, a question winding its way through courts was whether the Donald Trump administration could revive and expand immigration restrictions on anyone deemed likely to be a "public charge." These immigration rules would be applied to people seeking visas or permanent residency in much the same way that nineteenth-century local and state officials sought to scrutinize newcomers for their "likelihood" to need poor relief. "Likely to be chargeable." Those words would roll off the tongue of William Larned. He knew this language well. As much as has happened in two centuries, it is surprising how similar our words, our ideas, and our big questions are to those of William Larned, Cuff Roberts, "One-Eyed" Sarah, and their contemporaries.[17]

RECURRING IDEAS, PERSISTENT QUESTIONS

Can "One-Eyed" Sarah or William Fales answer these persistent questions for our own time? They can help. Knowing a few concrete stories about the history of American poor relief can give readers today some context and experience to draw on while facing poverty. Knowing how early Americans helped those in need will not give us a flawless road map to helping people here and now. It will, however, give us examples of how we might confront the challenges we face today. Whether struggling with a low income yourself, working with low-income people, or simply trying to understand the world today, these five microhistories teach important lessons.

First, the United States has a very *long* history of poverty and government assistance to the poor. Welfare is not a new invention. It was not created by Franklin Roosevelt. Both charity and welfare were practiced in the United States as soon as the country was founded. People, as individuals or through family, religious, or civic organizations, have been trying to help their neighbors for centuries upon centuries. This is true of Native nations before 1492, migrants after 1492, and Americans of all kinds since before independence. In the American context, though, charity has always been accompanied by government assistance to the poor. As the life of William Larned shows, local governments taxed and spent to help their neediest neighbors before, during, and after the American Revolution. This poor relief was expensive, usually amounting to the largest portion of an individual's tax burden before 1830.

Second, government poor relief gave local governments a lot of power, which could be used in unintended ways. As the life of Cuff Roberts shows, local government officials could use the poor laws to banish people, whether or not they were poor. Roberts, combat veteran of the Revolution, was repeatedly banished because he was "Black." Ostensibly race-neutral, poor law officials could use these powers to control where people lived, and to specifically target people of color. And they did, throughout the North, in the generations after the American Revolution. In spite of this, Roberts made a life for himself and his children. Appealing to the federal government, Roberts and many other veterans gained pensions, originally intended only for "poor" veterans like them—and Roberts also figured out how to assert citizenship rights to enter Providence in spite of hostile overseers of the poor. Surviving cold, combat, and almost to age seventy, Roberts found ways to protect his family from local government and his health from old age.

Third, healthcare was a part of government poor relief. Medicines, doctors, and nurses, all were paid for by overseers of the poor. "One-Eyed" Sarah's life demonstrates how overseers of the poor provided expensive, effective health care for townspeople who were ill and could not afford treatment themselves. Moreover, Sarah's life is just one example of how important women were to the hard, hands-on work of caring for the poor. A Native woman with her own family to care for, Sarah's life reminds us that poor law officials relied on local government relief contractors: the workers and merchants who supplied the poor with services and goods. Governments could not care for the needy without the paid labor of Sarah and others like her.

Fourth, unmarried women and their children have long been at the center of arguments over poor relief. As Lydia Bates's life shows, overseers of the poor had a great deal of power to separate children and their parents. Most likely, Bates was separated from hers. And when this book loses sight of her, Bates seemed to be separated from her daughter Rhoda. In ways that modern readers might find abhorrent, early American poor law officials thought it best to make poor children grow up without their parents. Lydia Bates's life also shows, as "One-Eyed" Sarah's did, that low-paid or unpaid women did a great deal of work caring for others.

Fifth, compared to Bates's life as a pauper in the 1810s and 1820s, the lives of paupers a generation later were less free and less connected to their communities. William Fales's experience in the poorhouse was both controlled and isolated in ways that Bates had not experienced. Poorhouses were supposed to be more "humane" than the kind of assistance Bates received, and were supposed to be cheaper. By and large, they were neither. Instead, they took paupers like Fales and kept them mostly out of touch with the townspeople around them. This change cut down not only on Fales's social life, but also on the ability of his neighbors to earn money as local government relief contractors. Town tax revenue went to pay for debt service on poor farms and salaries for poorhouse keepers instead. William Fales, in the end, was happier in a private home, belonging to two women who were paid to care for him. These women did work like the work "One-Eyed" Sarah had done, except that they were paid by private donors. A generation before, this hard work would have been paid for by the town, or done by a pauper, like Lydia Bates.

These five microhistories show how Americans took care of their poorest neighbors between independence and 1850. While these five life stories from Rhode Island cannot stand in for every experience of poor relief in the early United States, they teach big lessons with their specificity. They show different forms that poor relief could take. They show practices we might want to imitate, and others we might want to carefully avoid. Furthermore, they give us a clear picture of the past of American welfare, from the points of view of people who were closest to it. American governments have been trying to help the needy among us for centuries. Rarely have Americans been satisfied with how that is done. Americans have argued and argued, as "Howard" and "Shepherd" Tom Hazard did. Americans have done the hard work of nursing and housekeeping, like "One-Eyed" Sarah and Lydia Bates did. Americans have both helped—and discriminated against—each other, as William Larned did. Americans have endured and struggled against the poor law, as William Fales and Cuff Roberts did. We continue to debate and do the important work of helping those in need. Knowing the experiences of those who debated government assistance to the poor in the past, along with those who experienced it and those who made it happen, can give us perspective and courage for the work that still needs to be done.

NOTES

1. On begging as a crime, see Select Committee on House of Industry, *Majority and Minority Reports of the Select Committee on House of Industry* (Providence: Knowles, Anthony & Co., City Printers, 1859), 4 (emphasis in original). On carrying wood back and forth, see "Franklin," *Letters to the Secretary of State [of New York] on the Subject of Pauperism* (n.p., 1853), 105. On the conflation of immigrants with paupers and on deportation, see Hirota, *Expelling the Poor*, chaps. 3, 7.
2. On poor relief during the Civil War, see Trattner, *From Poor Law to Welfare State*, 77; Loiacono, "Poverty and Citizenship in Rhode Island, 1780–1870," chap. 5; Green, *This Business of Relief*, chap. 4; and Paul D. Escott, "'The Cry of the Sufferers': The Problem of Welfare in the Confederacy," *Civil War History* 23:3 (September 1977), 228–240.
3. On Dorothea Dix and the bill to use federal lands to fund hospitals for the mentally ill, see Trattner, *From Poor Law to Welfare State*, 66–67 and Philip R. Popple, *Social Work Practice and Social Welfare Policy in the United States: A History* (New York: Oxford University Press, 2018), 138–139. On the Bureau of Refugees, Freedmen, and Abandoned Lands, see Eric Foner, *Reconstruction: America's Unfinished Revolution, 1863–1877* (New York: HarperCollins, 1988), 142–153. On soldier's pensions, see Theda Skocpol, *Protecting Soldiers and Mothers: The Political Origins of Social Policy in the United States* (Cambridge: Harvard University Press, 1992), chap. 2, especially page 132. On Confederate soldier pensions, see Kathleen Gorman, "Confederate Pensions as Southern Social Welfare," in Elna C. Green, Ed., *Before the New Deal: Social Welfare in the South, 1830–1930* (Athens: University of George Press, 1999), 24–39.
4. For Rhode Island examples, see Loiacono, "Poverty and Citizenship in Rhode Island, 1780–1870," chap. 6. On National Conference of Charities and Corrections, see John E. Hansan, "National Conference of Charities and Correction (1874–1917): Forerunner of the National Conference of Social Welfare" in Virginia Commonwealth University, *Social Welfare History Project*, online at <https://socialwelfare.library.vcu.edu/organizations/national-conference-of-charities-and-correction-the-beginning/>
5. William Dean Howells, "Tribulations of a Cheerful Giver," in *Impressions & Experiences* (New York: Harper & Brothers, 1896), 151.
6. Katz, *In the Shadow of the Poorhouse*, chap. 4. Abramovitz, *Regulating the Lives of Women*, chap. 5. Amy Dru Stanley, *From Bondage to Contract: Wage Labor, Marriage, and the Market in the Age of Slave Emancipation* (Cambridge, U.K.: Cambridge University Press, 1998), chap. 3.
7. Wagner, *The Poorhouse*. Popple, *Social Work Practice and Social Work Policy in the United States: A History*, 135. Trattner, *From Poor Law to Welfare State*, chap. 10. Abramovitz, *Regulating the Lives of Women*, chap. 6.
8. Alice Kessler-Harris, "The Uneasy Promise of the Welfare State," in Alice Kessler-Harris and Maurizio Vaudagna, Eds., *Democracy and the Welfare State: The Two Wests in the Age of Austerity* (New York: Columbia University Press, 2018), 1–26. David Garland, *The Welfare State: A Very Short Introduction* (New York: Oxford University Press, 2016), chaps. 1, 4. Abramovitz, *Regulating the Lives of Women*, 24.
9. Garland, *The Welfare State*, 6. While no one had the title social worker in the early 1800s, overseers of the poor had some of the responsibilities social workers have today, including checking on the well-being of children and the elderly in their

town, arranging for outdoor relief for the elderly, and separating children and their parents when they deemed it appropriate.

10. Katz, *In the Shadow of the Poorhouse*, 213–225.
11. Katz, *In the Shadow of the Poorhouse*, 227, 242–255. Ira Katznelson, *Fear Itself: The New Deal and the Origins of Our Time* (New York: W. W. Norton, 2013), chap. 5. Abramovitz, *Regulating the Lives of Women*, 195–196, 242–243.
12. Katz, *In the Shadow of the Poorhouse*, 254.
13. On the "three glorious decades," see Kessler-Harris, "The Uneasy Promise of the Welfare State," 9–10. On the continuing power of local officials, see Karen M. Tani, *States of Dependency: Welfare, Rights, and American Governance, 1935–1972* (Cambridge, U.K.: Cambridge University Press, 2016), chap. 1.
14. Joseph E. Paull, "Recipients Aroused: The New Welfare Rights Movement," *Social Work* 12 (April 1967): 101–106, reprinted in Gwendolyn Mink and Rickie Solinger, *Welfare: A Documentary History of U.S. Policy and Politics* (New York: New York University Press, 2003), 264–268. Annelise Orleck, *Storming Caesars Palace: How Black Mothers Fought Their Own War On Poverty* (Boston: Beacon Press, 2005). Wilson Sherwin and Frances Fox Piven, "The Radical Feminist Legacy of the National Welfare Rights Organization," *WSQ: Women's Studies Quarterly* 47:3 (2019), 135–153.
15. For Reagan's stump speech, see 15 February 1976 *New York Times*, 51. For a recent take on Linda Taylor, believed to be the actual "woman in Chicago," see Josh Levin, *The Queen: The Forgotten Life Behind an American Myth* (New York: Little, Brown and Company, 2019). On underemployment, see William Julius Wilson, *When Work Disappears: The World of the New Urban Poor* (New York: Alfred A. Knopf, 1996), 25–26. On Reagan-era cuts, see Katz, *In the Shadow of the Poorhouse*, 296–299
16. The Personal Responsibility and Work Opportunity Reconciliation Act is online at https://www.congress.gov/104/plaws/publ193/PLAW-104publ193.pdf. On George W. Bush, see April 30, 2002 "Fact Sheet: Compassionate Conservatism," archived at https://georgewbush-whitehouse.archives.gov/news/releases/2002/04/20020430.html.
17. Susannah Luthi, "Supreme Court Allows Trump to Enforce 'Public Charge' Immigration Rule," *Politico* 27 January 2020, online at https://www.politico.com/news/2020/01/27/supreme-court-enforce-trump-immigration-rule-106520

ACKNOWLEDGMENTS

This book is dedicated to Caroline Cox. Before her career at the University of the Pacific, she was a recent Ph.D., and adjunct lecturer, at UC Berkeley, where she taught me historiography of colonial North America and oversaw my senior thesis. Her warmth, generosity, and scholarly knowhow made a big difference to me. She is much missed. Also, readers will find her scholarship cited in chapter 2.

I would not know a thing about Lydia Bates if it were not for Andrew Smith, archivist at the Rhode Island Supreme Judicial Court Records Center. I was looking for something else when Smith put the Lydia Bates case file in front of me. In the years since, as he discovered two more case files related to Lydia Bates, he mailed me copies of each page! Likewise, I learned much about William Fales by reading the website constructed about the Portsmouth Asylum by the Raytheon Employees Wildlife Habitat Committee.

Archivists at the Rhode Island Historical Society have been really helpful to me over the years, during my visits and over email. Among them have been Jennifer Galpern, Dana Signe K. Munroe, Kirsten Hammerstrom, and J.D. Kay. I have also benefited from the help of librarians and archivists at the American Antiquarian Society, the Library Company of Philadelphia, the Massachusetts Historical Society, the Mystic Seaport Collections Research Center, the Providence City Archives, the Rhode Island Black Heritage Society, the Rhode Island Geneaological Society, and the Rhode Island State Archives. Clerks and Clerk's office staff in town halls or city halls in or near Rhode Island were also helpful, especially in Central Falls (for Smithfield Town Records); Coventry, Pawtucket (for North Providence Town Records); Providence; Portsmouth; Uxbridge (Massachusetts); and Westerly. Margaret M. Long and her staff at the Scituate Town Building were both encouraging and helped me find unusual sources.

Librarians at UW Oshkosh's Polk Library have been wonderful, tracking down books, sleuthing for illustrations, helping me with genealogy. Among them are Jennifer Bumann, Marisa Finkey, Sam Goldben, Ron Hardy, Erin McArthur, Ted Mulvey, Sarah Neises, Joe Pirillo, Susan Raasch, Joshua Ranger, Matthew Reinhardt, Lin Schrottky, and Laura Zirbel.

Colleagues at UW Oshkosh have also been wonderfully supportive of my book writing. From all over campus, whether in STEM or business, education or the humanities and social sciences, my fellow scholars have patiently listened, read, and offered constructive feedback. Two formal settings in which this happened were a Dean's Symposium, with the support of John Koker, and a Women's Studies Brown Bag, with the support of Christie Launius. One informal setting for this has been the Noontime Basketball Association. I especially wish to thank my current and former colleagues in the History Department: Franca Barricelli, Kevin Boylan, Christie Demosthenous, Lane Earns, James Frey, Andrea Jakobs, Ana Kapelusz-Poppi, Stephen Kercher, Michelle Kuhl, Karl Loewenstein, Michelle Mouton, Kay Nordhaus, Jeff Pickron, Susan Rensing, Kimberly Rivers, Tom Rowland, Mick Rutz, and Gina Schiavone. In the Department of Social Work, James Brown, Carol Collien, Audra Eggum, Colleen Hansen, Jon Hudson, Jeff Marks, Nikki Millerd, Renee Pasewald, Jim Power, Matthew Ringenberg, Mary Weeden, and Amy Fischer Williams have all, in different ways, helped me to understand what social work is today, and how it is—and is not—similar to the work of overseers of the poor two hundred years ago. Historians in other disciplines, including Jodi Eichler-Levine, Michael Jasinski, Timothy Paulsen, Matt Richie, Dave Siemers, Bob Stelzer, Nathan Stuart, and Paul Van Auken, have all listened to me talk about this book a lot. So have my co-workers in the University Studies Program: Mary Chapin, Sue Fojtik, Mike Lueder, Debbie Gray Patton, Ken Price, and Tracy Slagter.

Another way UW Oshkosh has made this book possible is through Faculty Development grants. These grants supported much of the research and writing that went into this book. I am grateful to the Faculty Development Board readers and administrators for all their work, especially Cindy Maas and the College of Letters and Science Dean's office: Franca Barricelli, John Koker, Colleen McDermott, Kim Rivers, Jane Luker, Samie Anderson, and Erin Heiling. National Endowment for the Humanities Summer Seminars were also a great help: "The Problem of Governance in the Early Republic" led by John Larson and Michael Morrison at the Library Company of Philadelphia in 2011 and "The American Maritime Commons" led by Glenn Gordinier and Eric Roorda at Mystic Seaport's Munson Institute in 2018. I read a lot, researched and wrote, and all in the company of wonderful colleagues and seminar leaders from a variety of disciplines.

Thanks to the *New England Quarterly* for permitting me to use material published as part of "William Larned, Overseer of the Poor: Power and Precariousness in the Early Republic." Then editor Linda Rhoads and reader Cornelia Hughes Dayton both made that work better. Thanks also to the institutions which allowed me to use their images as illustrations: the American Antiquarian Society, the Anne S. K. Brown Military Manuscripts Collection (at Brown University), the Internet Archives, the Peabody Essex Museum, the Providence City Archives, the Rhode Island Historical Society, the Rhode Island Supreme Judicial Court Records Center, and the Smithsonian American Art Museum.

I have really enjoyed working with Oxford University Press on this book. So many of my favorite books come from this publisher, and I am excited to see mine join that list. Andrew Dominello, Stefano Imbert, and Dana Bliss found great readers, explained things clearly to me, and helped me think about how to make a book useful to historians and social workers, among others. Prabha Karunakaran and Michael Stein both improved this book with their attention to detail.

The historians and other scholars who have helped me make this book better over the years are too many to list. I will try anyway, knowing that I am likely missing someone important. As conference commentators, co-panelists, panelists on another panel, colleagues at seminars, askers of questions, answerers of questions, conversation partners, or just plain great examples, you were all a help to me: Susan Brandt, Richard D. Brown, Erik Chaput, Mark Cheatham, Christy Clark-Pujara, Matthew Crow, Laurel Daen, Robin Einhorn, John Fea, Craig Friend, Mary Fuhrer, Elna C. Green, Hidetaka Hirota, Stephen Kantrowitz, Mark Kelley, Angela Keysor, Jessica Lepler, Ann Little, Shira Lurie, Daniel Mandell, Kya Mangum, Joanne Pope Melish, Chad Montrie, Katy Morris, Alyssa Penick, Sharon Romeo, Nicole Schroeder, Billy G. Smith, Elyssa Tardif, Katrina Thompson, Zoltán Vajda, Kyle Volk, Gabriella Vöő, David Wagner, Jamin Wells, Kanisorn Wongsrichanalai, Ronald J. Zboray, Mary Zboray, and the whole room at the December 2019 Massachusetts Historical Society Pauline Maier Early American History seminar. A few of you I have not properly met, but I thank you anyhow.

In addition to Caroline Cox, a number of mentors over the years have shown me how to be a researcher, a storyteller, a teacher, and an academic. These include my dissertation adviser, Jacqueline Jones, who provides a great model of big thinking and of how to shepherd students to successes. Chris Beneke's example and good humor helped me see how I could be a professor. Michael Willrich's freewheeling class discussions and high standards were vital for me. Jane Kamensky's interest in her students, sense of fun, and focus on narrative history writing have shaped much of my career. My graduate training was also shaped, in very positive ways, by Joan Bryant, Denise Holladay Damico, David Engerman, David Hackett Fischer, Mark Hulliung, Kevin Kenny, Fr. David Michael, Eric Schlereth, Lindsay Silver Cohen, and Will Walker. Prior to that, Elizabeth Boles's mentorship in Washington, D.C., changed my life. My colleagues—and the visitors—at the National Mall and Memorial Parks, especially Michael Kelly, helped me think about the big project of sharing stories about the past.

While there are many scholars and history-tellers whose research and storymaking I admire, Cornelia Hughes Dayton, Ruth Wallis Herndon, Joanne Pope Melish, and Seth Rockman all know a great deal about the subjects on which I focus in this book. Over years, each has been very generous with their time and thoughts. I have learned much from each of them.

Ruth Wallis Herndon is not only a world-class expert in this subject, but has also been a mentor to me ever since Jackie Jones suggested I ask Ruth to be an outside reader for my dissertation. Ruth has been generous with her knowledge, and encouraging. She is also one of the people who read a whole draft of the book. Her comments saved me from errors big and small, and pointed out historiography that was very valuable.

I also owe much to each scholar or editor who read the entire book in draft form: Dana Bliss, Richard D. Brown, Philip Popple, and Eric Schlereth. Likewise, colleagues who read chapters helped me improve it. They include Cordelia Bowlus, Vivian Bruce Conger, Karl Loewenstein, Kim Rivers, Tom Rowland, Dave Siemers, Julie Winch, and seven anonymous readers for Oxford University Press. I assigned draft chapters to many of my undergraduate students, especially in a readings course with Jennifer Depew, the upper division course "Early American Republic, 1787–1828, and a course co-created with medievalist Kim Rivers, "Charity and Memory in England and the U.S.A.: 1066–1966." Each reading helped me avoid inaccurate or infelicitous phrases, missing citations, and lapses in clarity, among other problems. Thank you each! Any remaining errors or clunkiness, self-indulgent writing, understandable mistakes, or stupid mistakes are mine.

Thanks to my family. Jon Loiacono, Patrice Thompson, and Joey Loiacono have encouraged me, read chapters, recommended readings, drawn pictures, and been willing to listen to a great deal of this history. István Jakobs, Lilla Jakobs-Németh, Lilla Jakobs, Katalin Kiss, Carl Thompson, and Cecile Thompson have all given me places to sleep and work while writing this book. Cecile Thompson and Vincent Thompson and family have all traveled to listen to me talk about this subject. It has been nice to share the experience of academia with Katie Brion and family. Izabella was writing her own first book as I wrote mine, reminding me to delight in the varieties of language and to include alternate perspectives. Zita kindly lent me her desk for a final stretch of writing and inspires me to remember thick description. Helena asks good questions, urging me to explain things clearly. Andrea Jakobs celebrated every research find, shouldered additional responsibilities, asked questions, listened, and read chapters at every stage. I cannot thank her enough.

I sent up a lot of prayers over the years I was working on this book. I am pretty sure you were listening. Thanks for that and so much more.

Finally, thank you, dear reader, for giving these stories a read.

BIBLIOGRAPHY

PRIMARY SOURCES
Manuscript Primary Sources
Abbreviations

PCHA   Providence City Hall Archives, Providence, Rhode Island
RIHS   Rhode Island Historical Society, Providence, Rhode Island
RISJCRC   Rhode Island Supreme Judicial Court Records Center, Pawtucket,
          Rhode Island

Coventry, Town of. Land Records: Grantees Volumes 11, 13. Coventry Town Hall.
     Coventry, Rhode Island.
Coventry, Town of. Coventry Town Council Minutes 1805–1818. Coventry Town Hall.
     Coventry, Rhode Island.
Cranston, Town of. Cranston Town Records. MSS 193. RIHS.
Larned, Samuel. Samuel Larned Papers. MSS 81, Series 2. RIHS.
North Providence, Town of. North Providence Town Council and Probate Minutes.
     Pawtucket City Hall. Pawtucket, Rhode Island.
Portsmouth, Town of. Portsmouth Town Meeting Minutes. Portsmouth Town Hall.
     Portsmouth, Rhode Island.
Providence, Town of. Probate Records. PCHA.
Providence, Town of. Town Council Minutes. PCHA. *These minutes are more edited, final
     draft versions of the minutes, as noted in Herndon, "On and Off the Record."*
Providence, Town of. Town Council Minutes. MSS 214 sg 9. RIHS *These minutes seem
     to be the first draft of the minutes, as noted in Herndon, "On and Off the Record."*
Providence, Town of. Town Meeting Minutes. PCHA.
Providence, Town of. Providence Town Papers. MSS 214 sg 1, Series 3. RIHS.
Providence, Town of. Town Tax. MSS 214 sg 10. RIHS.
Revolutionary War Military Records. MSS 673 sg 2, Series 1, Sub-series A, Box 1, RIHS.
Rhode Island Supreme Judicial Court. Case File "Scituate v. Thomas T. Hill," September
     Term 1820. RISJCRC.
Rhode Island Supreme Judicial Court. Case File "Thomas T. Hill v. Overseers of the
     Poor of Scituate," March Term 1823. RISJCRC.
Rhode Island Supreme Judicial Court. Case File "Thomas T. Hill v. Overseers of the
     Poor of Scituate," September Term 1823. RISJCRC.
Rhode Island Supreme Judicial Court. Records Book Supreme Judicial Court No.
     8 1815–1821, Records Book Supreme Judicial Court. . . Book 9 Sept. 1819.
     RISJCRC.

Rhode Island Supreme Judicial Court. "State vs. Israel Phillips et al." In Superior Court Record Book No. 10 (September Term 1827). RISJCRC.

Scituate, Town of. Manuscript Back Pages of *Acts and Laws of the English Colony of Rhode-Island and Providence Plantations in New-England in America.* Newport: Samuel Hall, 1767. Scituate Town Archives. Scituate Town Building. Scituate, Rhode Island.

Scituate, Town of. Scituate Town Council Book. Scituate Archives. Scituate Town Building, Scituate, Rhode Island.

Scituate, Town of. Scituate Town Records. MSS 216. RIHS.

Smithfield, Town of. Council and Probate Journal Volume 3 1797–1822 Part 2 Smithfield. Central Falls City Hall, Central Falls, Rhode Island.

Smithfield, Town of. Probate Records Volume 3 1797–1819 Smithfield. Central Falls City Hall, Central Falls, Rhode Island.

Published Primary Sources:

Broadside: *Schedule of the Expences of the Town . . . from August 1, 1799 to August 1, 1800.* Providence, RI: Carter, 1800.

Hard=Scrabble Calendar, Report of the Trials of Oliver Cummins [et al] . . . . Providence: Printed for the Purchaser, 1824.

In Memory of Edwin Channing Larned. Chicago: A.C. McClurg & Co., 1886.

The Providence Directory. Providence: Brown and Danforth, 1824.

The Rhode-Island Clerk's Magazine or Civil Officer's Assistant. Providence: Printed by Nathaniel Heaton, Jun., For Henry Cushing, 1803.

Arnold, James Newell. *Rhode Island Vital Extracts, 1636–1850,* 21 volumes. Providence: Narragansett Historical Publishing Company, 1891–1912.

Bartlett, John R. *Census of the Inhabitants of the Colony of Rhode Island and Providence Plantations . . . 1774.* Providence: Knowles, Anthony & Co., 1858.

Bartlett, John. *Records of the State of Rhode Island and Providence Plantations in New England* Volume X, *1784 to 1792.* Providence: Providence Press Company, 1865.

Bureau of the Census. *Heads of Families at the First Census of the United States Taken in the Year 1790 Rhode Island.* Washington, DC: Government Printing Office, 1908. Accessed digitally at https://www2.census.gov/library/publications/decennial/1790/heads_of_families/rhode_island/1790j-02.pdf

Bureau of the Census. Reproductions of Manuscript Census Returns for Censuses of 1790, 1800, 1810, 1820, 1830, 1840, 1850. Accessed digitally via Ancestry.com. Provo: Ancestry.com Operations, Inc., 2010. Images reproduced by FamilySearch.

Bureau of the Census. *Return of the Whole Number of Persons. . . According to "An Act. . . " Passed March the First, One Thousand Seven Hundred and Ninety-One.* Philadelphia: N.P., 1793. Accessed digitally at https://www.census.gov/library/publications/1793/dec/number-of-persons.html.

Bureau of the Census. *Return of the Whole Number of Persons . . . According to . . . the second Census . . . of the United States.* Washington, DC: House of Representatives, 1801. Accessed digitally at https://www2.census.gov/prod2/decennial/documents/1800-return-whole-number-of-persons.pdf.

Bray, Robert C. and Paul E. Bushnell, Eds. *Diary of a Common Soldier in the American Revolution, 1775–1783: An Annotated Edition of the Military Journal of Jeremiah Greenman.* DeKalb: North Illinois University Press, 1978.

Brown, William J. *The Life of William J. Brown of Providence, Rhode Island.* Freeport, NY: Books for Libraries Press, 1971.

Brown, William J. *The Life of William J. Brown of Providence, R.I.*, edited by Joanne Pope Melish with a foreword by Rosalind Wiggins. Durham: University of New Hampshire Press, 2006.

Cushing, John D., Ed. *The First Laws of the State of Rhode Island*. Wilmington: Michael Glazier, Inc., 1983.

Fales, William R. *Memoir of William R. Fales, The Portsmouth Cripple*, Edited by S.H.L. Philadelphia: Lindsay & Blakiston, 1851.

Forbes, John, Alexander Tweedie, and John Connolly. *The Cyclopaedia of Practical Medicine*, Volume I. London: Sherwood, Gilbert, and Piper, and Baldwin and Cradock; Whitaker, Treacher, and Co., 1833.

"Franklin." *Letters to the Secretary of State [of New York] on the Subject of Pauperism*. N.P.: 1853.

Hazard, Thomas R. *Report on the Poor and Insane in Rhode-Island; Made to the General Assembly at Its January Session, 1851*. Providence: Joseph Knowles, State Printer, 1851.

Howells, William Dean. "Tribulations of a Cheerful Giver." In *Impressions & Experiences*. New York: Harper & Brothers, 1896.

Humphrey, Heman. *Miscellaneous Discourses and Reviews*. Amherst: J.S. and C. Adams, 1834.

MacGunnigle, Bruce C., Ed. *Regimental Book Rhode Island Regiment for 1781 &c*. East Greenwich: Rhode Island Society of the Sons of the American Revolution, 2011.

Mathew, Linda L., Ed. "Gleanings from Rhode Island Town Records: Providence Town Council Records, 1789–1801." In *Rhode Island Roots: Journal of the Rhode Island Geneaological Society*. Special Bonus Issue. April, 2007.

Rhode Island. *Public Laws of the State of Rhode Island and Providence Plantations*. Providence: Knowles and Vose, 1844.

Rhode Island Historical Society Librarian. *The Early Records of the Town of Portsmouth*. Providence: E.L. Freeman and Sons, 1901.

Rider, Sidney S. *Rhode Island Historical Tracts No. 10 An Historical Inquiry Concerning the Attempt to Raise a Regiment of Slaves in Rhode Island*. Providence: Providence Press Company, 1880.

Rockman, Seth. Ed. *Welfare Reform in the Early Republic: A Brief History with Documents*. Boston: Bedford/St. Martin's, 2003.

Secretary of State of Rhode Island. Digital Archives. https://sosri.access.preservica. com/home/.

Select Committee on House of Industry. *Majority and Minority Reports of the Select Committee on House of Industry*. Providence: Knowles, Anthony & Co., City Printers, 1859.

U.S. War Department. *Revolutionary War Pension and Bounty-Land Application Files*. National Archives. Microfilm.

U.S. War Department. *Revolutionary War Pension and Bounty-Land Warrant Application Files, 1800–1900*. Database online. Provo, UT: Ancestry.com Operations, Inc., 2010.

U.S. War Department. *Revolutionary War Rolls, 1775–1783*. Record Group 93. National Archives Microfilm Public M246. Database online. Provo, UT: Ancestry.com Operations, Inc., 2010.

Whipple, Frances Harriet, and Elleanor Eldridge. *Memoirs of Elleanor Eldridge*. Edited by Joycelyn K. Moody (Morgantown: West Virginia University Press, 2014).

Newspapers

Cadet and Statesman (Providence)
Columbian Phenix or Providence Patriot
The Columbian (New York)
Daily Advertiser (New York)
Impartial Observer (Providence)
Manufacturers' and Farmers' Journal (Providence)
Newport Mercury
New York Times
Providence Beacon
Providence Gazette and Country Journal
Providence Phoenix
Rhode Island American (Providence)
Rhode Island Republican (Newport)
United States Chronicle. (Providence)
I am grateful for access to the Readex *Early American Newspapers* database and Proquest *Historical New York Times* database for access to most of the newspapers mentioned above.

SECONDARY SOURCES

Abramovitz, Mimi. *Regulating the Lives of Women: Social Welfare Policy from Colonial Times to the Present.* Third Edition. New York: Routledge, 2018.

African Origins Project. *Voyages: The Trans-Atlantic Slave Trade Database. Online at slavevoyages.org.*

Balogh, Brian. *A Government Out of Sight: The Mystery of National Authority in Nineteenth-Century America.* Cambridge, U.K.: Cambridge University Press, 2009.

Baumgarten, Linda. *What Clothes Reveal: The Language of Clothing in Colonial and Federal America.* Williamsburg: Colonial Williamsburg Foundation, 2002.

Benes, Peter, Ed. *Life on the Streets and Commons, 1600 to the Present.* The Dublin Seminar for New England Folklife Annual Proceedings 2005. Boston: Boston University, 2007.

Blackie, Daniel. "Disability, Dependency, and the Family in the Early United States." In Michael A. Rembis and Susan Burch, Eds. *Disability Histories.* Urbana, Illinois: University of Illinois Press, 2014.

Bond, Edward L. "The Parish in Colonial Virginia." *Encyclopedia Virginia.* Available at <https://www.encyclopediavirginia.org/parish_in_colonial_virginia_the# start_entry>.

Brekke, Linzy A. "The 'Scourge of Fashion': Political Economy and the Politics of Consumption in the Early Republic." *Early American Studies* 3:1 (Spring 2005): 111–139.

Brown, Richard D. "Microhistory and the Post-Modern Challenge." In Hans Renders and Binne De Haan, Eds., *Theoretical Discussions of Biography: Approaches from History, Microhistory, and Life Writing,* Boston: Brill, 2014.

Brown, Richard D. *Revolutionary Politics in Massachusetts: The Boston Committee of Correspondence and the Towns, 1772–1774.* Cambridge, MA: Harvard University Press, 1970.

Brown, Irene Quenzler, and Richard D. Brown. *The Hanging of Ephraim Wheeler.* Cambridge, MA: Belknap Press, 2003.

Bourque, Monique. "Populating the Poorhouse: A Reassessment of Poor Relief in the Antebellum Delaware Valley." *Pennsylvania History: A Journal of Mid-Atlantic Studies* 70:4 (2003): 397–432.

Bourque, Monique. "Women and Work in the Philadelphia Almshouse, 1790–1840." *Journal of the Early Republic* 32:3 (Fall 2012): 383–414.

Cassedy, James H. *Medicine in America: A Short History*. Baltimore: Johns Hopkins University Press, 1991.

Ceppi, Elisabeth. *Invisible Masters: Gender, Race, and the Economy of Service in Early New England*. Hanover: Dartmouth College Press, 2018.

Chace, Henry Richmond. *Owners and Occupants of the Lots, Houses, and Shops in the Town of Providence, Rhode Island, in 1798*. Providence: Livermore & Knight, 1914.

Chambers, Clarke A. "Toward a Redefinition of Welfare History." *Journal of American History* 73:2 (September 1986): 407–433.

Clark-Pujara, Christy. *Dark Work: The Business of Slavery in Rhode Island*. New York: New York University Press, 2016.

Cobbett, William. *A Protestant Reformation in England and Ireland*. Charlotte: TAN Books, 2012. Originally Published in 1824 by London Charles Clement.

Conley, Patrick T. *The Makers of Modern Rhode Island*. Charleston: The History Press, 2012.

Conn, Steven, Ed. *To Promote the General Welfare: The Case for Big Government*. New York: Oxford University Press, 2012.

Cook, Edward M., Jr. *The Fathers of the Towns: Leadership and Community Structure in Eighteenth-Century New England*. Baltimore: Johns Hopkins University Press, 1976.

Coughtry, Jay. *Creative Survival: The Providence Black Community in the 19th Century*. Rhode Island Black Heritage Society, n.d.

Cox, Caroline. *Boy Soldiers of the American Revolution*. Chapel Hill: University of North Carolina Press, 2016.

Cox, Caroline. *A Proper Sense of Honor: Service and Sacrifice in George Washington's Army*. Chapel Hill: University of North Carolina, 2004.

Cray, Robert E., Jr. *Paupers and Poor Relief in New York City and Its Rural Environs, 1700–1830*. Philadelphia: Temple University Press, 1988.

Creech, Margaret. *Three Centuries of Poor Law Administration: A Study of Legislation in Rhode Island*. Chicago: University of Chicago Press, 1936.

Crouch, John. *Providence Newspapers and the Racist Riots of 1824 and 1831*. Providence: Cornerstone Books, 1999.

Daen, Laurel. "Revolutionary War Invalid Pensions and the Bureaucratic Language of Disability in the Early Republic." *Early American Literature* 52:1 (2017): 141–167.

Daen Laurel. "'To Board & Nurse a Stranger': Poverty, Disability, and Community in Eighteenth-Century Massachusetts." *Journal of Social History* 53:3 (Spring 2020): 1–26.

Danbom, David B. *Born in the Country: A History of Rural America*. Baltimore: Johns Hopkins University Press, 1995.

Daniels, Bruce C. "Poor Relief, Local Finance, and Town Government in Eighteenth-Century Rhode Island." *Rhode Island History* 40:3 (Aug. 1981): 75–87.

Davis, Natalie Zemon. *Women on the Margins: Three Seventeenth-Century Lives*. Cambridge, MA: Harvard University Press, 1995.

Dayton, Cornelia Hughes. "Rethinking Agency, Recovering Voices." *The American Historical Review* 109:3 (June 2004): 827–843.

Dayton, Cornelia Hughes. *Women before the Bar: Gender, Law, & Society in Connecticut, 1639–1789*. Chapel Hill: Institute of Early American History and Culture / University of North Carolina Press, 1995.

Dayton, Cornelia H. and Sharon V. Salinger. *Robert Love's Warnings: Searching for Strangers in Colonial Boston*. Philadelphia: University of Pennsylvania Press, 2014.

Demos, John. *The Unredeemed Captive: A Family Story from Early America*. New York: Vintage Books, 1995.

Desmond, Matthew. *Evicted: Poverty and Profit in the American City*. New York: Penguin Random House, 2016.

Doughton, Thomas L. "Unseen Neighbors: Native Americans of Central Massachusetts, A People Who Had 'Vanished'." In Colin G. Calloway, Ed. *After King Philip's War: Presence and Persistence in Indian New England*. Hanover, NH: Dartmouth University, 1997.

Dupre, Daniel. "The Panic of 1819 and the Political Economy of Sectionalism." In Cathy Matson, Ed. *The Economy of Early America: Historical Perspectives & New Directions*. University Park: Pennsylvania State University Press, 2005.

Einhorn, Robin. *American Taxation American Slavery*. Chicago: University of Chicago Press, 2006.

Englander, David. *Poverty and Poor Law Reform in 19th Century Britain, 1834–1914*. New York: Longman, 1998.

Escott, Paul D. "'The Cry of the Sufferers': The Problem of Welfare in the Confederacy." *Civil War History* 23:3 (Sept. 1977): 228–240.

Fenn, Elizabeth A. *Pox Americana: The Great Smallpox Epidemic of 1775–82*. New York: Hill and Wang, 2001.

Ferraro, William Michael. "Lives of Quiet Desperation: Community and Polity in New England Over Four Centuries: The Cases of Portsmouth and Foster, Rhode Island." PhD diss., Brown University, 1991.

Fideler, Paul A. *Social Welfare in Pre-Industrial England*. New York: Palgrave Macmillan, 2006.

Foner, Eric. *Reconstruction: America's Unfinished Revolution, 1863–1877*. New York: HarperCollins, 1988.

Freeman, Joanne B. *Affairs of Honor: National Politics in the New Republic*. New Haven: Yale University Press, 2001.

Frey, Sylvia R. *Water from the Rock: Black Resistance in a Revolutionary Age*. Princeton: Princeton University Press, 1991.

Friedman, Lawrence J., and Mark D. McGarvie, Eds. *Charity, Philanthropy, and Civility in American History*. Cambridge, U.K.: Cambridge University Press, 2003.

Garland, David. *The Welfare State: A Very Short Introduction*. New York: Oxford University Press, 2016.

Geake, Robert A., and Lorén M. Spears. *From Slaves to Soldiers: The First Rhode Island Regiment in the American Revolution*. Yardley: Westholme, 2016.

Gerstle, Gary. *Liberty and Coercion: The Paradox of American Government from the Founding to the Present*. Princeton: Princeton University Press, 2015.

Gerzina, Gretchen. *Mr. and Mrs. Prince: How an Extraordinary Eighteenth-Century Family Moved out of Slavery and Into Legend*. New York: Amistad, 2009.

Ginzburg, Carlo. "Microhistory: Two or Three Things That I Know About It." In Hans Renders and Binne De Haan, Eds. *Theoretical Discussions of Biography: Approaches from History, Microhistory, and Life Writing*. Boston: Brill, 2014.

Goldberg, Chad Alan. *Citizens and Paupers: Relief, Rights, and Race, from the Freedmen's Bureau to Workfare*. Chicago: University of Chicago Press, 2007.

Gordon, Linda. *Pitied But Not Entitled: Single Mothers and the History of Welfare, 1890–1935*. New York: Free Press, 1994.

Gordon, Linda. "Who Deserves Help? Who Must Provide?" *Annals of the American Academy of Political and Social Science* 577 (2001): 12–25.

Gorman, Kathleen. "Confederate Pensions as Southern Social Welfare." In Elna C. Green, Ed. *Before the New Deal: Social Welfare in the South, 1830–1930*. Athens: University of George Press, 1999.

Grandchamp, Robert. "'I have never heard of him since'—The Case of Scituate's James A. Matteson." *Small State Big History: The Online Review of Rhode Island History*. Online at http://smallstatebighistory.com/never-heard-since-case-scituates-james-matteson/.

Green, Elna C. *This Business of Relief: Confronting Poverty in a Southern City, 1740–1940*. Athens: University of Georgia Press, 2003.

Green, Shirley. "Freeborn Men of Color: The Franck Brothers in Revolutionary North America, 1755–1820." Ph.D diss., Bowling Green State University, 2011.

Grigg, Susan. "The Dependent Poor of Newburyport, 1800-1830." Ph.D diss., University of Wisconsin Madison, 1978.

Hamilton, Cynthia S. "Spreading the Word: The American Tract Society, *The Dairyman's Daughter*, and Mass Publishing." *Book History* 14 (2011): 25–57.

Hansan, John E. "National Conference of Charities and Correction (1874–1917): Forerunner of the National Conference of Social Welfare." In Virginia Commonwealth University, *Social Welfare History Project*. Online at <https://socialwelfare.library.vcu.edu/organizations/national-conference-of-charities-and-correction-the-beginning/>Hardesty, Ross. *Unfreedom: Slavery and Dependence in Eighteenth-Century Boston*. New York: New York University Press, 2016.

Haulman, Kate. *Politics of Fashion in Eighteenth-Century America*. Chapel Hill: University of North Carolina Press, 2011.

Hawke, David Freeman. *Everyday Life in Early America*. New York: Harper Perennial, 1989.

Henretta, James A. "The War for Independence and American Development." In Ronald Hoffman, John J. McCusker, Russel R. Menard, and Peter J. Albert, Eds., *The Economy of Early America: The Revolutionary Period, 1763–1790*. Charlottesville: United States Capitol Historical Society / University of Virginia, 1988.

Herndon, Ruth Wallis. "On and Off the Record: Town Clerks as Interpreters of Rhode Island History." *Rhode Island History* 50:4 (1992): 103–115.

Herndon, Ruth Wallis. *Unwelcome Americans: Living on the Margin in Early New England*. Philadelphia: University of Pennsylvania Press, 2001.

Herndon, Ruth Wallis. "Women as Symbols of Disorder in Early Rhode Island." In Tamara L. Hunt and Micheline R. Lessard, Eds., *Women and the Colonial Gaze*. New York: New York University, 2002.

Herndon, Ruth Wallis. "'Who Died an Expence to This Town': Poor Relief in Eighteenth-Century Rhode Island." In Billy G. Smith, Ed. *Down and Out in Early America*. University Park: Pennsylvania State University Press, 2004.

Herndon, Ruth Wallis. "Poor Women and the Boston Almshouse in the Early Republic," *Journal of the Early Republic* 32:3 (Fall 2012): 349–382.

Herndon, Ruth Wallis, and John E. Murray, Eds. *Children Bound To Labor: The Pauper Apprentice System in Early America*. Ithaca: Cornell University Press, 2009.

Herndon, Ruth Wallis, and Ella Wilcox Sekatau. "The Right to a Name: The Narragansett People and Rhode Island Officials in the Revolutionary Era." *Ethnohistory* 44:3 (Summer 1997): 433–462.

Herndon, Ruth Wallis, and Ella Wilcox Sekatau. "Colonizing the Children: Indian Youngsters in Servitude in Early Rhode Island." In Colin G. Calloway and Neal Salisbury, Eds., *Reinterpreting New England Indians and the Colonial Experience*. Boston: Colonial Society of Massachusetts, 2003, 137–173.

Himmelfarb, Gertrude. *The Idea of Poverty: England in the Early Industrial Age*. New York: Alfred A Knopf, 1984.

Hindle, Steve. *On the Parish? The Micro-Politics of Poor Relief in Rural England c. 1550–1750*. New York: Oxford University Press, 2004.

Hirota, Hidetaka. *Expelling the Poor: Atlantic Seaboard States & the 19th-Century Origins of American Immigration Policy*. New York: Oxford University Press, 2017.

Hitchcock, Tim. *Down and Out in Eighteenth-Century London*. London: Bloomsbury Publishing, 2005.

Holcombe, Randall G. and Donald J. Lacombe. "The Growth of Local Government in the United States from 1820 to 1870." *The Journal of Economic History* 61:1 (Mar 2001): 184–189.

Hurd, Henry M., et al. *The Institutional Care of the Insane in the United States and Canada*. Volume 3. Baltimore: Johns Hopkins Press, 1916.

Innes, Stephen. Ed. *Work and Labor in Early America*. Chapel Hill: Institute of Early American History and Culture, 1988.

James, Eugenia Learned. *The Learned Family in America, 1630–1967*. N.P.: Setco Printing Co., 1967.

Jensen, John. "Before the Surgeon General: Marine Hospitals in Mid-19th-Century America." *Public Health Reports* 112:6 (1997): 525–527.

Jones, Jacqueline. *American Work: Four Centuries of Black and White Labor*. New York: W.W. Norton & Company, 1998.

Jones, Jacqueline. *A Dreadful Deceit: The Myth of Race from the Colonial Era to Obama's America*. New York: Basic Books, 2013.

Jones, Martha S. *Birthright Citizens: A History of Race and Rights in Antebellum America*. Cambridge, U.K.: Cambridge University Press, 2018.

Journal of the Early Republic. Roundtable: "Poor Women." *Journal of the Early Republic* 32:3 (Fall 2012): 331–492.

Journal of the Early Republic. Roundtable: "Taking Stock of the State in Nineteenth-Century America." *Journal of the Early Republic* 38:1 (Spring 2018): 61–118.

Kamensky, Jane. *The Exchange Artist: A Tale of High-Flying Speculation and America's First Banking Collapse*. New York: Viking, 2008.

Katz, Michael B. *In the Shadow of the Poorhouse: A Social History of Welfare in America*. Tenth Anniversary Edition. New York: BasicBooks, 1996.

Katz, Michael B. Ed. *The "Underclass" Debate: Views from History*. Princeton: Princeton University Press, 1993.

Katznelson, Ira. *Fear Itself: The New Deal and the Origins of Our Time*. New York: W. W. Norton, 2013.

Kessler-Harris, Alice, and Maurizio Vaudagna, Eds. *Democracy and the Welfare State: The Two Wests in the Age of Austerity*. New York: Columbia University Press, 2018.

King, Steven. *Sickness, Medical Welfare and the English Poor 1750–1834*. Manchester: Manchester University Press, 2018.

Kudlick, Catherine J. "Disability History: Why We Need Another 'Other'." *The American Historical Review* 108:3 (June 2003): 763–793.

Larkin, Jack. *The Reshaping of Everyday Life, 1790–1840*. New York: Harper Perennial, 1989.

Learned, William Law. *The Learned Family*. Albany: Weed-Parsons Printing Company, 1898.

Legler, John B., Richard Sylla, and John J. Wallis. "U.S. City Finances and the Growth of Government, 1850–1902." *The Journal of Economic History* 48:2 (1988): 347–356.

Lemons, J. Stanley. *Retracing Baptists in Rhode Island: Identity, Formation, and History*. Waco: Baylor University Press, 2019.

Lepler, Jessica M. "Introduction: The Panic of 1819 by Any Other Name." *Journal of the Early Republic* 40:4 (Winter 2020): 665–670.

Lepore, Jill. "Historians Who Love Too Much: Reflections on Biography and Microhistory." *Journal of American History* 88:1 (June 2001): 129–144.

Levin, Josh. *The Queen: The Forgotten Life Behind an American Myth*. New York: Little, Brown and Company, 2019.

Levy, Barry. "Rediscovering the Lost City of American Welfare." *Reviews in American History* 38:3 (September 2010): 414–419.

Levy, Barry. *Town Born: The Political Economy in New England from its Founding to the Revolution*. Philadelphia: University of Pennsylvania Press, 2011.

Lockley, Timothy James. *Welfare and Charity in the Antebellum South*. Gainesville: University Press of Florida, 2007.

Loiacono, Gabriel "Economy and Isolation in Rhode Island Poorhouses, 1820–1850." *Rhode Island History* 65:2 (Summer 2007): 31–47.

Loiacono, Gabriel. "Poor Laws and the Construction of Race in Early Republican Providence, Rhode Island." *Journal of Policy History* 25:2 (2013): 264–287.

Loiacono, Gabriel. "Poverty and Citizenship in Rhode Island, 1780–1870." PhD diss., Brandeis University, 2008.

Loiacono. Gabriel "William Larned, Overseer of the Poor: Power and Precariousness in the Early Republic." *New England Quarterly* 88:2 (June 2015): 223–251.

Magnússon, Sigurður G. and István M. Szijártó. *What is Microhistory? Theory and Practice* New York: Routledge, 2013.

Mandell, Daniel. *Tribe, Race, History: Native Americans in Southern New England, 1780–1880*. Baltimore: Johns Hopkins University Press, 2008.

Marks, Rachel. "The Published Writings of Edith Abbott: A Bibliography." *Social Service Review* 32:1 (March 1958): 51–56.

Mays, Dorothy A. *Women in Early America: Struggle, Survival, and Freedom in a New World*. Santa Barbara: ABC-CLIO, 2004.

McBridge, Bunny and Harald E. L. Prins. "Walking the Medicine Line: Molly Ockett, a Pigwacket Doctor." In Robert S, Ed. Grumet, *Northeastern Indian Lives, 1632–1816* Amherst: University of Massachusetts Press, 1996.

McCarthy, Kathleen D. *American Creed: Philanthropy and the Rise of Civil Society, 1700–1865*. Chicago: University of Chicago Press, 2003.

McDonnell, Michael A., and Briony Neilson. "Reclaiming a Revolutionary Past: War Veterans, Pensions, and the Struggle for Recognition." *Journal Of The Early Republic* 39:3 (2019): 467–501.

McKee, Christopher. *Ungentle Goodnights: Life in a Home for Elderly and Disabled Naval Sailors and Marines and the Perilous Seafaring Careers That Brought Them There*. Annapolis: Naval Institute Press, 2018.

Measuring Worth Foundation, "Purchasing Power Today of a US Dollar Transaction in the Past." Online at https://www.measuringworth.com/calculators/ppowerus/index2.php.

Melish, Joanne Pope. *Disowning Slavery: Gradual Emancipation and "Race" in New England, 1780–1860*. Ithaca: Cornell University Press, 1998.

Melish, Joanne Pope. "Introduction." In *The Life of William J. Brown of Providence, R.I.*, edited by Rosalind C. Wiggins and Joanne Pope Melish. Durham: University of New Hampshire Press, 2006.

Melish, Joanne Pope. "The Racial Vernacular: Contesting the Black/White Binary in Nineteenth-Century Rhode Island." In James T. Campbell, Matthew Pratt Guterl, and Robert G. Lee, Eds., *Race, Nation, and Empire in American History*. Chapel Hill, University of North Carolina Press, 2007.

Melish, Joanne Pope. "The Manumission of Nab." *Rhode Island History* 68:1 (Winter/Spring 2010), 37–43.

Middlekauf, Robert. *The Glorious Cause: The American Revolution, 1763–1789*. New York: Oxford University Press, 1982.

Middleton, Simon and Billy G. Smith. "Class and Early America: An Introduction." *William and Mary Quarterly* 63:2 (Apr. 2006): 211–220.

Middleton, Simon, and Billy G. Smith, Eds. *Class Matters: Early North America and the Atlantic World*. Philadelphia: University of Pennsylvania Press, 2008.

Middleton, Stephen. *The Black Laws: Race and the Legal Process in Early Ohio*. Athens: Ohio University Press, 2005.

Mink, Gwendolyn. *Welfare's End*. Ithaca: Cornell University Press, 1998.

Mink, Gwendolyn and Rickie Solinger. *Welfare: A Documentary History of U.S. Policy and Politics*. New York: New York University Press, 2003.

Mohl, Raymond. *Poverty in New York, 1783–1825*. New York: Oxford University Press, 1971.

Nash, Gary. "Poverty and Politics in Early American History." In Billy G. Smith, Ed. *Down and Out in Early America*. University Park: Pennsylvania State University Press, 2004: 1–40.

Nash, Gary. *The Forgotten Fifth: African Americans in the Age of Revolution*. Cambridge, MA: Harvard University Press, 2006.

Nicolosi, Anthony S. "The Newport Asylum for the Poor: A Successful Nineteenth-Century Institutional Response to Social Dependency." *Rhode Island History* 47:1 (Winter 1989).

Novak, William J. "The Legal Transformation of Citizenship in Nineteenth-Century America." In Meg Jacobs, William Novak, and Julian Zelizer, *The Democratic Experiment: New Directions American Political History*. Princeton, NJ: Princeton University Press, 2003.

Novak, William J. "The Myth of the 'Weak' American State." *American Historical Review* 113:3 (June 2008): 752–772.

O'Brassil-Kulfan, Kristin. *Vagrants and Vagabonds: Poverty and Mobility in the Early Republic*. New York: New York University Press, 2019.

O'Brien, Jean M. "'Divorced' from the Land: Resistance and Survival of Indian Women in Eighteenth-Century New England." In Colin G. Calloway, Ed. *After King Philip's War: Presence and Persistence in Indian New England*. Hanover, NH.: Dartmouth University, 1997.

O'Malley, Gregory E. "Beyond the Middle Passage: Slave Migration from the Caribbean to North America, 1619–1807." *The William and Mary Quarterly* 66:1 (January 2009): 125–172.

O'Malley, Gregory E. "Balancing the Empirical and the Humane in Slave Trade Studies." *Uncommon Sense—The Blog of the Omohundro Institute of Early American History*

& *Culture* (January 2015). Online at https://blog.oieahc.wm.edu/balancing-the-empirical-and-the-humane-in-slave-trade-studies/./

Orleck, Annelise. *Storming Caesars Palace: How Black Mothers Fought Their Own War On Poverty*. Boston: Beacon Press, 2005.

Pagan, John Ruston. *Anne Orthwood's Bastard: Sex and Law in Early Virginia*. New York: Oxford University Press, 2003.

Parascandola, John. *Sex, Sin, and Science: A History of Syphilis in America*. Westport: Praeger, 2008.

Parker, Kunal. *Making Foreigners: Immigration and Citizenship Law in America, 1600–2000*. Cambridge, U.K.: Cambridge University Press, 2015.

Parrillo, Nicholas. *Against the Profit Motive: The Salary Revolution in American Government 1780-1940*. New Haven: Yale University Press, 2013.

Patterson, James T. "America's 'Underclasses,' Past and Present: A Historical Perspective." *Proceedings of the American Philosophical Society* 141:1 (Mar. 1997): 13–29.

Paull, Joseph E. "Recipients Aroused: The New Welfare Rights Movement," *Social Work* 12 (April 1967): 101–106. Reprinted in Gwendolyn Mink and Rickie Solinger, *Welfare: A Documentary History of U.S. Policy and Politics*. New York: New York University Press, 2003.

Peltonen, Matti. "What is Micro in Microhistory?" In Hans Renders and Binne De Haan, Eds. *Theoretical Discussions of Biography: Approaches from History, Microhistory, and Life Writing*. Boston: Brill, 2014.

Pestana, Carla Gardina, and Sharon V. Salinger, Eds. *Inequality in Early America*. Hanover: Dartmouth College, 1999.

Pierce, John T., Sr., Ed. *Historical Tracts of the Town of Portsmouth, Rhode Island*. Hamilton Print Co., 1991.

Pimpare, Stephen. "Toward a New Welfare History." *Journal of Policy History* 19:2 (2007): 234–252.

Pimpare, Stephen. *A People's History of Poverty in America*. New York: The New Press, 2008.

Piven, Frances Fox, and Richard A. Cloward. *Regulating the Poor: The Functions of Public Welfare*. Updated Edition. New York: Vintage, 1993.

Polta, Andrew T. "Disorderly House Keepers: Poor Women in Providence, Rhode Island, 1781–1832." Master's Thesis, University of Rhode Island, 2018.

Popek, Daniel M. *They " . . . fought bravely, but were unfortunate:" The True Story of Rhode Island's "Black Regiment" and the Failure of Segregation in Rhode Island's Continental Line*. Bloomington, Indiana: AuthorHouse, 2015.

Popple, Philip R. *Social Work Practice and Social Welfare Policy in the United States: A History*. New York: Oxford University Press, 2018.

Quigley, William P. "Rumblings of Reform: Northern Poor Relief Legislation in Antebellum America, 1820-1860." *Capital University Law Review* 26 (1997): 739–774.

Quigley, William P. "Reluctant Charity: Poor Laws in the Original Thirteen States." *University of Richmond Law Review* 31 (1997): 1–98.

Quigley, William P. "The Quicksands of The Poor Law: Poor Relief Legislation in a Growing Nation, 1790–1820." *Northern Illinois University Law Review* 18 (Fall 1997): 111–178.

Quigley, William P. "The Earliest Years of Federal Social Welfare Legislation: Federal Poor Relief Prior to the Civil War." *University of Detroit Mercy Law Review* 79 (Winter 2002): 157–188.

Ranlet, Philip. "The British, Slaves, and Smallpox in Revolutionary Virginia." *The Journal of Negro History* 84:3 (Summer 1999): 217–226.

Rao, Gautham. "Administering Entitlement: Governance, Public Health Care, and the Early American State." *Law & Social Inquiry* 37:3 (2012): 627–656.

Rath, Richard Cullen. *How Early America Sounded*. Ithaca: Cornell University Press, 2003.

Raytheon Employees Wildlife Habitat Committee. "Portsmouth Asylum: An Introduction." Online at: https://rewhc.org/townfarmintro.shtml.

Rediker, Marcus. *The Slave Ship: A Human History*. New York: Penguin, 2007.

Renders, Hans, and Binne De Haan, Eds. *Theoretical Discussions of Biography: Approaches from History, Microhistory, and Life Writing*. Boston: Brill, 2014.

Rockman, Seth, Ed. *Welfare Reform in the Early Republic: A Brief History with Documents*. Boston: Bedford/St. Martin's, 2003.

Rockman, Seth. "Work, Wages, and Welfare at the School of Industry." *Maryland Historical Magazine* 102 (Spring 2007): 575–611.

Rockman, Seth. *Scraping By: Wage Labor, Slavery, and Survival in Early Baltimore*. Baltimore: Johns Hopkins University Press, 2009.

Rockman, Seth. "Negro Cloth: Mastering the Market for Slave Clothing in Antebellum America." In Sven Beckert and Christine Desan, Eds., *American Capitalism: New Histories*. New York: Columbia University Press, 2018.

Rothbard, Murray N. *The Panic of 1819: Reactions and Policies*. New York: Columbia University Press, 1962.

Rothman, David J. *The Discovery of the Asylum: Social Order and Disorder in the New Republic*. Boston. Little Brown, 1971.

Salinger, Sharon V. "Review of Simon Newman, *Embodied History: The Lives of the Poor in Early Philadelphia*." *American Historical Review* 109:1 (February 2004): 176.

Salinger, Sharon V. *Taverns and Drinking in Early America*. Baltimore: Johns Hopkins University Press, 2002.

Schwartz, Joel. *Fighting Poverty With Virtue: Moral Reform and America's Urban Poor, 1825–2000*. Bloomington: Indiana University Press, 2000.

Schwartz, George. "Digging Up Salem's Golden Age: Ceramic Use Among the Merchant Class." *Ceramics in America*. 2011. Accessed via *chipstone.org*.

SenGupta, Gunja. *From Slavery to Poverty: The Racial Origins of Welfare in New York, 1840–1918*. New York: New York University Press, 2009.

Sherwin, Wilson, and Frances Fox Piven. "The Radical Feminist Legacy of the National Welfare Rights Organization." *WSQ: Women's Studies Quarterly* 47:3 (2019): 135–153.

Skocpol, Theda. *Protecting Soldiers and Mothers: The Political Origins of Social Policy in the United States*. Cambridge, MA: Harvard University Press, 1992.

Smith, Barbara Clark. "The Adequate Revolution." *William and Mary Quarterly* 51:4 (October 1994): 684–692.

Smith, Billy G. *The "Lower Sort": Philadelphia's Laboring People, 1750–1800*. Ithaca: Cornell University Press, 1990.

Smith, Billy, G., Ed. *Down and Out in Early America*. University Park: Pennsylvania University Press, 2004.

Sparrow, James T., Novak, William J., and Sawyer, Stephen W. *Boundaries of the State in US History*. Chicago, London: University of Chicago Press, 2015.

Stadum, Beverly, *Poor Women and their Families: Hard Working Charity Cases, 1900–1930*. Albany: State University of New York Press, 1992.

Stanley, Amy Dru. *From Bondage to Contract: Wage Labor, Marriage, and the Market in the Age of Slave Emancipation*. Cambridge, U.K.: Cambridge University Press, 1998.

Staples, William Read. *Annals of the Town of Providence from Its First Settlement to the Organization of the City Government in June 1832.* Providence: Knowles and Vose, 1843.

Stokes, Howard Kemble. *The Finances and Administration of Providence.* Baltimore: Johns Hopkins Press, 1903.

Sweet, John Wood. *Bodies Politic: Negotiating Race in the American North, 1730–1830.* Philadelphia: University of Pennsylvania Press, 2003.

Sylla, Richard. "Long-Term Trends in State and Local Finance: Sources and Uses of Funds in North Carolina, 1800–1977." In Stanley L. Engerman and Robert E. Gallman, Eds. *Long-Term Factors in American Economic Growth.* Chicago: University of Chicago Press, 1986: 819–868.

Sylla, Richard, and John J. Wallis. "Historical Economics: U.S. State and Local Government." *NBER Reporter* 14 (1995): 14–16.

Tani, Karen M. *States of Dependency: Welfare, Rights, and American Governance, 1935–1972.* Cambridge: Cambridge University Press, 2016.

Taylor, Alan. *American Revolutions: A Continental History, 1750–1804.* New York: W.W. Norton, 2016.

Thompson, Mary V. *In the Hands of a Good Providence: Religion in the Life of George Washington.* Charlottesville: University of Virginia Press, 2008.

Tiffany, Francis. *Life of Dorothea Lynde Dix.* Boston: Houghton Mifflin Company, 1890.

Trattner, Walter I. *From Poor Law to Welfare State: A History of Social Welfare in America.* Sixth Edition. New York: Free Press, 1999.

Ulrich, Laurel Thatcher, and Lois K. Stabler. "'Girling of It' in Eighteenth-Century New Hampshire." In Peter Benes, Ed. *Families and Children. Dublin Seminar for New England Foklife, Annual Proceedings, 1985.* Boston: Boston University, 1987.

Walker, Cyrus, and Town of Scituate Bicentennial Committee. *The History of Scituate, R.I. by Cyrus Walker.* Edited by Hedley Smith. N.P.: Racine Printing, 1976.

Wagner, David. *The Poorhouse: America's Forgotten Institution.* Lanham: Rowman & Littlefield, 2005.

Wagner, David. *Ordinary People: In and Out of Poverty in the Gilded Age.* Boulder: Paradigm Publishers, 2008.

Walton, Geri. "Medical Blistering in the Georgian Era." *Geri Walton: Unique History from the 18th and 19th Centuries* Online at <https://www.geriwalton.com/medical-blistering-in-georgian-era/>.

Watkinson, James D. "Rogues, Vagabonds, and Fit Objects: The Treatment of the Poor in Antebellum Virginia." *Virginia Cavalcade* 49:1 (Winter 2000): 16–29.

West, Edward Homer. *History of Portsmouth 1638–1936.* N.P. N.D.

Wiberley, Stephen Edward, Jr. "Four Cities: Public Poor Relief in Urban America, 1700–1775." PhD diss., New Haven, Yale University, 1975.

Williamson, Margaret. "Africa or Old Rome? Jamaican Slave Naming Revisited." *Slavery and Abolition* 38:1 (2017): 117–134.

Willrich, Michael. "Home Slackers: Men, the State, and Welfare in Modern America." *Journal of American History* 87:2 (September 2000): 460–489.

Wilson, William Julius. *When Work Disappears: The World of the New Urban Poor.* New York: Alfred A. Knopf, 1996.

Withey, Lynne. *Urban Growth in Colonial Rhode Island: Newport and Providence in the Eighteenth Century.* Albany: State University of New York Press, 1984.

Wolfe, S.J. "Dating American Tract Society Publications Through 1876 from External Evidences: A Series of Tables." Online at American Antiquarian Society: http://www.americanantiquarian.org/node/6693.

Wood, Gordon. *The Radicalism of the American Revolution.* New York: Alfred A. Knopf, 1991.

Wright, Conrad Edick. *The Transformation of Charity in Postrevolutionary New England.* Boston: Northeastern University Press, 1992.

Wright, Conrad Edick. "Review of Lawrence J. Friedman and Mark D. McGarvie, *Charity, Philanthropy, and Civility in American History.*" In *American Historical Review* 109:1 (February 2004): 172.

Wright, Meredith and Nancy Rexford. *Everyday Dress of Rural America, 1783–1800, With Instructions and Patterns.* New York: Dover Publications, 1992.

Wulf, Karin. "Gender and the Political Economy of Poor Relief in Colonial Philadelphia." In Billy G. Smith, Ed. *Down and Out in Early America.* University Park: Pennsylvania University Press, 2004.

Yokota, Kariann Akemi. *Unbecoming British: How Revolutionary America Became a Postcolonial Nation.* New York: Oxford University Press, 2011.

Zilversmit, Arthur. *The First Emancipation: The Abolition of Slavery in the North.* Chicago: University of Chicago Press, 1967.

INDEX

For the benefit of digital users, indexed terms that span two pages (e.g., 52–53) may, on occasion, appear on only one of those pages.

Figures are indicated by *f* following the page number

Printed in the USA
CPSIA information can be obtained
at www.ICGtesting.com
LVHW010024191123
764206LV00003B/12